thousand will suffice. If I idealize that audience slightly, it is to rid myself of old habits.

2

To BEGIN, THEN. At the age of sixty-five, after a month's stay in Holland and France, I returned to Berkeley in mid-July, where I settled down to gardening and reading, mainly works from around the year 1800. These were Goethe's *Wilhelm Meister* and *Elective Affinities*, both in English translation, and a volume of German Romantics in the Pléiade series. At the same time, I became distracted, or rather consumed, by the sort of thoughts inspired by my every trip to Paris—after Wilno, the second site of my ill-fated youth. Thirty years after the war, to Leśmian's question "Can economic well-being be achieved in a world of non-being?" Paris was answering unequivocally, without a quibble: "Yes, it can." But how did that affect me, I who had nothing to say to any Frenchman?

We are born on earth only once and we indulge in much mimicking and posing, dimly aware of the truth, but with pen in hand it is difficult to escape that awareness: then, at least, one wants to keep one's self-respect. As a young man I was struck by the magnitude of what was occurring in my century, a magnitude equaling, perhaps even surpassing the decline and fall of antiquity, so that I remained oblivious to, almost unconscious of, disputes over poetics, whether those of Skamander or the Avant-Garde; to the political comedies of the late thirties, and to the sort of literary debates promoted by Karol Irzykowski. How, then, at a later date, as a witness to what was under way, could I seriously have pursued a literary career, either in the People's Republic of Poland or abroad among the émigrés, as if nothing had happened? To whom, about what, was I to speak? Even after I had surfaced from my meditations on History, now investing them with a new tone and sense, and brought my thoughts to bear on language, on Polish poetry, and on individual poets, I was against narrowing the argument to questions of craft and thus ignoring the great paramount theme. Yet I lacked the tools to handle that theme, nor am I much better equipped now. Today I am awed by the violence of my prewar poetry, a violence of tone born of a disproportion between the matter conveyed and the imagery to match it. To have pursued a "literary career" would have signaled a retreat from far more dramatic urgencies. Even my switching of careers—from diplomat to a professorship in Berkeley—may have been a way of escaping literature. If I was to evade that highest calling, which only in a handful of poems I had managed not to betray, then let it be to a minimum, which consideration, along with my disdain for the laws of the marketplace, saved me from the frantic pursuit of fame and money. If my earlier conflicts with the literary profession had been ambivalent, condemning myself to the agonies of a civil servant had proved calamitous. My conflict with the market in the West, on the other hand, was clear and decisive, my arrogance blatant; and my persistence was rewarded, quite providentially, for, unlike the tedium of bureaucracy, working with young people can be meaningful and of mutual benefit. From the moment I became a "professor of Slavic literatures," I was relieved of having to attend to the success of my literary work; that is, I was again denied a writer's vocation, and this time happily so.

Those readings from around the year 1800 which occupied me during July and August of 1975 were in preparation for a fall course on Dostoevsky; but not only. Their choice alone testified to the gradual nurturing of this book's undertaking, one in which the Romantic era will rear its head more than once.

3

TO OBEY THE FREELY MOVING HAND . . . Is that possible? To forget that there may be other readers, not just Polish, and yet to write only in Polish, for an exclusively Polish audience? One of the most serious and frustrating dilemmas resulting from prolonged residence abroad is having to repress the constantly intruding thought: How would this sound in English? How construed by a foreign reader? I cannot stand writing in a foreign language; I am incapable of it. There was a time when I dreamed of an international role for myself, of world renown—guiltily, hesitantly so—and though my fantasies never took any definite shape, they were no less real. True, I did get a taste of that fame, even my share of foreign reviews, like those in Germany comparing me to Faulkner (?), or those in the United States acknowledging my influence on American poets of the younger generation, but seldom were they written with intelligence and even more seldom were they willing to grant me any originality. The din of the marketplace—I could not help thinking—part of the general clamor of voices and names that are quickly forgotten the next day. How glad I am now that I clung to my native language (for the simple reason that I was a Polish poet and could not have been otherwise); that I did not emulate those émigrés in France and the United States who shed one skin and language for another. I would not deny that my Polish served my pride by erecting a protective barrier between myself and a civilization in the throes of puerility (*qui sombre dans l'idiotie*), just as my "Westernness," my "universality," served me as a faithful ally in my revolt against "Polishness"—both when the word "Nation" was enthroned with a capital "N," and later, following its dethronement, when it was restored to full honors. Let my case stand as a lesson: behold the enduring image of a poet, ill at ease in one place, ill at ease in the other—"always and everywhere ill at ease"—who managed to distance himself by spinning, cocoon-like, his incomprehensible language. Sartre once wrote to Camus that in view of his distaste for political systems, he saw only one place for him: the Galápagos Islands. How often I have recalled those words, here, in California, which has been—for me, a Polish poet —my Galápagos; and how I grieved, even suffered guilt, over the forfeiture, until I accepted it and stopped feeling ashamed. What did I have to be ashamed of? That I was made of this very clay?

Nonetheless, I belong to the estate of Polish literature and to no other. What American writer feels himself a part of an American literary estate, especially when, in light of the different service to which the word is put here, the reality of that estate remains something tenuous? While the estate of Polish, Russian, and Czech literature is for me something visible, even palpable, I am not so sure but that the estate of French literature—notwithstanding its Academy, its annual awarding of prizes and honors (more reminiscent of some tribal contest)—has not gone to seed amid all the furor.

One would like to astound the world, to save the world, but one can do neither. We are summoned to deeds that are of moment only to our village, our Catalonias, our Waleses, and our Slovenias. Not that in defying Alfred Jarry's "Debraining Machine" I would now try to uphold a belief in Slavic idylls. But if I am to nourish the hope of writing with a free hand, with gaiety, and not under pressure, then I must proceed by keeping only a few Polish readers in mind.

4

How to accept that what is obvious to us may not be so for others? How many ways, on how many levels, do we discover the inaccessibility of another mind. And this makes for unease: if behind the words uttered in conversation lies another perception, another wisdom, then the words, although the same, must connote something different. Anyone who has ever taught in a school or a university knows it from experience—when casually invoking an unfamiliar name, or a Greek or Latin phrase which must be glossed before it can be understood. But such gaps in understanding, owing to a greater or lesser degree of literacy, are not the most grievous. We are beholden to our times, above all to the time of our youth; when that time turns out to be as remote and exotic for succeeding generations as the age of Philip the Fair, then our muteness begins to really press: how, in what words, to transmit the things witnessed, felt, things that for us are endowed with a horrifying concreteness?

An elderly gentleman, if he has known many famous people, endured many trials, been a spectator to great events, will not hesitate to sit down and reel off his memoirs. Memoir writing is popular today; there is even something moving in this disinterested need to bear witness to "the way it was." But not everyone is fated to compile his memoirs, least of all I. That is because mine is a pained, bruised, excoriated memory, and I am fearful of the past, as once I was fearful of a page in a natural-history book showing a hyena standing upright with its forepaws on a grave. Oh, to be one of those serene, mild-mannered gentlemen who can sit by the fireplace, with one gout-stricken leg propped on a stool brought up close to the fire, and muse philosophically about the past. Nor are external causes, historical horrors, etc., to blame for that lack of amiable cohabitation with my former self. Only my nature, my character is to blame, that condition known in moral theology as a "scrupulous conscience," a vulnerability to *delectatio morosa*, to brooding over the portion of one's sins. My life has seen an abundance of both joy and sorrow, of reason and folly, of good and evil, enough to make up a passable biography, if it were not that every pinprick had grown to a stab; moreover, a slow-healing one. "I picture you," Gombrowicz once remarked, "as a Lithuanian squire living in some backwater place miles from the nearest town, swatting flies and brooding over the fact that twenty years ago his wife served him plum rather than cherry *pirogi*, and wanting to know what it meant." An apt observation. Anyone prone to both melancholy and irascibility dwells on historical atrocities at the risk of compounding a private pain with a collective shame.

Memory was once regarded as the mother of the Muses: *Mnemosyne mater musarum.* I can testify that it is really so, that when perfection summons, it is untrappable except as the detail recalled: the polished wood of a handrail, towers glimpsed through a breach in the green, a sunbeam on a very particular lake bay. From what does ecstasy come—in a poem, in a painting—if not from the detail recaptured. And if distance is the essence of beauty, that distance by which reality is cleansed—of life's willing (*Lebenswillen*), of our grasping lust for power and possession, Schopenhauer, that great theoretician of art as contemplation, would have said—then there is also a distance to be gained by bodying forth the world in recollection. True—but the reverse is no less true. Because a moment is not movement, or duration, is in fact its opposite; and just as a group of men and women in a Giorgione painting is the more evocative for its being fixed, arrested, so it would lose much of its power as soon as it, their *moment*, were to speed by like a film frame. The past conceived as movement, as duration (be it the past of a nation, a continent, or a civilization, known to us secondhand, or our own past, that of an individual), is a realm where those who once lived are as shadows, so that the closing centuries of Assyria or Babylon, disposed of by Friedrich Hegel in a single page, might stand as a caricature of every past. And what power can restore life to shadows? It is here that imagination becomes embattled with movement, on behalf of the moment, and whatever is restored to brilliance becomes, so to speak, a moment torn from the throat of motion, a testament to the durability of even the most ephemeral instant, to the trickery of the nullifying memory. So perhaps it is another, more bountiful memory, one twinned with Imagination, which is the mother of the Muses. In victory, works drawn from the stuff of memories are a store of living images; in defeat a "re-creation" of movement, of characters' thoughts, emotional states, internal rhythms—"fiction," in other words—and unless an author expressly intends a fairy tale, the whole is sub-verted by that dullness proper to the pallid existence of shadows.

Enough. My memory, so faithful and rigorous when it comes to the detail, is so scarred that for fear of rekindling pain, it can turn years, whole periods into a void, a vacancy, so that I am scarcely even tempted by the memoir. And how could I make pretensions to "sincerity," I who go around in a corset, all self-discipline on the inside? As an anti-Freudian, I have never lain on a psychoanalyst's couch, though a psychoanalyst might find in me no mean case study; but then, the damage inflicted by such analysis might outweigh the good.

5

I AND GOMBROWICZ. Of two dissimilar, even contrary natures, we were yoked together rather by circumstances. The histories of nations have their mysteries, and the career of the Polish word, written across many borders, is such a mystery. As émigrés, wormwood-fed by the Polish emigration until praised by foreigners and visitors from Poland, we became lasting friends. I did not know him before the war, never sat at his café table, but while he was living in Argentina and I in France, we struck up an alliance, without ever corresponding, always alluding to each other with respect even in our quarrels in print. Later, in the spring of 1967, there were two months when we met every couple of days, usually the four of us: Gom-browicz, Janka, Rita, and I. I could not say whether

Gombrowicz appreciated me as an intellect or a poet, probably the former; I would not even swear that he had read my poetry. He urged me to write novels—a genre for which I had a proven talent, he said—to which I replied that I held neither the genre nor my novelistic abilities in very high esteem. Talking philosophy was his real passion, and his condescending attitude toward our colleagues in Poland was grounded in what he called their intellectual inferiority, in their lack of philosophical training. Our talks? Usually in French, out of consideration for Rita, and he once commented: "Odd, whenever we switch to Polish, you become fuzzy."

He used to chide me (he could not very well leave me unscathed) for corrupting the young, i.e., by teaching literature at the university. *What* literature? Was there even such a thing as "literature"? Let alone a "Polish literature"? He was unimpressed by modest achievements, whatever their merits, and when I once invoked Brzozowski's name, I heard: "What drivel! There's no such person!"—which is to say, for Gombrowicz the virtue of existence was not something to be readily conferred, and his mocking disdain for the philosophy of the Polish Romantic poets was, like his sarcasm in general, not without its serious underside. He offered me a way of redeeming my sins: I was to teach only one author, Gombrowicz, and in that way I would be doing full justice to Polish literature by teaching its most Polish writer. He did have a point there, because what other Polish writers could have been taught in America in the absence of any translations? Only Gombrowicz and Witkiewicz.

When I laughingly told him that I had edited an anthology of contemporary Polish poetry in English translation, and that I was preparing a history of Polish literature for publication, he winced in disgust. "Why waste your time on such trivia! Imagine Nietzsche editing anthologies!" Textbooks, he declared, were permissible, but only for money. Had I done it for money? All right, so I had (which was not the whole truth).

And yet, I am told, that hefty, handsomely printed, and generously illustrated volume, which came into his hands only a few days before his death, afforded him no little pleasure—he kept it by his bedside and used to leaf through it (he did not know English). In it was a large, page-size photograph of him, proof that he, too, the comical adolescent Gombrowicz, had joined the ranks of the exalted whom some future Professor Pimko was bound to revere as "prophets" to a man.

"Gombro" was sensitive enough to register the various shades of friendship. If he felt my wholly unaffected and unselfish respect, he must also have sensed a certain residue bespeaking the differences in our sensibilities, a hidden resistance, perhaps alloyed with some hard, brutal, even unworthy part of myself. I regarded Gombrowicz as a man incapable of friendship, of the emotional urge, and in his relations with people I noted a persistent self-obsession. Yet his egoism, just because it was open and somehow consistent, not only did not diminish, but even enhanced the courage of this man who had the audacity to appoint himself, his bodily self, as priest before the altar of Gombrowicz-the-artist. He was a rarity among writers; everything he wrote was of the highest caliber, which was reason enough for respect, yet I kept my own world private, convinced that there was little I could offer someone of his disposition, and it is quite possible that he sensed this reticence on my part.

Gombrowicz was a very rational man, endowed with abundant good sense and, appearances to the contrary, remarkably sane in his views. He struck me as quite well organized, in the sense that there was no contradiction between the things he wrote and said and his manner of behavior, quite the opposite of those savages who astonish us by the angelic tone of their art, or of those dainty thoroughbreds given to bloodthirsty visions. I could appreciate how long he must have labored to achieve that consistency, and I recognized this, his *virtù*, as his greatest asset. His life's misery, defeats, humiliations, on the other hand, the stuff of which he had fashioned himself, sacrificing Gombrowicz-the-man to Gombrowicz-the-artist, seemed less severe than they doubtless were—I could only imagine them, after all—which merely enhanced the impression of consistency.

We admire in others what we ourselves lack. I would not claim even a fraction of that rationality that was "the lunatic Gombrowicz's" strength; nor were the various tiers of my nature in concord with one another, reminding me always of that fairy-tale coach drawn by a lobster, a fish, and a swan.

6

HERE A DIGRESSION. Many years ago, the Wilno section of the Union of Polish Writers had its meeting place in the Basilian Monastery, on whose premises, if the records were not in error, was the corridor once lined with the cells of the Philomath prisoners, among them Mickiewicz's, nicknamed "Konrad's cell." It was there, in the monastery, that the so-called literary Wednesdays were held—sessions devoted to readings by local writers or by writers from out of town and abroad, to lectures and discussions, etc. In or around 1933, our group, Żagary, had a reading there. Seated in the front row were two from the editorial staff of the conservative *The Word* (thanks to its editor, Stanisław Mackiewicz, one of the leading Polish newspapers of the day, to which the history of Żagary owes much): Ksawery Pruszyński and Jerzy Wyszomirski. The first, who was not a local figure, I would come to know only much later. Cossack-like, with green eyes and the cheekbones of a Mongol, Pruszyński led a full if not very long life, which ended in circumstances as obscure as the obscurity that still surrounds many events of that time. In 1951, Pruszyński, then Poland's ambassador at The Hague, was driving alone by car to Warsaw, via Germany, when he fatally collided with a truck. Shortly before he left, he had received word from Warsaw that he was about to be charged with collaborating with the Polish Intelligence while on a journalistic assignment in Republican Spain. The message, believed to have come from a high-ranking official, was clear: "Do not return to Warsaw or you'll meet with an accident."

Wyszomirski, a neurotic, dwarfish, bespectacled man, too self-deprecating to tout himself as a poet, with only one volume of poetry to his name (*The Holocaust*), was *The Word*'s chief literary editor and hung out every night at the Wilno pubs, drowning his gloom in drink. Supposedly he was born into the family of a tsarist army officer stationed in one of the garrison towns, and indeed, he behaved altogether like a man of the nineteenth century. After the war he lived in Łódź, earning a living as a distinguished translator of Russian fiction. He took his own life in 1955—he had had enough of the system. So there they were, the two of them, seated in the front row opposite me as I read. When at one point Pruszyński leaned over to Wyszomirski, I cocked my ear and overheard him whisper: *"Baloven' sud'by."* The remark hurt, set me to brooding even in those days. Literally, the Russian meant "a plaything of fate," but I responded rather to its pejorative sense of man-as-puppet, of one duped and betrayed by fate. I was haunted by that epithet for a long time afterward. Two "worldly wise" men, eyeing with curiosity a talented upstart—boyishly good-looking, at that—had been fooled by appearances, as others were also to be deceived, marveling at how easily success came to me, envying me either fame or money. In reality, fate held much pain in store for me, and the admiration bestowed on me by those older literary colleagues, an admiration tinged with pity, somehow set the pattern for future misperceptions. Privately I acknowledged only their pity, feeling myself defenseless against fate's shrewd devices.

7

AMONG WRITERS WHO WERE my contemporaries, I have envied only one: the poet Julian Przyboś. Not his poetry so much as the territory he claimed for himself, his immunity to fits of indecision or hesitation. As a student of Polish literature in Cracow, he proclaimed a belief in science and technology, social progress, the twentieth century—in "the metropolis, the mass, and the machine." On this "literary materialism" he premised his relentlessly avant-garde theory of poetry, so rigorously applied in his own verse. And the times bore him out. Nature was deposed, automobiles and airplanes were multiplying, medicine was finding ways to prolong human life and lower the infant mortality rate; the lower classes were on the rise, migrating from the countryside to the cities, learning to read and write, being transformed from a race of starving earth-grubbers into a "mass" hungering for movies, appliances, amusements, fashions. As only socialism was destined to realize man's dreams, or so the disciples of progress had long been preaching, a benign History now became the refuge of hope in Poland. Even the village of Przyboś's childhood had borne witness to the changes for which he and, as he envisioned, all poets strove, poetry being for him a "rocketing to euphoria." Had not the Promethean human tribe already launched its flight to the stars when Przyboś was still a boy, a village herder? In poetry, too, above the snickering of a few Warsaw cafés and despite prophecies of a mass culture demanding a more accessible, more melodious, less precious kind of poetry, the new mode, of which Przyboś was the shining exemplar, had triumphed—a poetry of linguistic teasers, turned inward on grammatical and syntactical intricacies. If Przyboś had always been seriously committed to his vocation and role as trailblazer, then in his final years he was rewarded for his faith and perseverance. He became the subject of articles, monographs, dissertations; presided over new publications of his work, chaired conferences; an authority, a television celebrity. And he died as he had lived, in the service of poetry: while serving on the jury of a poetry award, he collapsed in his chair, and finis.

For Gombrowicz, Przyboś was one of the multitude of perennially avant-garde poets, whose poetry no one, except perhaps for coeds like Miss Youthful, cared to read. For such poets he prophesied a grim fate: "The end of your reign is at hand, that day when the mysterious finger of modernity will inscribe MANE TEKEL FARES on your tedious temple! Nonentity reaches out to you with open arms. Nullity, the most vacant Nullity, comes like a cat on the prowl, ready to devour your factory of metaphors and the stagecoach of your intellectual baggage."

Lucky Przyboś! He surely would not have known—assuming he had read Gombrowicz's "Against the Poets"—how to take that "nullity on the prowl." Pain is a tragedy, but so is the awareness of pain, and Gombrowicz, just because he knew the price paid for every evasion of reality, was not to be envied. Tragedy is also awareness of the philosophical deep, over which—and thanks to which—science and technology have erected their flimsy palaces. Here again, Gombrowicz was not to be envied. He was skeptical even when it came to his own work.

Let us not belabor the differences: Gombrowicz and Przyboś belong to the same chapter of Polish literature. Intellectual freedom in a Catholic country always goes hand in hand with atheism, and a comparison of Gombrowicz's aristocratic atheism with Przyboś's peasant atheism would make a splendid topic. As would the careers of other Polish atheists. The son of the devoutly Christian Apollo Korzeniowski, Joseph Conrad, could say: "The starry sky above me, the moral law within me"—and the inspiration for his areligious ethics need not have come from Kant; Seneca would have sufficed. Yet for those born at a later date—Witkiewicz, Przyboś, Gombrowicz—there could be only the proposition: "The starry sky above, *no* moral law within," morality having surrendered to a relativity born of ceaseless social flux, leaving only Art—even if written with a small "a." This was consistent with the nineteenth-century European tradition begun by Shelley's "Adonais" (1821), in which the poet, in mourning the death of Keats, became the true ancestor of our modern aestheticism: Man perishes entire and leaves no trace except a spark of beauty, provided he can trap it. Witkiewicz, Gombrowicz, and Przyboś each understood Art in his own way: Przyboś, as a "factory of metaphors"; Gombrowicz, in his quaint and comical fashion. Yet these three sensibilities, by excluding themselves from Christianity, as if not a single drop of holy water had ever been shed in Poland, are like dancers in a square dance, changing partners at random. Gombrowicz felt the terror of existence no less acutely than Witkiewicz, was no less sensitive to the demoniacal forces of history, and in the summer of 1939 he foresaw the depths into which mankind must descend—and which he was spared only by an act of providence. But Witkiewicz's ultimately apocalyptic vision was alien to Gombrowicz. Not only was he fascinated with youth, with the low, the vulgar, brought to the surface by a violent heave of the social mix, by an agitation of the masses, but he had hopes of capturing man's modern needs and emotional strivings ("Let a new music resound!"). To those who were horrified by the unrivaled specter of our century's barbarity and baseness, who prophesied an abrupt end to the earthly circus, he would caution, "Remember who you were," and begin enumerating all the epidemics, the natural calamities, the shorter lifespan, the filth, the superstition, and the obscurantism that were the lot of the human tribe until not so very long ago. On the tribe's future destiny he withheld judgment. Calamities, disasters, yes, but somehow people would cope. In many ways a conservative, dispassionate, apt to shrug at any stampede, Gombrowicz, to judge by his writings and by our conversations, did not assume that mankind was headed for the worst, but rather for the best, by which he meant not greater abundance but greater awareness. On this point, the progressive Przyboś would have taken greater cheer from Gombrowicz than from the "catastrophist" Witkiewicz.

8

To pursue a "literary career" means (would that it were otherwise) to cultivate the art of begging, and Gombrowicz must have endured much humiliation, particularly in the twenty-odd years of his Argentinian exile. The routine jobs, along with the bulk of his correspondence, were aimed only at ensuring him a minimum subsistence (he was a man of modest needs) and at promoting his work. In retrospect, these defensive "tactics" assume rather the appearance of a planned strategy, of a campaign which was finally, if belatedly, crowned with success; namely, with money and world fame.

How seriously did Gombrowicz regard his fame, his genius, and did he ever achieve genuine renown? His emergence abroad both gratified me and took me by surprise. Despite his somewhat tendentious views on the use of lowbrow forms to seduce the reader, I have always felt his writing to be of the exquisite, aristocratic variety. And world-famous, with a name like his? And how did he go equipped into the marketplace? Like a count with a fencing foil, thrust among gangsters wielding blackjacks and machine guns, i.e., into a marketplace ruled by violence and pornography. Nabokov, after all, would have remained an unknown if not for *Lolita*, after which his novels were pounced upon by the publishers. Gombrowicz never willfully indulged in such strategies, but then neither was he granted even a quarter of Nabokov's fame, having been promoted largely by highbrows. Then again, the banalities written about his work in the French, British, and American literary press did not persuade one that the more urbane critics were any better at grasping his meaning. To make matters worse, his novels did not sell; of his three plays, one, *The Marriage*, was too difficult, while another, *Operetta*, was too demanding in terms of stage production; much of his oeuvre (i.e., *Trans-Atlantic*) was too "Polish," and his *Diaries* too voluminous. Financial success, due chiefly to a few theatrical productions, came suddenly, which did not spare Gombrowicz from again falling on hard times in his final years, caused not through any personal extravagance of his own.

I did my best to promote the Gombrowicz cult, devoting many classroom lectures to his work, and with generally favorable results: among young Americans, it gained a number of enthusiasts, though not before its deeper meaning was elucidated. And the very fact that such laborious commentary was needed to explicate Gombrowicz's more recondite elements began to make me skeptical about him as an author of international stature, and not because he was insufficiently "universal." In his personal struggle with the Polish tradition and the Polish ethos, in his historical rootedness, in his brilliant buffoonery, in his stylistic polish and control, he was not below international standards but, at least for his intended audience, above; and his own stance—that air of imperiousness toward the West, derived from a peculiarly Polish juvenility-inferiority—has been vindicated beyond expectation. Gombrowicz's presence on the shelves of American bookstores in the same land where Polish-American newspapers circulate is a sign that the traditional spread in Polish culture, between the elegant and the crude, has attained truly bizarre proportions.

Gombrowicz seemed to stake his future as an international writer on the next spin of the wheel, on mankind's future course; and if he hazarded no predictions, neither did he dismiss the prospect of total "scientification," the end of the humanities, the obsolescence of his and every other kind of writing (although he did express the hope that it would never come to that). His efforts to explain himself to his readers (in, for example, his *Conversations with Dominique de Roux* [in English, *A Kind of Testament*]) suggest that he had little confidence in the astuteness of foreign critics. And who knows whether he did not privately admit to having triumphed, obliquely and paradoxically, in gaining only a permanent place in Polish literature. In Poland, above all, his work should have been read in its entirety, including his *Diaries*, for only there could it be truly appreciated.

My propagandizing efforts were partially dictated by a sense of regret, of the sort a doctor or lawyer, let us say, if he were something of an artist *manqué*, might feel toward a cousin who was risking his all. Gombrowicz, in my opinion, was a pitiable man, just as there was something pitiable about his work. To "court one's own fame" seemed to me as sad as it was moving. I have never consciously promoted my work, not for lack of ambition, but simply because there was nothing to promote. I have written only one novel worthy of the name, *The Issa Valley* (which is, in fact, a work of fiction and not a "childhood memoir"), no plays, leaving only poetry and essays—and how could a poet from a Slavic country hope for anything more than a chamber audience confined to a few universities? We all entertain our illusions, but not when they overstep the bounds of reason.

How do I personally rate the writer Gombrowicz? I regard his work to be of the highest distinction, but only for the Land of Ulro, whence it comes. The term "Ulro" will be explained in the chapters to follow.

9

MUCH OF WHAT I AM recording here first takes shape in my head during my morning strolls, around eight, along our Grizzly Peak Boulevard. It is a residential district made up of wood-framed, single-family homes, each in a different architectural style and model. The downslope on one side is so steep that many of the houses are built on stilts and their gardens visible from higher up: rhododendrons, camellias, English laurel, and fuchsias that grow to tree size. The street, it is no exaggeration to say, runs along the westernmost rim of the North American continent, because directly to the west, beyond the city of Berkeley nudging the Bay below, and farther out, beyond the Golden Gate Bridge suspended at the Bay's entrance, there is only the Pacific. The seaward view is different every morning; sometimes the fog blankets everything, revealing only a sliver of ocean off in the distance; other times, it stands banked against the jutting San Francisco skyscrapers on the spit to the south; or it may settle like a cloud on the spit across the way, on the slopes of Mount Tamalpais, at which time I have before me: a vast panorama, blue water running out to the ocean, three bridges, and San Francisco practically at my feet.

After this exercise in *paysage*, as if I were about to begin a novel in the Flaubertian manner, I shall address a crippling disability of mine, lest anyone envy me what is truly one of the most spectacular vistas in the world. I recall the feelings of despair and revolt that once were mine on this street. No more running around, no more anticipating, no more being active, mixing, conversing—stranded in a zone of absolute alienation. A nightmare for me was the fate of the painter Norblin and his wife, the actress, Lena Żelichowska, both of whom committed suicide in San Francisco, or even that of Wacław Lednicki, who used to walk his dog a few streets away from here. I longed for companions, for my brothers-in-arms, better or worse, but brothers—or as Wikta (Prof. Dr. Med.) would have said: I longed for pals with whom to dabble in the muck. Whenever I tried my hand at fiction, what invariably came out was a grim Kafkaesque tale about a man imprisoned on an island; there were towns on the island but no pedestrians, only stuffed animals, with glowing buttons for eyes, visible through the windows. Good that I gave it up; such stuff is morose, hence immoral. It happened once that I met Herbert Marcuse in San Diego at the home of some acquaintance. Marcuse stood by the window and said: "This is a city inhabited by animals." How well I understood his contempt for those aphilosophical creatures, who were content only to live, but that same contempt for people, that intellectual arrogance of his, made me realize how much meanness of spirit resided in me as well.

I stepped on the throat of my anger—to travesty the Russian bard Mayakovsky. And now I know that it is right with me. The world isn't to your liking? Can't abide one side or the other? All right, we'll find something else for you: a mountain above the clouds and the sea, a place to meditate to your heart's content. But be careful, this time it's for keeps; either you'll make something of the gift or you won't: no more squeamishness for you. Even the continent stops here.

Then I went to work. Above all, fight becoming a split personality: one half a workaday drudge who earns his bread at the academic grind, the other a darling of the Muses who gapes at the clouds in his spare time and maybe gets off a poem or two—a kind of Gombrowicz at the Banco Polaco in Argentina. To the extent that I have been able to integrate both of these activities, the one feeding and fructifying the other, there is no denying that mine has been a fairly cozy academic career. Nor should I neglect to mention that I enjoyed certain advantages: an above-average high school, better than those attended by most Americans in the humanities, and graduation from a respectable university. Two of my professors, the youngest, are still alive—Wiktor Sukiennicki (philosophy of law) and Stanisław Swaniewicz (economics). Sukiennicki once reminded me of my graduating examination—exceptional, he said—and how impressed he had been by my knowledge of eighteenth-century British philosophers. By then I had lost all recollection of that examination, even the names he recited to prompt me had faded from memory, along with all my other academic feats (the feats of a dog acrobat trained in hoop jumping). It was not the wealth of knowledge I had accumulated so much as the awakening of a historical sense, inspired both by my studies and by the force of historical event. The lack of such a sense is a serious handicap for apprenticing American academics; he who is blessed with it, on the other hand, holds a decided advantage. In my case, such assets had to compensate for a serious debility: the lack of an academic degree, since a master's degree, in law no less, hardly counted for much.

Talk to people, mix with people: to influence and be influenced. This was my only protection against the melancholy of the émigré who lives on memories. My ambition was at least partially realized, as attested by this book joining past and present but which is, in fact, a book addressed to the future, if not my own, then that of others. By enlisting twenty-year-olds as my interlocutors, I had to have my doubts—how many of our words meet with innate obtuseness or deficiencies in education—and I could count myself lucky if one out of ten showed some sign of recognition. I began almost every course wondering whether I would manage it, whether I would rouse them, make a breach in those minds nurtured on television—and with each successive year I felt like a magician who goes on pulling rabbits from his top hat, never quite knowing from one performance to the next whether the trick will come off. Among my professors in Wilno, there were those who never bothered about student rapport. They mumbled in their beards, reciting their notes in a patter audible only to those in the front rows, in a lecture auditorium that sat two to three hundred students—there were no microphones in those days. Even Lednicki, who was already retired by the time I arrived in Berkeley, treated his classes with disdain, calling them a "captive audience." Possibly I was moved to pity mixed with revulsion by his patronizing attitude and his resulting isolation. On second thought, it was not his patronizing attitude which disturbed me. We delude ourselves by insisting on "audience response," when our real purpose is the cultivation of our own resources; and we are dependent on the eyes and ears of others, however few in number, as a measure of what is dead and what alive in us. Lednicki bestowed a fixed knowledge, never seeking to renew it, to set the shuttle in motion, back and forth between the most intimate thought of a given moment and the hours of classroom lecturing. The mere possibility that I might follow his example appalled me.

Ora et labora. Pray and work. *Nulla dies sine linea,* never a day without a line, as that master draftsman, Apelles, enjoined himself (not in Latin, of course, since he was Greek). These ancient maxims still adorned the walls when I was enrolled in the lower classes of the Sigismund Augustus Gymnasium. Determination alone will not get you very far; the secret was submission, not force. Meaning, above all, submission to those instincts which first manifested themselves at the age of sixteen; the willed gratification of those intellectual impulses that were once only vaguely intuited. The describing of a great arc with which to bind early youth with maturity. To put it another way, our mind's history is like a jigsaw puzzle; it has to be assembled slowly, little by little, from an array of scattered pieces. Only that way do we make alliance with our passion, do we accede to it, and the long hours of labor become lightened. My Berkeley years have been a time of self-education, in areas waiting for me since early adolescence, as it were, in which enterprise the lecture hall has served as a stimulus, consuming only a portion of that professional competence requisite for my own private life.

Our ambivalences, uncertainties, disenchantments, renewed probings gradually form a pattern more logical than we may assume. Here I would list the three motifs, the three axes around which my lecturing and research have been gathered. *Unde malum*—wherefrom evil, or the old, all-embracing question of whether the world was the work of some malicious demiurge—led me from our school textbook on Church history to my later readings in theology and the history of religious doctrines, and ultimately, years later, to my course on Manichaeanism. The latter was listed, *faut de mieux*, as a Slavic literature course only because it related to the Bogomils, to Russian sectarianism, and to the presence of Manichaean elements in certain Russian writers; but in fact it went back to the very roots, to the gnostics of Alexandria and Rome of the second century A.D. Nor were my ongoing readings in and about Dostoevsky unrelated to this intrinsic problem, and here a new motif intrudes: nineteenth-century intellectual history, the background sources, in other words—where did men such as Dostoevsky and Nietzsche come from? why did they turn out to be so prophetic?—the key to which, naturally, was to be sought in the Enlightenment and in early Romanticism. Hence the course on Dostoevsky. And the third, finally, that of Polish literature: an obligatory survey course, rather of the culture than of the literature; and the moderns. Neither Polish poets nor Gombrowicz himself can therefore reproach me for omitting them. These, briefly summarized, are the fruits of my labors.

No, I had not anticipated that my professorial duties would bear so directly on my internal life, that they would become a bridge spanning the earlier and the later passions. Just as I never suspected that Gombrowicz would serve as an agent of self-definition. And is not this precisely the service he performs for us? If I were now writing in English, how frustrating not to be able to invoke such shorthand names!

10

WHEN I WAS SIX, my mother bought me a wooden squirrel at a market square. This was in Tartu, then called Dorpat. The little animal, or rather its flat, plywood replica, was auburn-enameled. A trinket. Yet through it I came to know the power of Eros, and even if I never had beheld a woman's face—my insides wrought, swollen with vague longing or, who knew, with more than longing—I could still have sung the praises of that robust god. I fell in love, simply, and such was the fervor of my emotion then that I still treat it with respect, as something very much above ridicule.

An enigma. Or maybe not so enigmatic; the scientific truths fed me by civilization have never persuaded me. The sexual drive, in all its subliminal forms—how can a primitive urge compare with such a mighty, imperious deity that makes a mockery of men's minds? As if, like a shoal-lined river, a powerful element were borne along, continually carving out new beds, and one of its many currents were taken as the source of all the others. In love with a wooden squirrel! Later, it was with a book illustration, a bird, a poet; a line of words, rhythmically linked. I would even risk the proposition that my Eros was jealous when I addressed my emotions to human beings, that it wished to make me its absolute servant, in love with all things existing, discretely and collectively, much as Constantin Güys, that *"peintre de la vie moderne"* sung by Baudelaire, was said to be.

Later, by my native Niewiaża, I discovered tucked inside a Lithuanian missal—most likely Barbara's, the steward's wife's, or Anusia's, the cook's—some holy pictures, one of which pierced me with love's arrow. It was an image of the Mother of God, draped in blue, on a field of gold—gold stars—and warm rust tones. The origin of such devotional articles is hard to trace; this one could have been a copy of an original done by one of the Sienese school, facsimiles being cheaper to come by, or a work modeled on the Madonnas of Siena.

The sequel came much later—"midway life's journey." I acquired my English in wartime Warsaw—self-taught, but enough to read the poets. In one anthology, I came across a few of Blake's poems, and I recognized them at once: the poems evoked the very same thing as that holy picture, had nearly the same tonality. I was not privy to Blake's art then, nor could I have been, as the reproductions of his work came much later. Looking at them today, I realize just how sound my intuition was. In those times and in that landscape so inhospitable to a child's awe before the miraculous, Blake restored me to my earlier raptures, perhaps to my true vocation, that of lover.

My conversion to Blake was, at that time, an emotional one, for my understanding failed me the moment I began to ponder the meaning of individual poems and lines; and yet that obscurity, so unlike that cultivated in the poetry of my contemporaries, was part of the magic. I made several more attempts at deciphering him, but only in recent years have I delved in earnest. So that today, whenever I confer with American Blakeans, a clan dedicated to an almost hermetic science, I realize—after having read many of the conflicting commentaries on his poetry and art, after having learned to distinguish the true from the spurious— that I have attained to the middle stage of initiation (with Blake, there can be no final stage). I was led to Blake by my childhood Eros, but my intellectual fascination is so fundamental that I choose to leave it for later chapters. For now, let me say only that it would be an injustice to place Blake in the company of other English Romantic poets: as one of a handful of figures to emerge in the last couple of centuries, he can hardly be contained by the word "literature." He has been justly studied, with varying success, by historians of art, religious scholars, theologians, psychologists, and cultural historians. Yet, one might counter, what sort of poet is Blake if not even a five-hundred-page glossary of his symbols—compiled by S. F. Damon—is adequate to elucidate the esoterica in his *Prophetic Books*, paintings, and engravings? That of course depends on how one defines the mission of the writer-artist.

The name Ulro is from Blake. It denotes that realm of spiritual pain such as is borne and must be borne by the crippled man. Blake himself was not one of its inhabitants, unlike the scientists, those proponents of Newtonian physics, the philosophers, and most other poets and artists of his day. And that goes for their descendants in the nine-teenth and twentieth centuries, up to and including the present.

11

BRIX (we shall refer to him by that pseudonym) is writing a dissertation on Gombrowicz. For me, as his advisor, it has been the occasion of some interesting observations. In mining the philosophical bedrock of Gombrowicz's vision, Brix has come up with, in the first instance, the name of Schopenhauer, and aptly so, I believe. Polish literature has been profusely subdivided by force of political event; the Moderna, or Young Poland, ends in 1918, followed by the period 1919–39, and so on. Yet a more vital current, heed-less of such partitions, may course underneath. The real crisis of the Moderna, i.e., the traumatic experience of positivism and biological evolutionism (tempered by the Positivists through a moralizing didacticism and diluted religiosity), did not, for lack of sufficient intellectual and verbal maturity, receive full expression until the time of Leśmian, Schulz, Witkiewicz, and Gombrowicz, none of whom are "officially" affiliated with the Moderna. It was Schopenhauer, long relegated to the shadows even in his own country, who proved a cousin to the despair-ridden Moderns, a precursor, particularly in his view of Nature (long before Darwin's time, a reminder that Darwin was merely shuffling an already cut deck). *The World as Will and Idea* said, in essence, that there was only a *Natura devorans* and a *Natura devorata*: a Nature that devours and a Nature devoured. For Gombrowicz, man is both Will and pain, a solitary monad that seeks mastery over others, that struggles *to be* at the expense of others' being. For Schopenhauer, the infernal circle of Will, of being-born-to-be-devoured, is transcended only through art, which cleanses will through distance, and through holiness, which altruistically relinquishes power over others. Gombrowicz rejected the latter and recognized only art, though not without defiling somewhat the image of "our mistress and mediatrix"—so worshipped by poets of the Moderna —by acknowledging its dual aspect: the artist's will uses art to triumph over others, to dominate, to command obedience and surrender, while the artist's other half, through distance, militates against his selfish instincts. The writer emerges, therefore, not as some pure and noble figure in the ministry of art (however much a brute in real life), but as overtly aggressive (if inwardly torn).

By emphasizing the element of struggle, I simplify, of course: Gombrowicz is no naturalist, nor do his monads exist in isolation, since they engender something through reciprocity. Then, too, for him that struggle is conducted on the level of grimaces, gestures, glances: one masters, or is oneself mastered, by means of a tyrannizing glance. Still, the biological element in Gombrowicz cannot be dismissed, and the natural sciences, the modernists' true obsession, exert a constant presence in his work.

Through careful analysis of the texts, Brix, fully appreciative of Gombrowicz's artistry, concluded that behind the ingenious plotting, behind the seductive humor and levity of style, there poses a somber vision, an insidious mockery of everything that makes us human and that makes life possible in a humane society—kindness, fraternity, friendship, unselfish devotion. The Gombrowiczian enterprise, realized in work after work, Brix takes to be fundamentally misanthropic. Gombrowicz's chief strategy is a willfully blasphemous parody of time-honored customs and rituals, notably the rites of Catholic liturgy, for it is on the ruins of religion that Gombrowicz would erect his "interhuman church." It is not accidental that *The Marriage* opens against the landscape of a church in ruins; that the priest's matrimonial power is transmuted into a regal, dictatorial power. Again, in Gombrowicz's earlier work, we find parodies of the Mass, of the Eucharistic supper, whose celebrants are united by their partaking of the sacrificial offering. The parody is seen, for example, in the banquet given by Countess Kotłubay (in the story "Countess Kotłubay's Banquet"), at which the guests, all aristocrats, consume a dish of cauliflower, that is, the flesh of Cauliflower, a peasant lad who perished from hunger. In *Ivona, Princess of Burgundia*, it is again a supper that unites the residents of the palace, because Ivona's death— the court conspires to have her choke on a bony fish—is also a sacrificial death, freeing them from various shameful obsessions. In *Pornografia*, the godless priest, Frederick, succeeds in joining a young couple through a jointly perpetrated murder. Early in the novel, he "spoils" a Mass; later he triumphs over the religiosity of the Catholic matron, Amelia, whose virtuousness is revealed as a need for approbation—hence her deathbed concentration on Frederick, her using of him to "test" her own faith, as only man can be a god for man. The last of Gombrowicz's novels, *Cosmos*, is also liturgical, only here, argues Brix, the priest-figure, Leon, is cast as a priest of masturbation. Gombrowicz's misanthropy, he claims, is manifested in a gratuitous, even capricious cruelty, in the nonchalance with which his characters commit acts of murder, almost "for kicks"; in their detachment and loneliness; in their author's impotence to create objective characters that are not merely different versions of himself. Even his philosophical bias, the persistence with which he argued that we can know nothing of the world—either its existence or nonexistence—except our perceptions of it, was the sign of a moral crippling, in that it elevated the deprecation of others and the exaltation of self to the sole means of perception.

Brix's discoveries came as no revelation to me. Gombrowicz's humanistic pronouncements had often struck me as hollow. "Man is for man a god"—lovely: Ludwig Feuerbach, Anno Domini 1841. But what if this is superseded by another maxim: Man is for man a wolf. Which is it to be, then, a god or a wolf? "Well, what are you waiting for? Slug away!" Gombrowicz would exhort at the sight of two men in company, one bearded and the other clean-shaven, and of the contradiction they embodied. No, he was not the most sanguine of thinkers, and when in his dissertation Brix alludes to the formidable influence of Dostoevsky, we are apt to say, "Warmer, warmer . . ." This, in effect, would put Gombrowicz among the great poets of Will and Self-will: on the one hand, Schopenhauer and his disciple, Nietzsche, and, on the other, pursuing the same track on his own, Dostoevsky. In his youth, stirred by high ideals and professing a faith in mankind, Dostoevsky was a

Fourierist who heralded the coming age of universal bliss. But from those four years in the Omsk labor camp, among peasants convicted of ordinary crimes and among hardened criminals, men whom he admired, was born the dilemma at the center of his greatest works: Can man love his fellow man? To which, in *Notes from the Underground*, he replied: No. There the narrator proclaims his indifference to the fate of his fellow humans, declaring that all mankind could perish, so long as he might enjoy his tea in peace. The *Notes* pose a philosophical equation so artfully contrived as to defy solution or simplification. In his later novels, Dostoevsky would desperately try to solve the equation, and would succeed only by invoking religious faith. By their sheer complexity, the *Notes* anticipate by many decades the whole existentialist argument. When read together with Bakhtin's study of Dostoevsky's poetics, a work dating from the 1920s, they will be found to embody the whole notion of a "dialectics of perception," by which a subject (the "I") transforms another into an object—a concept to be later extended, simultaneously but separately, by the philosopher Sartre and the writer Gombrowicz. The affinity of these two, along with their common ancestry in the *Notes*, testifies to the virulence—

Here it is I who am elaborating on Brix's own arguments in order to give them credence. What jarred me were not his insights so much as the strong censure they provoked. It suddenly made me querulous. Why should someone such as himself, an American liberal, feel morally affronted and not I? Was it because we Poles were heir to a different sensibility, one that made us double up with laughter at the sight of a man hanged, decapitated, or knifed—a more macabre sense of humor that blinded us to certain perplexities? If so, where did it come from? A baroque tradition? Dire dreams conferred on us by history?

The childish abandon with which we read Sienkiewicz? Maybe one did not have to be raised on a violent television, as Americans of Brix's generation had been, to forfeit one's moral sensitivity.

But it was not just that. The reason lay in a more serious disparity. Brix, a humanitarian and progressive, would assent to man's innate goodness, which, if protected from the corrupting effects of an evil society, must suffice as the only foundation of ethics, an ethics free of religious sanctions. I would even say that Brix, more than a hundred years after Chernyshevsky, is in many ways descended from that noble dreamer, whose passionate longing for a resplendent future, whose vision of man inhabiting a "crystal palace" Dostoevsky would ridicule in his *Notes from the Underground*. If Gombrowicz were a man given to religious impulses, his pessimism might be pardonable. But, because he was an atheist, his mockery of human coexistence, exposed by him as mutual aggression, made him something of a deserter, one who betrayed the secret hopes of the secular priest such as Brix was by nature.

Was there perhaps not a simpler reason why I was not outraged by Gombrowicz? If Brix found Gombrowicz bleak, could I not be accused of an even starker bleakness? Gombrowicz in his *Diaries* speaks of me as of one made naked, divested by history of faith in any values. Was then our macabre humor not a sign of our divestiture? But invoking the meat grinder of history strikes me as only partially valid. My pessimistic vision of the world was formed early in life, around the age of fifteen; and if I am sensitive to the Schopenhauerian impulse in Gombrowicz and the Moderns, it is because as a boy I was initiated into Nature's reckless indifference by Nusbaum-Hilarowicz's book on Darwin and natural selection. Nor was my early fascination with the Manichaean heresy merely incidental.

How to explain an extreme pessimism coupled with ecstatic praise, with hymns of ecstasy? Who knows whether this contradiction, so full of import, does not constitute the proper theme of this book. At any rate, I have always been hostile to the "dark" tradition in twentieth-century literature; its mockery, sarcasm, and profanations have seemed cheap to me when compared to the power of Evil that is within every man's experience. There is, I have detected, something inherently servile in the courting of various demonic and profane tendencies. Then why does Gombrowicz fail to shock me as well he ought—in the way, say, that I have been revulsed by what Alexander Wat once labeled as "striptease literature"?

Were I and others occasionally so charmed by Gombrowicz, so manipulated by him, made so attentive to the naked king's vestments as not to see that his works were, in fact, a rather hackneyed version of the nihilistic enterprise so universally in favor? Or was I simply a hypocrite, affecting admiration only because he and I were obliged to make common cause in the face of an émigré audience unable to comprehend us?

12

AND YET BRIX WAS WRONG, and I warned him that he was heading down a blind alley. He was intent on wringing a philosophy out of Gombrowicz like juice from a lemon and then serving it to us in a glass. Bitter to the taste, eh? And just as surely as the juice is intrinsic to the lemon, so, too, when we behold those stark and round yellow shapes ripening in folds of green, we are not likely to be thinking of their utility. How can Gombrowicz's thought be wrenched from his form, from the play of conventions, the laughter, the fun? I asked Brix what he took to be the nature of comedy; I asked him how many instances of comedy he could cite that would not violate his rather exalted notions of human dignity. Was it so charitable of Cervantes to amuse us at the expense of his demented knight? Or of Gogol to mock poor psychopaths like Akaky Akakievich, a man obsessed with love for his own overcoat? Laughter, if we accept Baudelaire's definition (*"De l'essence du rire"*), is akin to cruelty; it stems from a feeling of superiority, and even children's laughter, because children are "devils in embryo" (*"des Satans en herbe"*), is distinct from expressions of a strictly animal enjoyment. I had no illusions that I would persuade my doctoral student by invoking Baudelaire. To say, as the French poet does, that laughter is satanic and therefore profoundly human is to assume man's infinite inferiority relative to pure Being and man's infinite superiority in relation to animals. For Baudelaire, the purest, most sublime form of comedy was the grotesque, which comes of a feeling of superiority not of man over man but of man over Nature (and hence our own materiality). In tracing the origin of comedy to this fundamental cleavage—between the limitless aspirations of a creature in pursuit of its ideal image and the knowledge of its own foul carnality—Baudelaire went so far as to suggest that true comedy arose only with the advent of Christianity.

All right, I said, I won't press the point. But I then carried the argument a step further, no study of Gombrowicz can omit the name of Rabelais. Not only because Gombrowicz celebrated him as a writer who obeyed his own fancy as freely and uninhibitedly as a child peeing behind a tree. But also because Rabelais, the proclaimed spokesman of modern man's revolt against the Middle Ages, was the quintessence of a comic tradition that went back centuries, an argument advanced by Mikhail Bakhtin, whose book on Rabelais I recommended to Brix. By dividing man in half, from the waist up and the waist down—to speak in shorthand—the Middle Ages had manifested its true spirit. The more man aspired to the spiritual with his upper half, the more he laughed at the functions of the lower; hence that medieval ribaldry which exulted in words for stuffing the belly, copulating, and excreting, making the Rabelaisian hero, who floods the town with his pissing, a true child of the Middle Ages. This laughter—the laughter of the Mardi Gras, of carnival attractions—provided a release for energies contained during the liturgical year; the license permitted during Mardi Gras festivities, bold even by today's standards, could extend even to parodies of the Mass, of matrimonial and coronation rites. And not only was the sacred character of such rites not thereby diminished; it was enhanced, through parody, as if man had need of two masks—one solemn, the other comical. This duality is suggested by the bearing of medieval devils, whose horns and tails, whose drollery and vindictiveness, however grotesque, in no way detracted from their more serious role, that of evil spirits from the Gospels. That was why, I explained, my Roman Catholic soul was so little offended by Gombrowicz's profanations. If indeed they were meant as such; more likely the feasting and marital rites recur in his work for the simple reason that the wedding and the feast are highly formal rituals in the life of the civilization from which he came. I advised Brix to concentrate rather on Gombrowicz's celebration of the game, of the word, because Gombrowicz, although in many respects crippled, showed himself human in his capacity for creative festivity. To bear in mind that

Gombrowicz was a writer of the twentieth century, and to consider those qualities that set him apart from others, both kindred and rivals.

That was the point. My blood runs cold when I pronounce the words: the twentieth century. Vast territories of silence. In the din of language, in the millions of words per minute, in the excrescence of press, film, and television, there looms another, unmediated reality; and the first, which is mediated, cannot keep pace with the second, even less so than in the last century. The matter of which I speak is known to all who have felt awed by the passing of historical moments, situations, climates; of people and even of whole nations; and I was one of the many who, having lived it firsthand, regret they were able to capture so little of it. Its intractable nature (by now engrained in us) destroyed the idea of the novel as a "mirror in the roadway"; and instead of pursuing the truth of our epoch in a horde of "realistic" novels, which somehow repel by their falsity, we have recourse to the fable, poetic distillation, metonymy, or we shun art and literature altogether in favor of memoirs and nonfiction.

Given such an obstacle, the quality of a writer is measured by his resilience, by his bounce on the trampoline; and Gombrowicz, who was nurtured in the decades between the wars, would have plodded away at the realistic or psychological novel had he not vaulted into the realm of clowning. And, as in the case of Witkiewicz, that clowning act proved closer—even if unfaithful, abstract—to reality. Although Gombrowicz's philosophy left me unsatisfied, although its "difficulty" often intruded on its reception by the reader, I will grant it this much: thanks to that philosophy, Gombrowicz was able to surmount the fate of his comrades who remained glued to the flypaper. But am I not guilty of the same fallacy as Brix in severing the substance from the form, only here in reverse? Not really. The duality is there in Gombrowicz, so that while the tone of his writing is crystal-bright, vivacious, gleefully proclaiming its form, the tone of intellect is somber, grim. But then, was he not a child of the epoch? Still, when compared to such like-minded writers as Kafka, Beckett, Sartre, Ionesco, there is something in his inflection, a note of triumph and geniality, rooted perhaps in that sanity and measure which he held in such high regard, to set him apart. This may explain why I prefer his *Diaries* to his novels and plays, because there, in the *Diaries*, he reveals himself at his most imperious, his most openly and cheerfully pugnacious.

But if the writing and the thought are one, then Gombrowicz's thought is bright-bleak. Whenever he plays destroyer and ironist, he joins the company of writers who for decades have been letting their ears freeze just to spite their mommies, even as mommy—read the cosmos—ignored their tantrums.

Gombrowicz's "interhuman church" is premised on the notion that our actions derive not from within, from some mysterious center of our person, but in response to the behavior of others, in a specific and constantly shifting pattern. He called on the twentieth century as his witness, a century that has seen respectable persons, caught in a pattern of mutual agitation and incitement, become butchers. Given our lack of sovereignty, Gombrowicz counseled humility; instead of "I assume" or "I think," we should rather say, "It is assumed me," "It is thought me." Yet for centuries civilization has sustained itself through a belief in the uniqueness of the individual human soul as the source of our decisions; through the belief that the soul's good or evil intention would tip the scale on the Day of Judgment. Now it was no longer I who willed good or evil, because I was a captive of others. Alas, Gombrowicz's "interhuman church" seems an illustration of the theory of those behaviorists who proclaim the model society to be one of absolute slavery—a state that can be achieved when human animals, those statistical units making up the genus Homo, become so trained as to look upon slavery as freedom perfected. And if, in fact, we were to translate Gombrowicz's vision (so curiously vaunted by him) into the language of psychology, severing it from the living body of his work, we would be left with either a truism or an inauspicious draft.

For a long time I was perplexed by Gombrowicz, until William Blake came to my assistance. Blake, in his England at the turn of the last century, was appalled by the concept of a moral law equal in rigor to the strictness of Newtonian physics. A Christianity reduced to a set of rules, terrifying sufferers with the fires of Hell for the least transgression, seemed to him a monstrous parody, a prison guardhouse. Yet Blake, anxious as he was to liberate man from the tyranny of prohibitions (as well as of despots), was no cousin to Rousseau; no vision here of a return to the innocence of natural man. On the contrary, Blake's natural man *already* bore the mark of the Fall. But if each was accountable, if each was punishable and yet not punishable —for it was written: "Judge not, that ye be not judged"— where was the way out? The problem that engaged Blake would loom increasingly larger, in both range and magnitude, up to the present: the fact that the Particular has been consumed by the Universal. If man is but a fleeting fleck of foam on a wave, then he can be easily absolved, since what matters is the wave and not the foam. All of Blake's work is a violent assault on the Universal in defense of the "Minute Particulars." For what is sin if not a *state*, like zones of hot and cold, sunshine and cloud, traversed by a bird; and it is not human existence, unique no matter how much it shares in the sinful states of others, but those states which are to stand judgment and be delivered to the fires of Hell.

By invoking Blake, I was able to reconcile the Gombrowiczian idea of collective self-invention with the numerous statements of the preacher Gombrowicz, ardent defender of the individual. Whether or how he himself reconciled them is irrelevant here. His intention strikes me as having been genuinely moral ("Don't make a petty demon out of me"), aimed at the debunking of every sort of fanaticism through a revelation of the process by which it is born; and at making less severe our pronouncements of guilt, whether our own or that of others. That he conceived of everything as ritual, as the liturgy of people building an enclosed space through their own gestures, then however unmoved I am by his heroes and their rituals, I nonetheless value his attempt to show man as a creature of ritual. First there was Homo sapiens, later Homo faber and, above all, in our own time, Homo ritualis.

13

THE FIRST POEM to excite me, enthrall me, and enlist me in the service of incantation has left no words in my memory, only images and a certain aura. As a child of five—this would have been in Russia, around 1916—I would listen as they read to me from a large book, published, if I am not mistaken, by the Idzikowski Bookstore in Kiev and written, in all probability, by a poet in exile trying to earn a little money (shudder, colleagues of the feather, at the responsibility borne by the writer!). It was a tale in verse about an orphan who returns to his native village and finds it in ashes. Futilely he wanders through the weeds and nettles in search of his mother's grave, when suddenly he is entwined in the thorny arms of some blackberry bushes—the boy's mother, detaining him at her burial place. I gulped down my tears, and the melodrama has since become archetypal, traces of which I would go on discovering in myself in the years to come. The things read early in life remain opaque, only faintly illumined. Literally, too, as during those dark Lithuanian winters when, as a boy of eight or nine, in the flicker of a home-made candle and to the whirr of black cockroaches teeming in the corners, I would read anything I could lay my hands on—annuals bearing such titles as *A Children's Companion, Gleanings, Family Nights, A Literary Feast*. The only family atlas bore an imprint from the mid-nineteenth century—Africa still showed a big blank spot in the middle. A child rummages indiscriminately for the stuff, the particulars of fate, in kitschy sentimental romances, in adaptations of boys' and girls' classics, in illustrateds; but what most roused my appetite were bound periodicals from around the year 1840 (Polish? French?), with their colored woodcuts of exotic plants and animals, savages presented in all their sumptuous nakedness, side by side with ladies' gowns that might have been lifted from a fashion journal. I have the sensation of standing before a curtain, of parting it, only to stand before another, equally opaque curtain, yielding only the vaguest outlines and the scent of mystery: I am unable to name the effect on me of those striated Negroid bodies, of those sky-blue crinolines and soft pink ribbons, all bathed in the effluvia of musty, rust-stained pages. There is my ancestry, there among titles inscribed on the spines of volumes that are rarities today, works such as Strumiłło's *Gardens of the North,* Giżycki's *An Economic-Technical Guide to a Herbarium,* a first edition (as now seems clear to me) of Mickiewicz's *Ballads and Romances.* It would be only too easy, in retrospect, to see a pattern at work here, but as any genealogy would have to note also the influence of James Fenimore Cooper, Mayne Reid, and later, of Polish Romantic poetry, the effort seems hardly worth the risk. Indeed, I can no longer tell whether at the time, as an adolescent in Wilno, I was a reader of, or a participant in, Słowacki's *An Hour of Thought*—caused, no doubt, by my associations with Jaszuny, to whose railway station I used to travel in a one-horse wagon from Raudonka (from the Lithuanian *raudonas*—red), situated between the Lithuanian village of Mariampol and the Byelorussian village of Czernica. But the reasons why I am part of *An Hour of Thought,* why I feel almost a contemporary of Słowacki, that Wilno dreamer "erecting his palaces on the books of Swedenborg," lie deeper.

For some, reading and writing are a passion, The Way, in the sense in which the word is used by the Taoists. Why that is so is a subject worthy of a separate study. There is a species of people who feel the compulsion more than others, people for whom reality is too painful as long as it remains anarchic, untrappable, and who feel continually obliged to give it order, a language. The invention of the printing press did not beget this breed. The recitation of the office and of litanies, Gregorian chant, the daily reading of the breviary and the lives of the saints provided ample nourishment—or what I would call an "ordering rhythm"—for both the clergy and much of the laity. Among the clergy and members of religious orders, there were doubtless many who would have felt more comfortable as laymen, whereas the truly chosen would probably have found it hard to imagine any other life for themselves. In our century, the conduct of this tribe is a matter of personal and painstaking discovery; yoga manuals may abound, but try to find a practical guide to the sort of discipline required of all who have been chosen independently of their will. Today I look upon the whole of my conscious life as a series of revolts against coercion. These revolts have ended in a return to a strict, even monastic regimen. Let me add that this category, that of people given to verbal incantation, is introduced not as a concession to what is termed the "psychology of art"; it is not coincident with the category of "poets" and "artists."

Language. After having spent several decades among foreigners, my ear's fidelity to Polish not only has not slackened but—so it seems to me—registers the language even more cleanly. It is doubtful whether the books we read in foreign languages can affect our own internal rhythm, one of the many rhythmic variants afforded by our native tongue. Admittedly, my Polish was continually subverted by the other languages heard around me, and possibly my own "rhythm" has been shaped through defiance. Not to mention that my childhood Polish was quite idiosyncratic, both lexically and accentually, being layered with Lithuanian and Byelorussian borrowings. And my Russian? Its acquisition is still a mystery, most likely picked up in Russia, not an acquired language. And then seven years of Latin in school. Two forceful languages, Russian and Latin, both encouraging emulation through their syntactic rigor and classicizing tendencies. French, acquired in my last years at school, passably competent, was to become the language of my intellectual training, though initially I was exposed to its formal aspect—my first exercises in versification (rather skilled, judging by what I can remember of them) were done under the sign of Joachim du Bellay. A parenthetic remark: The substandard nature of the region's vernacular, both urban and rural, a common phenomenon in ethnically mixed regions, may also have had a "Latinizing" effect on my Polish.

By the time I learned English during the war years, my "rhythm" was already fixed, and although I may have borrowed this or that from English poetry, of which I was then getting my first taste, the extent of that borrowing was minimal and did not run very deep. When I later had occasion to translate that poetry into Polish, people imputed various affiliations, all nonexistent—this despite my conviction that things read in a foreign language are appropriated in a purely intellectual way, even when the glass through which we look at foreign lines is pristinely transparent.

A knowledge of several foreign languages can be a cause for silently lamenting the inadequacy of language in general. When we hesitate to use a word native to us, our memory may suggest another, one more precise or felicitous, from a foreign language. The temptation to cultivate an imaginary, composite dialect then becomes very real. Yet the very fear of yielding to temptation may compel us to exercise an even stricter control over our native tongue.

As one directly descended from Mickiewicz, as one raised on all sorts of Romantic gimcrack, I can readily concur with Stanisław Brzozowski when he says, in his *Studies on the Crisis of European Culture*, that the entire period from the eighteenth century to the Moderna is deserving of one name: Romanticism. Today, basing my judgment on abundant observations of the postwar era, I am more inclined to speak of a "crisis" that has been under way for the past couple of centuries, with no end in sight. It is to this crisis, to the tapping of its roots, that my knowledge of foreign languages has been applied.

By reading the poets? Yes and no. To compare texts of French, English, Polish, and Russian Romantic poetry in the original is to discover that the term "Romanticism" signifies in each a different verbal medium. A child, on his first encounter with rhymed poetry of the sort written not for children but for adults, senses something artificial about it, a kind of verbal gushing forth; later he is taught that it is something worthy of veneration. For each literary language there is a corresponding level of artificiality; the smaller the distance between the sense and the signs— the closer the "poetic" speech to the vernacular, in other words—the lower the level; whereas the greater the distance, the higher the level. Only exceptional poets like Mickiewicz knew how to raise the vernacular to the poetic. For a long time I found Słowacki comical, and let's face it, though much of him will endure, he is excessively literary, even if that literariness went unnoticed by generations blinded by his magic. So, for reasons I would not elaborate on here, Shelley's "level of artificiality" is higher than Słowacki's, as is that of Coleridge, Keats, and even Wordsworth, that most "natural" of poets. Byron, so revered in Slavic lands, will survive through his legend—on condition that he is read in translation. Among the French, the level of artificiality, though qualitatively different because of the inheritance of classicism, is no less high, and that goes for Victor Hugo as much as for Lamartine, Musset, and de Vigny. Younger generations, immune to the magic, are repelled by the artificiality of language, all the more must a foreign reader be repelled; for me, as well, reading that kind of poetry was always a chore. My resistance to foreign influence is worth stressing—first, so no one will doubt that

I am most of all indebted to the poetry of my native tongue; and second, so that my weakness for Blake will be judged an exception and the extraliterary reasons for it made evident.

14

FOR A SLAVISTS' CONFERENCE held in Atlanta, one of whose sections was devoted to a panel discussion of Dostoevsky's religious thought, I prepared a short paper which—I now realize—belongs to the present narrative. My strategy, I might as well confess, is to keep adding new pebbles to the mosaic until a definite pattern begins to form, one in which the present chapter will be seen to have its place. Addressed to an audience of specialists, it has the disadvantage of containing a number of abbreviated thoughts, though perhaps I will have a chance to expand here and there.

Dostoevsky and the Religious Imagination of the West

1. Dostoevsky's religious thought marks a critical moment in the history of the only civilization that has conquered the entire planet Earth. Originally confined to a small Western European peninsula, that civilization elaborated its philosophy and science by modifying concepts of Christian theology. Since the eighteenth century, it has turned openly against its Christian sources.

2. Russia of the nineteenth century cannot be considered an integral part of that civilization, but Russian literature, a product of the educated, was a mutation of its Western counterpart. And no French, English, or German novelist achieved what was achieved by Dostoevsky, who made use of fiction to render the fundamental antinomy facing modern man. This raises the question of the cultural roles of the center and the peripheries, respectively.

3. Owing to their specific social structure, educated Russians assimilated in a few decades ideas that had taken two or three centuries to mature in the West. As with those diseases that remain harmless for natives but become lethal when transplanted abroad, the dilemma—philosophy and science versus religion—acquired an exceptional virulence in Russian minds. Thus, while the extreme boldness of Friedrich Nietzsche may be ascribed to his personal isolation and incurable illness, Dostoevsky's daring adheres to a certain cultural pattern. Within that pattern, the presence of an Orthodox Christian peasantry was a serious complicating factor.

4. It is strange now, nearly a hundred years after his death, to read a reformulation of the Dostoevskian dilemma by a Nobel Prize winner, the geneticist Jacques Monod, a man of no religious inclinations whatever. In *Chance and Necessity*, he says:

> No society before ours was ever rent by contradictions so agonizing. In both primitive and classical cultures the animistic tradition saw knowledge and values stemming from the same source. For the first time in history a civilization is trying to shape itself while clinging desperately to the animistic tradition to justify its values, and at the same time abandoning it as the source of knowledge, of *truth*.

Another quotation:

> Just as an initial "choice" in the biological evolution of a species can be binding upon its entire future, so the choice of scientific practice, an unconscious choice in the beginning, has launched the evolution of culture on a one-way path; onto a track which nineteenth-century scientism saw leading infallibly upward to an empyrean noon hour for mankind, whereas what we see opening before us today is an abyss of darkness.

5. In 1875, Dostoevsky noted: "Science in our century refutes everything formerly held in regard. Your every sin has been brought about by your unsatisfied needs, which are completely natural and therefore must be satisfied. A radical refutation of Christianity and its morality. Christ was not acquainted with science, they say" (*The Unpublished Dostoevsky: Diaries and Notebooks 1860–81*, Vol. II, trans. by A. Boyer and C. Proffer). Earlier, in his famous letter of 1854 to Fonvizina, Dostoevsky says: "Had I to choose between Christ and truth, I would choose Christ." A desperate statement, of far-reaching implications. I would advance the thesis that Dostoevsky's religious thought distills the leading Western controversy of the seventeenth and eighteenth centuries. At that time the assault on religion in the name of so-called objective truth entailed a threefold negation: the denial of Original Sin, the rejection of the Incarnation, and the secularization of Christian eschatology. Western defenders of the Christian religion who reacted to the assault used tactics similar to those used later by Dostoevsky.

6. The denial of Original Sin was predicated upon the good and reasonable nature of man. The defenders of Christianity stressed, on the contrary, the utter misery of

man, and identified the Fall with the victory of Self-love, which causes man infinite anguish. This was the line taken by Blaise Pascal ("*Le moi est haïssable*"). This was also the line taken by two great visionaries of the eighteenth century, Emanuel Swedenborg and William Blake. Swedenborg found the origin of *cosmic* Evil in man's *proprium*; Blake fixed on the universe as the Fall and on the "spectral" character of the Selfhood. Dostoevsky's *Notes from the Underground* is a culmination of the same line.

7. The Incarnation of God into man can be expressed only in the language of symbol and myth. The habit of relying on a language which appeals to what is presumed to be self-evident made the Incarnation utterly incomprehensible. Moreover, the vision of innumerable planets whirling in an absolute, Newtonian space had challenged the assumption of the special privilege granted by God to one of them. While God the Father was turned into an abstraction by the Deists, the "reasonable" approach to Christianity cast Jesus as a preacher and, at best, an ethical ideal. That is why the Christian faith, always strongly anthropocentric, searched for a new vision to compete with the new, atheistic idea of the Man-god who was to be his own redeemer. In the eighteenth century an extraordinary concept makes its appearance, one possibly related to that of the Adam Kadmon, the primordial, pre-cosmic man of the Cabala. For Swedenborg, God in Heaven has a *human* form; Christ's humanity is thus a perfect fulfillment of the Godhead. "The Human Form Divine" and the God-man as the only God were taken from Swedenborg by William Blake. For a while these two antithetical concepts—Divine Humanity and Human Divinity—converged, to the extent that today some scholars erroneously interpret Blake as a kind of poetic Hegel.

Dostoevsky was, so to speak, deprived of God the Father,

and his only hope was to cling to Christ. The opposition of the Man-god to the God-man is neatly drawn in his work and exemplified by his biography. From a belief in the Man-god held at the time of his belonging to the Petrashevsky circle, he progressed to a belief in the God-man. Yet he was never able to resolve the contradiction contained in his statement on the choice between Christ and truth.

8. The idea of three stages in the history of man—before the Fall, after the Fall, and finally, the restored harmony of the Kingdom—was borrowed from the Bible by secular philosophers of the eighteenth century and transmuted into the idea of an immanent, progressive movement. The number 3 was preserved. This dynamism, in turn, inspired new versions of Christian historiosophy. In the late eighteenth and early nineteenth centuries, many doctrines appear, all focusing on the Last Judgment and on the imminent advent of the third era, the era of the Spirit. Dostoevsky (as we know from *The Unpublished Dostoevsky*) was also a believer in the three stages: (*a*) before civilization, (*b*) civilization, i.e., the intermediary stage, and (*c*) after civilization, a final perfect harmony. Eschatology was his passion and obsession. The immediate future horrified him. We should take him seriously when he records in his notebooks: "All depends on the next century" (*"Vsyo v budushchem stoletii"*). We should also heed the testimony of O. Pochinkovskaya, who worked with him in the editorial office of *The Citizen* in 1873: "He struck the table with his fist so that I started, and raising his voice, exclaimed like a mullah in his minaret: The Antichrist is coming! Coming! And the end of the world is near, nearer than is believed."

9. Why, as related by Nadezhda Mandelstam in her *Hope Abandoned*, did Anna Akhmatova call Dostoevsky a

"heresiarch"? His heresy derived from his love of Russia and his concern for the future of Christianity. If educated Russians telescoped the intellectual developments of several Western European centuries into a few decades, they also, it would seem, outstripped the West and, through the mouth of Dostoevsky, posited a dilemma that was to be discovered by the West only much later. And that dilemma was: either social justice at the price of terror, lies, and slavery, or freedom, unbearable because demanded by an absent God and a non-intervening Christ, as stated in the *Legend of the Grand Inquisitor*. Dostoevsky was convinced that all of Western civilization would choose a belief in *man* as redeemer and, consequently, finish in slavery. Did he not call the Pope a leader of communism? But he also observed the rejection of Christianity by the Russian Westernized intelligentsia. Cornered, he sought a solution to a situation which he himself judged to be irresolvable. He was seduced by his passion for eschatology and placed his faith in the Christian Russian peasantry as the only hope for mankind. His heresy, that of the Russian Christ, meant that while he resisted all other temptations to make things easier for himself, he could not resist the messianic-nationalistic temptation.

10. Today, however, we cannot treat Dostoevsky's religious thought as a relic of the past. He has been vindicated by the grave consequences of the antinomy between science and the world of values. What in his time was regarded as an objective, scientific truth has often revealed its hidden metaphysical premises; and our civilization seems to be confronted by an option not between faith and reason but between two sets of values, disguised or not. Perhaps biologists such as Jacques Monod go too far when they postulate that the "animist tradition" forms part of the genetic code of our species. Yet even if we ignore

genetics, the experience of the twentieth century seems to corroborate the equation made by Dostoevsky in the *Legend of the Grand Inquisitor*. Grim. The equation boils down to this: try as he may, man has no alternative but to choose between God and the devil.

15

THE TEXT JUST CITED is dense enough that every statement might stand comment. I shall limit myself to only a few. By quoting Jacques Monod, who was awarded the Nobel Prize for his discovery of DNA, I do not mean to imply that I am competent in molecular ontogenesis and other related disciplines. I have quoted him because seldom has a scientific mind stood for so radical a rejection of everything that cannot be scientifically verified. By "animism" Monod means the projection of our human need for order and design, a function of our nervous system, onto a Nature governed entirely by chance and necessity, whereby we surrender to the "anthropocentric illusion." In the "animistic tradition" he places all religions as well as those systems premised on a "providential" evolution, such as dialectical materialism and Teilhardism. In the last chapter of his book, *Chance and Necessity*, Monod, a rigorous materialist, indulges in a scientific moralizing, clearly contradicting himself or perhaps inadvertently giving credence to his own thesis that the need for values is genetically prescribed. But this is somewhat peripheral to my theme.

Dostoevsky—forced to choose between Christ and truth. Something of a breakthrough, and not quite the same as the age-old quarrel between faith and reason. Those who endowed reason with diabolical attributes elected faith as the repository of truth ("I am the way, the truth, and the life" [John 14:6]). Others (Simone Weil, for example), whose contribution is not to be ignored, denied that there was, or ever could be, a conflict between a belief in Christ and the evidence of rational inquiry (assuming a conscientious mind, in the sense of truth-loving). The "truth" which Dostoevsky guarded against is synonymous with Monod's "scientific truth"; namely, the truth which holds that ascribing a benign will to the universe, whether today or tomorrow, is an illusion—leaving man alone, with a need of the heart which cries "No!" to the unfeeling machine that levels like a steamroller every living thing. The comparison of Nature to a machine, one frequently invoked by Dostoevsky, corresponds to Monod's image of biological organisms as living machines, which, thanks to a genetic instruction, are capable of duplicating themselves. Dostoevsky was shocked by Holbein's painting, which he had seen in Basel, because of that artist's naturalistic rendering of the buried Christ as a cadaver. Two of Dostoevsky's intellectual *raisonneurs*, Ippolit Terentiev in *The Idiot* and Kirilov in *The Possessed*, speak obsessively of Nature's triumph over the most priceless Being ever born on Earth: if such a man was deluded in prophesying his own resurrection, then the world was indeed a "devil's vaudeville" bereft of any values.

The *Notes from the Underground* and the *Legend of the Grand Inquisitor* are cited because they are the quintessence of Dostoevsky's religious thought and rank among the great philosophical works. The narrator of the first wants to lay bare the truth, defined as both mathematically certain (two times two equals four) and grim. His sarcasm directed at contemporaries like Chernyshevsky, who believed in a "crystal palace" erected on the foundation of man's innate self-interest, is akin to the sarcasm of a Monod who, some hundred years later, on the strength of biological evidence, debunked the notion of a beneficent, preordained fate for the human race. For Dostoevsky, individual will (egoism) and self-will (license) are destructive forces that delight in cruelty. At the same time, every individual wills *to be*, yet the moment an individual is resigned to the truth, when he says "That's life," two times two equals four, then he must accept that he is *not*. Hence the affliction of the riven mind. "I think, therefore I am" becomes "I think (can an objective mind think?), therefore I am not"—which is to say, I accept that I am a statistic, a supererogatory number. So the narrator declares "No!" to the cosmic order, but because he lacks anything with which to refute that order, the *Notes* become, finally, an endorsement of the "truth." The censors deleted the chapter in which Dostoevsky sought to balance the argument. Of its substance we know nothing except that the author argued as a Christian. He never restored the chapter in the book edition, and it has been irretrievably lost.

The *Notes* are so freighted with themes that by giving prominence to only one of them, however central, I might be accused of being arbitrarily selective. The strategy is nonetheless valid when, as in this case, that theme stands at the very core. The same holds for the *Legend of the Grand Inquisitor*, which can be reduced to the question: Who was right—the Christ tempted in the desert, or his tempter? The Legend, Ivan's parable (hence to be judged within the context of *The Brothers Karamazov*), answers that question: the Prince of this World, the Spirit of the Earth, was right. Ivan, it will be recalled, cannot admit to God the Father's providential rule, since Nature, a machine governed by its own necessities, is morally untenable.

Only Christ, if He was the Son of God, can alter the natural course of things. But Christ refused to turn stones into bread, by which refusal he symbolically surrendered to earthly powers the task of ministering to the hungry. He refused to exercise His divine authority by hurling himself from the pinnacle, and thus refute the inevitable consequence, that of physical destruction. He refused power over earthly kingdoms, even though He might have turned it to man's benefit. Ivan's parable betrays ancient Manichaean elements: the belief that God the Father is responsible for the suffering of living matter; that because He is something of an inferior demiurge His existence or nonexistence is immaterial. This leaves only the God of Light to roam the earth—but, alas, He too refuses to wield the scepter. The Grand Inquisitor is therefore justified in organizing a society of children, in professing the need for deception (which is the substance of Ivan's dream, the dream of a Russian intellectual, with himself cast as dictator). The Grand Inquisitor abides with his secret and with his private suffering: deliberately, out of human compassion, he has chosen to collaborate with the devil, because "objective" truth is on the side of evil.

Why, in Dostoevsky, is "objective" truth—the truth of science, the only truth acknowledged by Monod and his predecessors—endowed with diabolical properties? The Underground Man flouts the scientist's grandiose certitude, and even if two times two equals four, he says: I will have none of it. A reality borne in upon man as inviolable necessity is, by human standards, unacceptable. Everything in us rebels against existence-as-pain, against death. The Underground Man is no more a cynic or egoist than is Ivan Karamazov, who commiserates with the suffering of children; his protest against the proposition "two times two equals four" is tantamount to Ivan's famous declaration: "I give back my entrance ticket." Once we cease to view creation as the work of a good God, we are left with few alternatives. Either we remain underground and chew our nails, or we become a Grand Inquisitor to better organize society.

In *The Brothers Karamazov*, Dostoevsky failed to counterbalance Ivan's argument, and I am not alone in that judgment. This view is shared by the distinguished Russian mind, Lev Shestov, to whom my interpretation is greatly indebted. It would appear that Dostoevsky's last great novel, admittedly only its first volume, suffers at the expense of its author's political-religious heresy. It culminated, as is customary among the Slavs, in messianism, in a belief in a collective redeemer, as if it had not been messianists who sentenced Christ to death ("It is expedient for us, that one man should die for the people, and that the whole nation perish not" [John 11:50]).

The Western religious mind of the seventeenth and eighteenth centuries. Of relevance here are not concepts so much as images of the cosmos, which is why I prefer to speak of the religious *imagination*. The role of science in shaping the imagination was immense, that of post-Tridentine Catholicism rather negligible; and it is perhaps appropriate that I cite, among Catholics, the mathematician Pascal. In the Age of Enlightenment, that frontier where the religious and scientific imagination skirmished was represented by various forms of nondenominational religion, by "mystical lodges" as well as by Voltairian lodges—by that whole movement summarized by the French scholar Viatte as *"les sources occultes du romantisme."* The names of Swedenborg and Blake also belong here.

I might add that the concept of Godmanhood, so crucial

to Swedenborg and Blake, was not so far removed from the Christian tradition. At Chartres, on a statue showing the creation of Adam, God bears Christ's face and fashions Adam from clay in His own image and likeness.

16

THE PRECEDING CHAPTERS are no more than background to the main task at hand, which is the story of a man who discovered a treasure in a field and who kept it buried there after failing to turn its riches to profit. That man was myself, but the story of my discovery is indebted to my distant cousin, Oscar Władysław Miłosz, who wrote under the name of O. V. de L. Milosz. He was born in 1877, died in the spring of 1939—however, let us begin not with his biography but with his place in French literature today. From the bibliographies, both of his work and of the works on him, it is evident that even in his lifetime he was surrounded by an impressive circle of admirers. This is attested by the appearance shortly after his death, in the adverse conditions of the war, of a number of literary journals, among them *Poésie 42*, published in Lyons, of which he was the featured poet. A circle impressive not so much for its size as for its quality, for the fervor of its commitment. One who belonged to that circle was Armand Godoy, Swiss banker, amateur poet, a Milosz devotee and benefactor, and author of the pioneering study, *Milosz, poète de l'amour*. In Lausanne, during the war, Godoy launched the first collected edition of his idol's work, which, though not definitive (the project was subsequently realized by the Parisian publisher, André Silvaire), nonetheless gathered together the major work. And even though the Oscar Milosz cult was promoted by such influential Parisian men of letters as Jean Cassou, the loyal friend of his youth; even though my namesake left his mark in the literary-social chronicles as a habitué of the famous salon of the American Natalie Clifford Barney—every time his fame appeared to gather momentum, a new set of circumstances arose to block it, followed by yet another groundswell, and so on, as if a vigilant fate had forsworn granting him wider renown. If he was never among those poets hoisted to fame by the elevator of politics, neither was he counted among the exponents of any "movements" or trends, among those whose names were treated like playing chips and hence always on display. Even outsiders like St.-John Perse could strike a familiar chord, whereas no one knew quite what to make of my cousin.

I was a spectator to one of these groundswells in the late fifties. To be paid the following tribute by a Parisian critic (André Blanchet in *Etudes*, 1958) is no trifling matter:

> In 1939, barely twenty years ago, a stranger was buried in the Fontainebleau cemetery: one of the truest, loftiest poets ever to write in our tongue or in any other tongue. One of the most demanding of poets, and one of the most dismal failures. But it was a failure worthy of Nerval and Baudelaire, of Rimbaud and Verlaine. A failure worthy of Van Gogh. Forgive us, Milosz. You are one of those whom France ignores unto their dying breath, only to exult later in their careers, which are the more poignant for being tragically neglected; of those to whose voices she remains deaf while they are alive and to which she never ceases to attend later.

It was around this time that the Théâtre des Champs-Elysées staged Milosz's mystery play *Miguel Mañara*, and this production, successful enough to enjoy a run of a dozen or so performances, proved only that Paris was no place for such a poet. Shrill, vulgar, conceived rather as a vehicle for a theater idol (despite an avant-garde mise-en-scène), the staging aroused considerable skepticism as to a kind of sensitivity, or what passes for sensitivity, in our time. I still could recall Tadeusz Byrski's dignified Polish version, performed for the radio series "Theater of the Imagination" in Wilno before the war, and Juliusz Osterwa's Warsaw reading in the spring of 1939. By contrast, the Paris staging showed an utter inconsistency of language and delivery, as if the author, with his exquisite command of French, had written only a pseudo-French, as if he were suppressing another language, a sort of esoteric, hieratical Latin. The production only made apparent that the use to which he put language would find few actors capable of matching his special tone. The same applied to recitations of his verse, at least those I was able to hear on French radio and television and on recordings; to judge by these readings, few would have granted him major stature.

Despite the fact that two composers have written operatic scores for *Miguel Mañara*; despite the commercial success enjoyed by a new edition of his novel *L'Amoureuse Initiation*; despite all the foreign translations of his poetry— Milosz remains, more or less, what he was at the time of his death: a writer neither acclaimed nor forgotten.* A curious instance. There have been studies devoted to him, there is a society in Paris called La Société des Amis de Milosz

---

* *Fourteen Poems* by O.V. de L. Milosz, translated by Kenneth Rexroth, is now available (Copper Canyon Press, Port Townsend, Washington, 1984). See, also, copyright page for Lindisfarne Press edition of work by Oscar Milosz in English.

which publishes its own bulletin, there is even a tiny square in Fontainebleau that bears his name; yet, for all that, he remains the property of a closed circle. And not even it can agree on which of his works is more praiseworthy. Among the many reasons for his persistent neglect, not least is the multifaceted character of the work itself, the diversity of genres. The early poetry still finds its occasional admirers, yet those for whom he stands as one of the great French poets, and not merely of this century, point to the poetry written during his brief period of maturity, before he "fell silent." One novel. One stage play in verse, *Miguel Mañara*, plus two other poetic dramas, both of dubious stageability. And, finally, the work produced during the last decade or so of his life: those writings he called "metaphysical poems," in prose—hugely obscure and recondite—and Biblical exegeses, which prompted speculation that their author was suffering from a mental disorder. Yet these same "metaphysical poems" are a prime source for students of his philosophy. And if there were those who considered him "a great Catholic poet," why was his name omitted from the Catholic encyclopedias, while a generous article was consecrated to him in the Encyclopedia Judaica? A cabalist? A Catholic? Who, indeed, was he?

Nor was the matter of author's rights left untouched by adversity. Oscar Milosz died suddenly of a heart attack, without a will. I have reason to suspect that he would have appointed myself or one of his French acquaintances as his executor. His only legal heirs, by reason of kinship, were Adam Milosz and his sister, Emilia, residents of Warsaw and descended from the Druja side of the family, with which he had no personal contact. They, ironically, were made his literary executors. After the war I suggested that I be given executory powers; suspicious, always resentful of the Samogitian branch, and doubly so of me, a leftist, they preferred to settle the matter in their own fashion. So it happened that a certain Pole in Paris fell heir to the estate, admittedly modest in terms of worldly property, consisting of a small house in Fontainebleau and a library, but decisive with regard to the disposition of author's rights. To demonstrate how this affected the fate of his books would be to repeat various incriminating and vindictive charges made by members of the French publishing community; by their account, the effect was calamitous.

Those who have studied the secondary literature—dissertations on Milosz appear not only in France but in the French departments of American universities—must infer that if fate has taken such pains to shelter the work of this writer, it has been for one reason only: to ban him from a century he could not tolerate. Ultimately, he himself was to blame for his own neglect: from the very beginning, he refused to be cast as a symbol of the age, as an Apollinaire, Breton, or Michaux. Yet an absence of notoriety does not mean a lack of scholarly interest; indeed, there is a wealth of literary documentation on him, including articles, published correspondence, fragments of poems, multiple drafts, biographical material, not to speak of monographs.

I must have been thirteen when I read my first Milosz poem, in Polish—a copy of his *Selected Poems* (in Bronisława Ostrowska's translation, published in 1919) stood on the shelves of our flat in Wilno. The volume contained, among other things, *Miguel Mañara*, the first drama in verse, aside from *Forefathers' Eve*, which did not move me to laughter in the way that Słowacki's did. This marked the beginning of an acquaintance, of a personal as much as of a literary nature, that would be nurtured over many decades. Nor has my interest faded with his passing, now so distant in time, as I have kept up with all the publications in "Miloszology." My vivid recollection of the man and of our conversations, together with what I know of his native region, to which few Western scholars have access, would qualify me to add yet another literary-historical study to the list, yet such has never been my desire.

Two well-documented monographs have appeared since I took up residence in California. At the Sorbonne, a young scholar, Jacques Buge, submitted a dissertation which was later published, in 1963, under the title *Milosz, en quête du divin* (*Milosz, in Quest of the Divine*). In 1960, André Lebois, an established scholar of the older generation, published his *L'Oeuvre de Milosz*. At one time I tried to locate a dissertation written in French by an American, Stanley Guise, but it was never published, and I was never able to get a photocopy. Finally, while on holiday in Paris, I settled into one of the Sorbonne Library's alcoves (dust dating back three hundred years, the creak of wooden stairs) and read it from cover to cover. Entitled *La sensibilité ésotérique de Milosz*, it is essentially a collection of unpublished correspondence and marginalia from the poet's own private library, the originals of which are stored in the Collection Doucet, an archive devoted to twentieth-century poets and housed in a wing of that least twentieth-century of institutions, the Bibliothèque Sainte Geneviève.

Not only has my living in America not diverted me from my namesake's spiritual legacy, but it has even intensified my interest, giving me a new perspective with which to view many facts of his biography and many of his hitherto arcane pronouncements. Nor could I abstain from contributing something to Miloszology. Recalling Oscar Milosz's friendship with Christian Gauss, a once prominent Princeton dean and secretly a poet, I came to discover in the Princeton University Library (where the former dean's papers are stored) some nineteen letters, dating from 1900 to 1930, addressed by Milosz to Gauss. They had met as students in Paris in 1899, and what a melancholy portrait of a man, of that whole age known as la Belle Epoque, is evoked by those letters!

Finally—why not admit it—I have even translated several of Milosz's works, namely, those to which he himself gave prime importance—not into Polish but into English. What moved me to translate them? And why not into Polish? Indeed, what could have inspired me to such diligence in the first place? Was it because we bore the same surname? Sentimentality? Family snobbery? What follows should provide an answer.

17

WHEN I WAS A STUDENT, my classmates used to tease me about "the uncle in Paris"; the Student Puppet Theater even featured a puppet, bearing my likeness, that sang of "Uncle Oscar of the generous checkbook." Having a cousin, however distant, basking in the glamour of a city that by force of habit was still renowned as the capital of the world must have lent me a snobbish air. That awe for everything Western, so indigenous to both Sarmatian tribes, to Poles and Russians, could take many forms. Admittedly, among the Poles, that awe was tempered by a mocking contempt for German pedantry and for the Germans generally, with the result that their love of the West has traditionally been more Italian- and later French-oriented, so that when we were taught that the greatest Polish poetry was born in Paris, it was naturally taken for granted. Wilno, in all frankness, belonged to the provinces, a refuge of nineteenth-century customs and attitudes, and in rebelling against parochialism, in courting the New in every domain, I suffered from the acute snobbery of a provincial fop. I was even awed by Warsaw, though it was an awe mixed with terror, as of a Babylon. I was to be severely punished for that snobbery, condemned to the life of an émigré from the time I left Wilno, being gradually driven westward, all the way to the Wild West.

But there is another kind of snobbery to be addressed, and here again I summon Gombrowicz to my aid. To understand Polish culture one must take note of certain "class divisions," though not in the modern sense of the term. Mickiewicz's *Pan Tadeusz* presents a manorial society in all its class distinctions, a fabric made even more intricate by events of the ensuing hundred years. The landscape of *Pan Tadeusz* is Lithuanian, while the changes wreaked by national conflicts, impoverishment of the gentry, etc., only served to make that region even more insulated. In my province the "landed gentry" was much less prominent than, for instance, in the Kujawy and Sandomierz districts, where it was merging not so much with the white-collar as with the entrepreneurial class, with the owners of factories and apartment houses. Compared to Gombrowicz, by birth my social superior twice removed, the product of excellent breeding and so at ease in good society, I was a barbarian.

His affectations of genteel snobbery, it would appear, concealed a genuine snobbery, or a regret for not having been even "better born." Here, care must be taken to distinguish between origin and ancestry, even if these are sometimes confused. In Gombrowicz's milieu, to be called "a person of distinction" meant that you were a person of pedigree. The concept of pedigree was wholly foreign to me, and its absence in Lithuania, a country not otherwise neglectful of ancestry, is sociologically significant. As a democrat, I was slightly ashamed of my gentry stock (the squires had been exploiters). Social climbing? From home I had inherited the notion that I was of fitting and sufficiently high birth. No one whom I knew aspired to higher station. Of the Miloszes from Druja and Czereja—of those, in other words, who had emigrated to Byelorussia and who were not exactly immune to aristocratic airs—it was sarcastically said that wealth had made them swellheaded.

Still, I considered myself "better born" than Gombrowicz. For the simple reason that he was born in an inferior country. Once, in Vence, I reminded him that he came from central Poland. It was a devastating thrust. The knight Gombrowicz swayed in the saddle and was nearly unhorsed, but at the last moment he parried the blow, declaring that, on the contrary, his family had sprung from Samogitia, from the shores of my native Niewiaża, and that it was not until his grandfather's time, until after the 1863 uprising, that the family had emigrated.

If Gombrowicz had ever personally laid eyes on the Niewiaża Valley, he might have taken even greater pride in his ancestry. Its image, as immortalized by the pen of Father Ludwik Jucewicz in the first half of the last century, is known to every Lithuanian from his school reader (even if the text is a translation from the Polish). The Niewiaża Valley is revered as the heart of Lithuania, as its most idyllic district, and deservedly so. I shall never revisit that landscape, never verify the changes worked by time. The summers there were distinctive for the dark lush foliage of the parks along the river slopes, some so steeply inclined they reached down to the shoreline, and the white manor houses were spaced every few kilometers apart, each with its own riverside park, largely of ancient lindens, ash, and fir. Sometimes two manors and their parks would be situated so that they faced one another across the river; so, for example, the park in my native Šeteiniai overlooked Kalnoberże on the other side, once the property of Minister Stolypin before the First World War (I am not in the least surprised that he took such a liking to one of the Empire's loveliest provinces).

Rather than expand on the disparity between origin and birth, it will be enough to give a brief sketch of one such manor, typical of those along the Niewiaża, this one from my own district and even neighborhood. The time would have been 1925, a year in which I spent the summer there. Living on this particular manor were three of the Wojnowski clan. It was said that after the passing of the mother, Mrs. Wojnowski, the estate had gone to rack and ruin; and the rickety porch chairs, the shoddy upkeep, the calashes and plows parked in front of the house—showing to what extent the distinction between "manorial" and "agrarian" had become blurred—testified eloquently to its decline. Of the three sons, all confirmed bachelors, one was mildly demented, which was of little note in a region that had always abounded in eccentrics. The second, a gentle, slightly bovine man, ran the farm, which the Lithuanian Land Reform had trimmed to a property of modest size. What the third, a burly Romeo type, did, I could not say, only that he hung about the district capital in Kovno, mainly to wrangle with the bureaucrats. Domestics were few—one girl, in fact, rather free and bossy by the looks of it, who used to set the table with chipped plates and bent spoons. Later, as I recall, the farm's proprietor married an energetic woman of gentry stock and much was changed. But if the Wojnowskis were in no way inferior to Gombrowicz, neither could they be considered peers of that "gentry" from Sandomierz. I imagine Gombrowicz's milieu as having been roughly similar to that of Żeromski's fictitious manor in Nawłoć, which is to say, as something exotic beyond words.

The Niewiaża has exerted a manifestly obsessive hold on the literary imagination. That Sienkiewicz, in his novel *The Deluge*, made it the setting of his ideal "gentlemen's nest," should have predisposed me favorably toward him, were it not for my earlier disaffection with that writer. The river's special magnetic attraction might also account for a certain pilgrimage made to the river region of Kedainiai (as a child I used to contemplate, from the granary's upper windows, the distant towers of the Kedainiai parish church). In a silence disturbed only by an occasional creak in the parquet flooring, I read of that pilgrimage in a wing of the Bibliothèque Sainte Geneviève. It was as follows. One summer day in 1922, three people were aboard the Berlin–Königsberg–Kovno train: Count Maurice Prozor, his daughter Greta (it was her memoir I was reading), and Oscar Władysław Miłosz. Most probably they had conversed in French, the language favored by both men in their everyday speech and literary work; although they certainly knew Polish, one may presume that among the younger generation, to which Greta Prozor belonged, it was dying out. Count Prozor, born in Wilno but raised in France, was a French translator of Ibsen and the author of several literary studies. He and Oscar Milosz, who was many years his junior, were naturally joined in friendship by virtue of their common background. Indeed, not one of Milosz's French reviewers has shown himself capable of the sort of insights brought to bear by Prozor in his study of Milosz's poetry, and for this he earned the poet's gratitude. By way of a digression, as I momentarily abandon our threesome on their train journey, I quote from a Milosz letter (dated October 28, 1920) addressed to Prozor on the occasion of the publication of his study:

. . . I will not speak of my admiration for you as an artist, a psychologist, or a critic, only of the emotion, the deeply human emotion, stirred by the analogies which you so subtly, and rightly, draw between us: two Lithuanian artists, exiled from our physical homeland—both in the historical sense, such as has existed for centuries, and personally, such as we have been for decades—and forced to invent one of the spirit, no less Lithuanian but located in a past and future so remote as to be almost imaginary. When you mention a hotel on the rue de Rivoli, my memory evokes another from the past, this one on the rue Helder in 1889, and the mirage of distant childhood, which suffuses the pages you devote to me with such nostalgia, haunts me too, because I am a man who wills for the future and lives always in the past. No Frenchman has ever understood this—you alone, having yourself borne the tribulations imposed by social, national, and personal circumstances unknown among the Latins, have captured it with a poignancy that has touched me deeply. The more sensitive critics have placed me, with greater or lesser accuracy, in a certain spiritual setting, among a certain tribe of artists. By allying me with my own tribe, with my ancient people, you have cast my personality in striking perspective, filling a void which I myself have labored so hard to fill. You alone have appreciated that need of mine for a genuine homeland, a need which is the primary impulse of my work; by assigning me a fixed place on earth, you have physically grounded my art and work.

Historically exiled for centuries . . . The Prozors came from up around the Niewiaża, where neither Maurice nor Greta had ever set foot. Nor had Oscar Milosz, born in far-off Byelorussia, in Czereja, ever seen his ancestral Lithuania. Yet they took themselves to be "Lithuanian artists." Then, in 1918, Lithuania was back on the map again— true, a smaller Lithuania, now reduced to a fraction of the former Grand Duchy, but a Lithuania all the same. It was then that the Prozors and Oscar Milosz had sworn allegiance to the new state, and their expedition in 1922 was a journey in quest (*en quête*) of their ancestral land.

For Oscar Milosz, the trip had served practical, official aims as well. For several years he had been Lithuanian chargé d'affaires in Paris and Brussels. Before 1918 he had known nothing either of the nationalist movement in Lithuania or of the language itself; in fact, it would be no exaggeration to say that his choice of citizenship was prompted by indignation on hearing that Poland, itself a subjugated nation for many decades, had refused to grant Lithuania's claim to independence. He concedes as much in one of his letters to Christian Gauss, from which we learn that his decision was guided by a moral motive: a desire to serve his fellow man in a capacity that might atone for his egoistic solitude. Diplomatic service in defense of Lithuania would become the means of that atonement.

After crossing the German–Lithuanian border at Wierzbolów, the travelers found themselves in what might have been a remote outpost of old tsarist Russia: railway cars dating back to prewar times, sleepy train depots, something known as the *konka*, or horse tram, in Kovno; towns built around a single, broad, cobblestoned street. Above all, notes Greta Prozor, their curiosity was roused by the height of the police, giants towering two meters high.

After their arrival in Kovno, the travelers visited the former Prozor property in the Niewiaża Valley, and from there they made their way to Labunowo. When Oscar

Milosz began to write under the name of O. V. de L. Milosz, the final initial was meant to signify "de Labunowo," after the place which he had always been told was the Miloszes' ancestral estate. When no one at Labunowo (or Labunava in Lithuanian) could shed any light on his ancestry, they had recourse to the parish priest. Despite a hospitable reception and a night-long conversation held at the rectory (in Polish, what else?), they came away unenlightened.

A city-bred gentleman might stroll up to a Polish rube sitting in worn-out breeches before the cottage door, and begin inquiring about the man's great- and great-great-grandparents—a Polish peasant, after all, is descended from the legendary Piast and Rzepicha . . . But here? A scratching of the head and a drawling "Eh . . ." It was true that ancient ways had endured—like a fly embedded in amber—longer in Lithuania than elsewhere. Jucewicz records how, as late as the early nineteenth century, the peasant homes of northern Samogitia were still hung with swords and armor, the relics of their warrior-ancestors (which suggests that the Lithuanian military campaigns of old had been tribal in nature and not confined to one knightly caste). Strictly speaking, the Labunowo estate had never been the property of the Miloszes, which, again, was merely a question of title: the medium-size estates once owned by the family—Hanusewicze and Serbiny—lay in such close proximity to Labunowo as to be collectively designated by the same name. But the family records went back only as far as the sixteenth century, and our branch of the family tended to shrug off such ancestral searches. Incredulity also surrounds the legend of the family's Lusatian origin, although, for all anyone knew, there may have been some substance to it, judging by the presence of what was known as "the Sorbian cemetery" on the Serbiny property. Why were the Miloszes from Byelorussia so covetous of ancient titles? Even if Oscar Milosz had been able to establish the family's seat at Labunowo or to trace his lineage back to those Lusatian lords, I would be more inclined to see it, not as a sign of eccentricity, but as a means toward an end, as a strategy of self-defense in his exacerbating relations with the French. How many Poles have tried to aggrandize themselves by appending a "de" to their name! Even Guillaume Apollinaire used to sign his name Wilhelm de Kostrowitzky. By writing under the name O. V. de L. Milosz, my blood relation adopted a kind of pseudonym designed to create an air of mystery among the French. It was not until the First World War, and then only ironically, in correspondence with friends, that he began to use it; his earliest works and the bulk of his prewar letters all bear the signature O. W. Miłosz. Another incentive may have been his suddenly discovered "Lithuanian identity," and the Gallicized version only spared him the necessity of changing Milosz to Milašius. The initial "L," on the other hand, later came to signify Lubicz, which was indeed the Milosz coat of arms, whose emblem graces the book-plates in the works of Oscar Milosz's private library.

These somewhat embarrassing details should be placed in their proper context, that of the late twentieth century. Exile, before it became a phenomenon of the age, was once relatively rare; only later did it grow to the dimensions of a universal condition. The fate of Oscar Milosz, no longer exceptional when viewed from the present, from my American perspective, was only a dramatic foreglimpse of that great melting pot of the future. This French poet, born a subject of the tsarist Empire, one-quarter Italian on his grandmother's side (Natalia Tasistro), half Jewish on his mother's (née Maria Rosenthal, Warsaw-born), differed from today's cosmopolitan tribe in that he never rejected his inheritance of mixed blood. His insistence on his Lithuanian ancestry might be interpreted as a sham, yet he was no less insistent on his Jewishness, which he admitted was a source of many hardships—as evidenced not only by his study of Hebrew and later of the Cabala, but by his request to Christian Gauss urging him to visit his mother's relatives who had emigrated to the United States. Nor did he neglect his Italian side, which he claimed decisive, and in his writings there are frequent allusions to "the dead lady from Vercelli."

Note that in reflecting on his life he discovered a symbolic equivalence of his vision and his ancestry. Homelessness, in the tribal as well as the geographical sense, became a *correspondence* of the spiritual exile of modern man, and his own quest for a homeland, for *place*, acquired a double meaning. That the notion of homeland is born of the same realm as myth and fable we, above all, can appreciate—we as readers of *Pan Tadeusz*, a work that, paradoxically, can be said to "reflect" reality only on the sociological, novelistic plane. (Even as a student at the Gymnasium, I was sensitive to the work's license in its treatment of the Lithuanian landscape, until I finally understood it for what it was: a realized fairy tale.) Milosz's avowed aspiration for a "genuine homeland" suggests a conscious playing with a self-created myth, and not surprisingly the two volumes of Lithuanian fairy tales which he adapted are full of a charming humor. But fairy tales and myths do not lie—and Maurice Prozor was not lying when he portrayed both himself and Oscar Milosz as exiles of the century.

Not all who are homeless wish to remain so, and we are presently witnesses to a nostalgic revival on behalf of the regional homeland—whether it be a Wales, Brittany, or Provence. Yet those in Carcassonne who publish novels in *langue d'oc* must be aware of the mythmaking, legend-making aspect of the enterprise. I can sympathize with them; indeed, it seems to me now, when my own exile compares in many ways to that of Oscar Milosz, that even as a Wilno schoolboy in sympathy with the "regionalists," I understood that a homeland was both very much a need and a product of the imagination.

Oscar Milosz described himself as a man who lived always in the past. That it could hardly have been otherwise is borne out by the following passage, excerpted from his own writings:

> Music is love's cry; poetry its thought . . . One is the ecstasy of a given moment, and it sings "I live and love"; the other, a surrendering to the power of memory, and it seems to say "I have lived, I have loved," even as it seeks to render the most real and immediate love. That is why these two noble-minded sisters, once joined in art, were bound to part company.

Because, alas, the mind's awareness has lured poetry into its chambers. Between his word and the world that is both inside and outside him, the poet creates a distance, knowing in advance that every moment just lived recedes into the past, because it has become the poet's material; thus the prompting voice of irony, "Thou forgest a drama," is heard not only by the Romantic poet. Yet the compulsion to assume the role of spectator in the *theatrum mundi*, on whose stage the poet is also cast as a marionette, seems born of the very need for purification. Says Simone Weil, "Distance is the soul of beauty," and then cites Proust, the poet of memory, as an example. But this compulsion to render things past is no prescription for poetry. Every poet would experience the fullness of life, would body himself forth in music rather than serve the letter, and so he checks the urge to do so. The nature and intensity of that resistance may vary, depending on the style prevailing in a given epoch. In the case of Oscar Milosz, a man resolutely fixed on the past, I did not prize his melancholy, but I had always to forgive him for it.

18

Standing high on a shady hilltop rimmed by a deep moat, a relic of feudal times, Haunted House conjured up those sprawling, fortified nests spun by storks, the guardian spirits of Slavic lands, in the crowns of ancient trees. The hill, when surveyed from the endlessly trailing lane of silvery willows joining the hill to the Wilno highroad, loomed up like a leafy mass, somber and inert; but the closer one drew to the ancestral house of the Biała lords, the more the dark massif lost its semblance to a virgin forest and became a lovely English park, one that a couple of weeks of earnest pruning might have thinned of its rank weeds and shrubs. The old manor house came into view from the foot of the rise: its long, gray-green, moss-encrusted roof, its mansard windows, wistfully iridescent and weathered by the rains of a bygone era. A rust-eaten gate greeted the visitor with a sepulchral whine; a lane of weeping willows, sighing mysteriously, ushered him to the main entrance whose strangely chalked panels were crowned by three spike-size nails, arranged triangularly, that at one time must have impaled the wings of some pitiful bat, now long since turned to dust.

The door—the gruesome, shabbily whitewashed door of an ancestral tomb—opened on a dark vestibule, where the visitor, with one foot barely inside, was choked by the odor of musty decay. The faded countenances of innumerable Zborowskis, some wearing traditional Polish robes and costumes, and others of more recent date, periwigged and decked out in the French style, adorned the cobwebbed walls. A double door, stripped of its panels, in the wall facing the entrance opened on a lovely suite of rooms with tall windows and low ceilings, rooms full of a mysterious and quiet solemnity. One's gaze was immediately drawn to an incredible array of felt-topped game tables, presenting to the captivated eye every conceivable shade of green: one tea-spattered, another vodka-drenched, one wine-spattered, another mead-soaked. One look at this woeful meadow trampled by card playing was enough to conjure up, with poignant precision, the country's entire melancholy past. How many generations of vigorous and heroic noblemen had squandered time, fortune, and health in these grandiose rooms painted blue, red, and gold, under these vibrant windows, among tattered cards and wineglasses shattered against the wall in an ebullience of toasts proclaimed in Latin!

My wonder was equally aroused by the presence of ancient French monarchs and notables jostling with the portraits of Polish kings and Lithuanian Grand Dukes. The Slavic sister's true veneration for her French sister found here a more vivid and striking expression than in any of the scholarly histories of Henryk Walezy, a Frenchman by birth, or of Sobieski, Leszczyński, and Poniatowski, all Frenchmen at heart. The portraits must have been used at one time for target practice by some Swedish or Muscovite invader because their austere brows and expansive chests were riddled with bullet holes of every caliber, which now and then served as a corridor for some golden moth, iron-gray wood louse, or ancient spider shimmering with a sinister, diamondlike luster. The corners of the dim and dusty rooms were occupied either by faience-tiled stoves, cavernous enough to accommodate a cartload of firewood with their gaping maws, or by massive armoires whose glass doors lined with faded cloth joined the ornate parquet flooring to the ceiling's cracked murals.

The broad, deep shelves of the worm-eaten cabinets were nearly obscured by piles of sundry objects, and this bizarre assemblage might have provoked laughter were it not for the common scent of oblivion, death, and silence suffusing it. Old artificial flowers garlanded the barrel of a blunderbuss tinged a rusty red; rolls of parchment bearing the signatures of the famous and ponderous wax seals lay stacked in a cage resembling a Japanese pagoda with bells; a stuffed bullfinch, the pet charm of some great-aunt or other, crowned the burnished-gold forehead of some august and slightly decrepit notable; a mirror, the confidant of so many extinguished smiles, mimicked the ironic grin of its neighbor, a dank and sickly skull, half shrouded by issues of *Journal des Dames et des Modes*, published in French in the free city of Frankfurt am Main. Old Italian operas, diligently copied by a delicate hand on soft vellum paper edged in faded gold, testified to the zealous devotion of the musical Teresa; the imposing shakos, decorated with giant silver Polish eagles, the sprawling, now frayed epaulettes, and the precious firearms and grave-looking crutches spoke of Ludwik's glorious and tragic career; the restless litter of gnawed and yellowed folios, arcane instruments, and multi-shaped retorts containing the residue of evaporated salts evoked the shade of some mysterious ancestor who, in the time of the Vasas, had labored in chimerical pursuit of a nostrum or the philosophers' stone.

So begins Oscar Milosz's novel, *Le Majorat*, announced (*sous presse*) in the first edition of his Biblical drama

Mephiboseth in 1914. The novel bears the subtitle *Souvenirs d'un Anglais exilé en Russie*. It was not soon published, nor has the manuscript survived (its author was not in the habit of making copies). One can easily recognize the Czereja manor in the description of Haunted House, and the gardens of the author's secluded childhood in that "lovely English park." Yet it should not be assumed, from the poet's nostalgia for the lost world of childhood, that Milosz, who was brought to Paris by his parents when he was eleven, never returned to Byelorussia. He returned many times, in fact, and as a man in his late twenties he even spent a couple of years there, off and on, between 1902 and 1906.

Memoirs of the period pay tribute to a special felicity of life observable in the years preceding the First World War, at least in France, where the expression la Belle Epoque was coined. Yet, judging by the mental state reflected in Milosz's works and correspondence of the time, one might just as well have celebrated a fecund Sahara. On February 1, 1901, at eleven in the evening, Oscar Milosz, calmly and deliberately, with a cigarette dangling from his mouth, shot himself in the heart. The surgeon, the finest in all of Paris, refused to operate, believing him too weak to survive such an operation. I have no desire to play biographer; whatever the motives for this act—a hereditary predisposition, personal imbroglios, the terror of a new century veiled by beautiful illusion, or just the loneliness of a man who was always and everywhere an outsider—they are best left in obscurity. That he survived is cause for reflecting on the coming and going of certain individuals, and on the power that decides: fate or chance. If I accepted the latter, I would have to grant that it was merely by chance that he survived, by chance that he later wrote certain works, and by chance that we shared the same surname, which in turn led me to the discovery of his writings, and so on, culminating in the final link in the chain, in the reading of these words—by you, the reader, be you kind or malicious.

Between the Café des Deux Magots and Czereja. For an insight into the poet's life at Czereja, we again turn to his correspondence with Gauss, to those letters dated 1904. He was detained there, he writes, "by affairs neglected for the past forty years, the physical burden of which has fallen on my frail *Geisterseher*'s shoulders. I ride horseback in summer and versify lines by the thousands; in winter I go sleigh riding and reread Kant, Schopenhauer, and Plato while smoking my pipe. Occasionally I go on a trip with my two friends—with Don Quixote to Spain and with Heinrich Heine to Italy. One can get used to anything; above all, the less time spent in the 'world of reality,' the better." He speaks of his "solitary life in an ancient—three-centuries-old—house, surrounded by brooding lakes and forests, in the company of my horses, cats, and books."

Czereja, situated in the Sienno district, in the Mohylev region, had once belonged to the Sapiehas. Oscar Milosz was most likely negotiating the sale of properties scheduled for redistribution among the landless peasants. Of the manor, to which he will invite Gauss, he writes: "You [*Vous*] will see a land hardly imaginable to a foreigner— the dirtiest, coldest, most pathetic land on earth, a nordic land that would appeal to a northern poet like yourself. Alas, the house of my ancestors is old almost beyond re- pair owing to the family's prolonged residency in France —now it is up to me, the most impractical of men, to restore the manor [*château*] and put things right. In two years I shall have a small but new manor, so you will have to spend a few months with me—your summer holidays; in a land where the peasants are quite wild and whose great lakes and forests should prove inspirational to a poet. I wouldn't dare invite a Frenchman—the French are much too cynical; but a man of the north will always be more tolerant of nordic climes. Meanwhile, I look forward to seeing you in France, to our traveling together in Italy and elsewhere—traveling anywhere with you is a pleasure. Incidentally, have you ever read Henryk Sienkiewicz, our *national* glory (hence mediocrity)? They're putting on *Fire and Sword* at Sarah Bernhardt's in Paris—yet another claim to distinction!"

In another letter from Czereja, also dated 1904, he informs Gauss of his literary plans, about a new volume of poetry scheduled to appear in Paris. And about something unsuspected by any of his biographers: his work in Polish. "There will appear in Warsaw, around the same time as the French volume, a book of my Polish poems, with which I am quite pleased, even though the language is not quite pure: the long stay in Paris has Frenchified me a little." This second book was never printed and no one has ever succeeded in tracing the manuscript; nor did its author ever speak of it in his conversations with me. He missed Paris while in Czereja. Yet hardly had he returned when he complained of the sham and perfunctory cordiality prevailing in literary circles, and escaped to Germany, then to Switzerland and Italy. Of his great love in Venice his biographers know little except the girl's initials. His mother, it is believed, stood in the way of their marriage. He stayed a longer time in England, where he acquired an excellent command of English (he had a high regard for English poetry), somewhere in the interval between 1907 and 1910. The year 1910 can be said to mark the beginning of his literary coming-of-age, because this was the year in which his novel, *L'Amoureuse Initiation*, was published. Implicitly contained in it are all the motifs found in the passages cited above: a nostalgic return to the past, poetry as memory, an abhorrence for twentieth-century realities, a sense of humor verging on the sarcastic and melancholic, an affection for Italy ("Eventually, after the sale of my Lithuanian properties, I plan to settle in Italy. Italy may be my true homeland, because on the side of my paternal grandmother, a highly talented musician to whom I bear a striking resemblance, I am the last descendant of a very old Genoese family, which has helped me to understand much about my type of mind and sensibility"—from a letter to Gauss, dated 1906). The novel is set in eighteenth-century Venice; nor is the narration conducted in the "objective" style typical of a "novel of verisimilitude." Rather, it takes the form of a poetic monologue: the poor Sassolo Sinibaldi recounts to a young Danish nobleman, Benjamin, the story of his love for the deceitful Clarissa Annalena, which story becomes part of Benjamin's memoir (Benjamin is one of Clarissa's subsequent lovers). The book's theme can be formulated in one word: insatiability. Sassolo's love for Annalena is a passion for the All; that he cannot possess her fully (Rogozhin, in Dostoevsky's *Idiot*, can fully possess Nastasya Filippovna only by killing her) impresses on him the immensity of his desires, which nothing on earth can ever slake. The eighteenth-century setting, the evocation of cosmopolitan Venice, the narrative structure of a memoir-within-a-memoir, love as a curtain opening to "another dimension"—are we not here in the realm of German Romantic prose? Oscar Milosz, I would argue, was by choice a man from the turn of the eighteenth century. Imagine a character from Goethe's *Wilhelm Meister* and you would have a fair portrait of the man. Goethe was indeed his "spiritual master," to use his own words, and written in the margin of his copy of

Wilhelm Meister are three words summarizing the object of the trials to which the Master—and Oscar Milosz—was subjected: "Respect! Respect! Respect!" From Goethe, Milosz inherited a belief in mystery as the essence of art (one of his letters to Prozor speaks of "the perilous pull toward the mystery, almost inseparable from the love of poetry"). Often categorized as a Symbolist, even he tended to view his early work as Neo-Romantic. His favorite poets, besides Goethe (and Dante), were Byron, Lamartine, and Heine. The following passage, excerpted from a letter to Gauss (May 1914), should erase any doubts as to where, in which European time setting, he belongs:

> Speaking of pure and liberated poetry, I would alert you to a poet, Friedrich Hölderlin, who, though Goethe's contemporary, is not well known, not even in Germany. Two years ago, a German critic told me about him, but distrusting the critics, I gave it no further thought. Then last year I was in Munich, alone, dreadfully bored (loneliness, so much more bearable in my younger years, scares me now, and I envy you the wisdom of becoming a father!). So I went for a browse in the bookstores in the charming city of Munich. In one, I caught sight of Hölderlin's collected works; yawning, I stuffed the package under my arm, went back, stretched out on the couch, and opened the first volume: *Gedichte*. Ah, my friend, what a delight, what a revelation! For a year now, Hölderlin has been my bible: You must read this devil [*ce gaillard*], his lyrical novel, *Hyperion*, his poetry, his play *Empedokles*, his translations of Sophocles—for the first time, thanks to him, I now understand what Greek tragedy is! Dear Gauss, if you don't know this fellow, or if you can't get hold of him in America, I'll send him to you from Germany this summer. A poet like you cannot possibly ignore an ancestor like Hölderlin.

His is pure poetry, poetry incarnate; it has an undefinable, unforgettable quality to it, at times that of a more Olympic Baudelaire, other times that of a more human Goethe, or of Shelley if he quit being a girl and sang like a bearded Homer, or Byron if he came down from his throne and mingled with the humble crowd—it is wonderfully fine. And Hölderlin's story is equally fine—went mad at thirty-four and died a madman at seventy! In a word, your kind of poet, my kind, our kind!

Nearly a half century later, the literary historian André Lebois would write: "Milosz is our Hölderlin, and that assures him his rightful place in world literature." The comparison with Hölderlin is surely more apt than treating him as another Claudel, although, never having studied German, I cannot presume to judge.

19

BACK TO MY ESTATE. Before I elaborate, as promised, on certain intricacies, I must first introduce a few concepts —even laws—that have wide application. I shall begin with a tactless admission: I believe in the existence of a human nature. Such a concept is passé today, the mark of an ugly conservatism, wholly inconsistent with a progressive cast of mind. Today the search for what is durably, intrinsically human (other than "man is what he is not" and "man is not what he is") is treated as a vestigial custom acquired at a time when Nature was thought to be fixed, immutable. No one would ever accuse Marx of being a conservative. Yet here is Leszek Kołakowski, speaking in volume one of his *Main Currents of Marxism*:

> The idea of man's recovery of his own self is in fact comprised in that of alienation, which Marx continued to employ: for alienation is nothing but a process in which man deprives himself of what he truly is, of his own humanity. To speak in these terms implies, of course, that we know what man "truly" is, as opposed to what he empirically is: what the content of human nature is, conceived of not as a set of features empirically ascertained but as a set of requirements that must be fulfilled in order to make human beings genuinely human. Without some such standard, vague though it may be, "alienation" has no meaning.

But scholarly social analyses, the glossing of names and theories are not to my purpose here; to believe in human nature, it is enough to see it violated and debased, day by day, in its most primal, but by no means animal, needs.

Next, the concept of hierarchy. Wherever we have to do with the human mind and heart, equality is a fiction; inequality, the general rule. And just because the mind and heart are so palpably felt in art, poets and artists are obsessed with rank, with the promoting of some and demoting of others. But behind the vanity contest, behind all the comedy (of the weak judging the weak) and sheer ordinary folly, the longing for greatness, however misguided, must be acknowledged. Nor is the admirer of man's achievements in philosophy, art, and science a true partisan of equality, regardless of his or her politics. Since mention has been made of Hölderlin, I would here cite his "Hierarchy, Fraternity, Freedom." Let us note the order in which the three are placed. However much politicians may appropriate, even pervert such a catch phrase, the truth remains: we salute it continually in the kingdom of art and science.

With the law of hierarchy goes the law of travesty and parody. There is no inspiration, no idea, or discovery that, when mirrored in a lower intelligence, at a lower level of the "interhuman church," does not lose proportionately in value. If only something of the original, however weakened, however dimmed, would endure! But since the difference of degree is often one of absolute quality, the diluted version becomes a parody of the higher. Inspiration, its parody, and the parody of its parody: they surround us in constant and clamorous collision. Or, to use another metaphor, everything of substance is undermined, hollowed out by the termites of inferiority. By endowing masks and façades with a real existence, we find ourselves one day the victims of an illusion. A priest nurtured on the Freudian–Marxian–Chardinian dregs will be a priest in name only; a teacher, though able to read and write, an illiterate and a corruptor; a politician, an outlaw; artists and poets, the helpers of circus managers who stage spectacles with real blood and live copulation, exactly as in those Roman circus-theaters described by Tertullian.

Next, the law of triumphant banality—crucial, in my view, to an understanding of the history of this century's avant-garde. Without that moment of genuine infatuation with the new, there would be no succession of "movements" and schools. Those with long enough memories will recall having been captivated, at one time or another, by a bold color or verbal combination, a revelatory distortion, a jarring syntax. It was a thrall bespeaking another, more fantastic reality and, beneath the forms, a shimmering mystery and profundity. But our century's frenzied pace has been particularly hard on such works, turning the extraordinary into the ordinary, the sublime into the vulgar, the fantastic into the real, the most savage grotesque into a middle-class comedy of "manners and morals." Like that fairy-tale pile of gold discovered at night in the forest and revealed by day as wood rot. Not all of this century's art and literature has been dealt such a fate, but how little is salvageable.

Weathered by time, the transitory and the spurious fade into gray banality; but they may also lose their appeal when confronted by a more powerful beauty, one more abundant in *being*. Works less abundant in being are put to death, not by critics or canonical pronouncements, but by works of greater abundance. Which raises the question of whether a work kept in a drawer, or a painting condemned never to leave the artist's workshop, can be said to have the same power. In my view, they do—and this brings us, finally, to the law of magical intervention through unseen communion.

20

AGING IS A CURIOUS EXPERIENCE. Except for moments when the will is temporarily released from the matters at hand, I think of the past less often than I had feared. The past is an immense album whose images are blurred, elusive—protean in their inconstancy and therefore embarrassing. Memory consoles with its balancing of gains and losses, because not all is on the debit side; the passage of years bestows a sense of architectonics, and the purity of arch, the crystalline contour can compensate for the fading of warm colors. It also teaches futility, because we know now that the distance between the world and the word, contrary to all our previous expectations, remains unbridgeable.

Who of us has not seen himself as he once was—in an old photo, in someone else's portrayal? It happened to me in 1969, when I picked up Oscar Milosz's *Soixante-quinze lettres inédites* (*Seventy-five Unpublished Letters*), a volume of correspondence with the Vogts, just published in Paris. In one letter, dated November 11, 1931, I came across the following:

> This summer, to my great joy, I met my nephew, so called in former times, a direct descendant of one of my great-grandfather's brothers. I was expecting an ogre, a monster like all the rest of that family of grandees and warriors become rotten philistines [*sales bourgeoises*]. Imagine my surprise when I was confronted by a handsome young man of nineteen, a poet as passionate as he is poised [*très pondéré*], full of deference toward me because of my work, loyal to the monarchic, Catholic and aristocratic tradition in its more intelligent and nobler aspects, with enough of the communist in him to be of service to this incredible age of ours—in a word, a young cavalier [*jeune cavalier*], whom I regard a little as my own son. He has now returned to Wilno for his third year of law. Intelligence is such a glorious thing! Especially when it turns up in places where, by all the rules of logic, one would expect a beast full of reactionary or absurdly progressive views. However repelled I am by my family, I am glad to see that the thirteenth-century family line is to be perpetuated, thanks to this young man, who is bound to do it honor (at last), and to his brother, a mere fourteen-year-old. Excuse me for entertaining you at such length about *Monsieur le Cavalier*.

This portrait afforded me the sort of pleasure gained from self-recognition—even when the portrayal strikes us as too flattering. A possibly amusing footnote: his invective is at the expense of the Druja side of the family, referred to in our house as "the endees" (National Democrats), an epithet no more affectionate than *sales bourgeoises* —to which sociopolitical nuance I refer the historians.

The spiritual father-son relationship struck on my first trip to Paris proved durable, indeed. Now, many years later, I can better analyze the nature of this willing submission to a figure of paternal authority. I had made approaches earlier, before the war, but they were unsuccessful, most likely creating the impression of someone eager to aggrandize a French poet for purely selfish motives. The main obstacle was language, linguistically as well as intellectually. Oscar Milosz spoke Polish as fluently as I, so well, in fact, that I never once saw him grope for a word or phrase. Among the marginalia in the works from his private library, the more emotionally charged interjections are in Polish. Yet his literary French is quite distinct from his Polish, so distinct as to be nearly untranslatable. Its difficulty may well spring from a sensitivity to language, first exercised in Polish, during childhood, and later followed by a peculiar sort of transfer that proved highly amenable to the genius of his adopted language. Milosz's nouns, even when they signify abstract concepts, are endowed with great substantiality, even with personality, that may be a Slavic inheritance. But Polish is particularly deficient in native words denoting abstractions, and if a whole sentence can be nuanced by the grammatical gender of a given noun, as it so often is in Milosz's work, a translator has little recourse but to introduce words of foreign derivation. Some examples: *L'Affirmation, La Manifestation* (connoting not a public demonstration so much as an "incarnation"), *La Connaissance* (connoting not knowledge but "perception");

l'orgueil, whose masculine article sets it apart from the feminine *duma* or *pycha* in Polish. My Polish translations of Milosz were only partially successful, and when I tried my hand at the more difficult Milosz texts, I realized it was hopeless; in a language as non-abstract as Polish, they would have been turned to mush.

A more serious obstacle was my deficiency in the realm of ideas, which revealed itself when I tried to convey my admiration to Polish readers. Not only had I not mastered Milosz, at best a quarter of what I had read, but I had yet to master my own ambivalent feelings. The subject was one that had been sufficiently discredited, thanks to Polish Romanticism, and even travestied through Modernist rhetoric—namely, that terrain circumscribed by the term "mysticism." Suddenly, notwithstanding my antipathy toward Romantic and Modernist excesses, I was being forced to add a plus sign where I had always placed a minus. As I knew of no one in Poland to assist me in resolving these ambivalences, I let myself be guided by instinct, and in the process made a significant discovery: if a thing improperly stated is a betrayal of that thing, then better to remain silent than to commit a betrayal. Oscar Milosz only abetted my isolation, because now I began to suspect that something was ailing modern literature, indeed, the modern age itself. It happens sometimes that we enter a subway car without thinking, only to discover, after we have already boarded, that we have chosen the wrong line. If Oscar Milosz was right, the choice had been made long ago, not in the twentieth century and not by us, but it was a choice portending a calamity of cosmic dimensions. Or was he simply wrong?

I could not begin to reconstruct precisely the periods in which he exerted a greater or lesser influence on me. Today I think of it rather as a musical motif, sometimes superimposed by others, muted, yet one whose resonance grows stronger with time. This suggests a different approach: rather than chart my mind's evolution let me show its complexion today, placing Oscar Milosz in a certain context in which other names are brought to bear on his meaning. If the barriers posed by language are no less insurmountable today, then at least the ideas that were once lacking are now a little more within reach. Nonetheless, my text will have to contend with the inherent resistance of the Polish language vis-à-vis certain themes.

Not so long ago, I overheard someone remark in English: "There are two Miloszes, one a Pole, the other a Frenchman; the Pole is the better of the two." That anyone should have compared me to Oscar Milosz I found outrageous. I have never treated him as my poetic master, nor sought to imitate him or compete with him, being fully aware that every generation is given to its own stylistic manner, that every literature and literary language obeys its own laws. His influence on me has extended only obliquely to the "writer's craft," while to judge a poet "better" or "worse" exclusively as a poet means little to me. The law of hierarchy, properly exercised, does not apply here.

21

WE HAVE TO GO BACK to that time in Europe when human fate still hung in the balance. To Goethe. Since my own knowledge of Goethe's work is slight, I must rely on the American professor of German literature, Erich Heller, possibly because Heller, who was born in 1911, corroborates more or less the thesis advanced by Stanisław Brzozowski—who died in 1911 and about whom Heller has probably never heard—concerning "the Romantic crisis of European culture." Heller's essay "Goethe and the Idea of Scientific Truth" (in the collection *The Disinherited Mind*) addresses Goethe's "Thirty Years' War against Newton" and the poet's efforts to construct a science distinct from that established by Newtonian physics, to which science Goethe's own theory of color and *Urpflanze* was meant to contribute. Writes Heller:

> No, Goethe was not afraid of the first chapter of Genesis being discredited as a set book by the Honours schools of geology, biology and anthropology; but he was terrified that experimental science in alliance with a mechanistic philosophy of nature, so successful in posing and answering questions about the "How" of things, so prolific in establishing expected and unexpected *relationships between* this, that or the other, might finally abolish in the world all creative interest in *what* this, that or the other *are* and *mean*. For Darwin's theory was bound to feed the body of superstitious beliefs that had grown rampant ever since medieval scholasticism suffered its final defeat at the hands of Francis Bacon.

Heller takes up the dichotomy between the world of scientific laws—cold, indifferent to human values—and man's inner world. Coming into prominence only in the late eighteenth century, this split would later form the essence of the "Romantic crisis." Goethe attributed it to the alternative elected by science, and foresaw the consequences. "He appointed himself," states Heller, "a kind of emissary of Being in a territory of the human mind which had given itself up to the alluring mechanics of becoming, evolving and revolving." Goethe strenuously sought to avoid the cleavage, hence his experiments in search of another science consistent with "his faith in a perfect correspondence" between the human soul and the universe. In his lifetime he had witnessed the emergence of the "disinherited mind" in the ontological sense, of a mind torn between the certainty of man's insignificance in the immensity of a hostile universe, and an urge, born of wounded pride, to endow man with preeminence. The "incessant struggle between arrogance and humiliation" that ensued was one that would define the whole of modern literature, from Nietzsche to Kafka, Proust, Sartre, and so on.

Heller admires in Goethe his rejection of a "life of poetry" separate from a "poetry of life," and regards his failure in science as commendable:

> Goethe's science has contributed nothing substantial to the scientific progress between his time and ours, and nothing whatsoever to the advancement of techniques for the mastery and exploitation of Nature; but he did, by his opposition to contemporary science, lay bare in his time, with remarkable precision, the very roots of that crisis and revolution in scientific methods in which the twentieth-century scientist finds himself involved. In the history of science from Newton to Einstein, Goethe the scientist plays a Cinderella part, showing up the success and splendour of his rich relations, but also the potential *hubris* inherent in their pursuits. There may come a day when this Cinderella story will find the conclusion proper to such tales—but perhaps not before the new ecclesia of technology has had its consummate triumph by bringing to their explosive fusion the iciest mathematical abstractions and hot appetite for power.

I repeat that I make no claim to any professional competence in Goethe criticism, and I have invoked Heller's commentary primarily for the issues it raises. I cannot resist a final quotation, one especially congenial to my purpose:

> The anxiety that the world, in the course of its increasing analytical disruption, may approach the point where it would become poetically useless, and a barren place for human affections to dwell in, informs Goethe's scientific motives and makes him persist in an activity which, for a long period, to the detriment of his poetic creativeness and to his own dismay, "absorbs all my inner faculties." William Blake, unknown to Goethe, but his brother-in-arms against Newton, found things easier. He was a medieval peasant compared with Goethe, who had so big a share in mundane sophistication. For Blake the inventor of modern physics was simply party to a conspiracy of spiritual sin, a mythological ambassador, the second person in the Trinity of Evil, flanked by Bacon and Locke. But then, Blake saw angels in pear-trees, Goethe only "ideas." For him it could not be enough to say that modern physics was wicked; it had to be proven wrong by experimental methods.

Heller errs in calling Blake a "medieval peasant." Such a view may have been possible in 1911, though even at that time there were those, Brzozowski among others, who perceived in Blake something more complex than the visionary fantasies of a village shaman. But Heller is entirely correct in yoking Goethe and Blake in their conscious opposition to the dichotomy. It is, finally, what makes their place in Romanticism, a movement which conceded the split, so unique.

22

This brings us to Mickiewicz's ballad, "The Romantic":

"Silly girl, listen!"
But she doesn't listen
While the village roofs glisten,
Bright in the sun.
"Silly girl, what do you do there,
As if there were someone to view there,
A face to gaze on and greet there,
A live form warmly to meet there,
When there is no one, none, do you hear!"
But she doesn't hear.

Like a dead stone
She stands there alone,
Staring ahead of her, peering around
For something that has to be found
Till, suddenly spying it,
She touches it, clutches it,
Laughing and crying.

Is it you, my Johnny, my true love, my dear?
I knew you would never forget me,
Even in death! Come with me, let me
Show you the way now! Hold your breath, though,
And tiptoe lest stepmother hear!

What can she hear? They have made him
A grave, two years ago laid him
Away with the dead.
Save me, Mother of God! I'm afraid.
But why? Why should I flee you now?
What do I dread?

Not Johnny! My Johnny won't hurt me.
It is my Johnny! I see you now,
Your eyes, your white shirt.

But it's pale as linen you are,
Cold as winter you are!
Let my lips take the cold from you,
Kiss the chill of the mould from you.

Dearest love, let me die with you,
In the deep earth lie with you,
For this world is dark and dreary,
I am lonely and weary!

Alone among the unkind ones
Who mock at my vision,
My tears their derision,
Seeing nothing, the blind ones!

Dear God! A cock is crowing,
Whitely glimmers the dawn.
Johnny! Where are you going?
Don't leave me! I am forlorn!

So, caressing, talking aloud to her
Lover, she stumbles and falls,
And her cry of anguish calls
A pitying crowd to her.

"Cross yourselves! It is, surely,
Her Johnny come back from the grave:
While he lived, he loved her entirely.
May God his soul now save!"

Hearing what they are saying,
I, too, start praying.

"The girl is out of her senses!"
Shouts a man with a learned air,
"My eye and my lenses
Know there's nothing there.

Ghosts are a myth
Of ale-wife and blacksmith.
Clodhoppers! This is treason
Against King Reason!"

"Yet the girl loves," I reply diffidently,
"And the people believe reverently:
Faith and love are more discerning
Than lenses or learning.

You know the dead truths, not the living,
The world of things, not the world of loving.
Where does any miracle start?
Cold eye, look in your heart!"

[*Translated by W. H. Auden*]

Was Mickiewicz right in this ballad? If he was, if we are
to trust in "faith and love" rather than in "lenses and
learning," then why, after lectures exhorting us to exult
in this poem, were we herded into the natural-sciences lab
for instruction in the use of a microscope? Now, as I look
back on the time of our adolescence, I realize the extent to
which we were served a Mickiewicz tamed by clichés, a
cotton-wrapped Mickiewicz. And poems like "The Romantic" proved ideally suited to the taming process. The
poem is set in a village, but hardly a real village, not even
a remote gentry village, such as existed in the Grand
Duchy of Lithuania; it could just as easily be a village
in a Grimm fairy tale. And who exactly is that "crowd"?
How dressed? In typical fairy-tale costume, no doubt. And
the "man with a learned air," who in the name of Reason
declares the maiden "out of her senses," is imagined not
in the style of a Wilno professor but as the stock fairy-tale
figure that he is—adorned, most likely, with the peaked
cap of the astrologist or physician, which effectively dis-
tances us from the conflict: Ha, what does he know! In

the ballad's closing stanzas, the quarrel between crowd and savant is joined by the poet, presumably cast as a young wanderer who just happens through the village, yet sufficiently divested of any reality by the preceding stanzas that his dictum "Cold eye, look in your heart" is immediately read as the fable's moral.

My purpose here is to convey an image of Mickiewicz tamed and adulterated for curricular and extracurricular use. Man should indeed have a heart, should not immure himself with "dead truths"; he should indeed indulge in dreams, fantasies—what were once called "visions"—for without poetic fancy, as even the most practical-minded of the Positivists used to say, man would be but a reptile. Mickiewicz was a great poet, towering over others by the power of his emotion and by his ability to commune with the popular spirit, whose folk beliefs and legends served as inspiration for the water nymphs and ghosts of his *Ballads and Romances*, not to mention all the supernatural marvels of *Forefathers' Eve*: spirits dramatized on stage, souls heard atoning in a desk or dry log, angels, devils, "choruses on the left" and "choruses on the right" . . . True, Mickiewicz fell silent after *Pan Tadeusz* (1834), but it was a pardonable silence, as it amounted to a repudiation of poetry in favor of action. Less pardonable was his obsession with the occultism of Towiański, which caused him to lose his chair at the Collège de France and ruined his course, Lectures on Slavic Literatures. Well, that was just a phase, and by no means the last, as shown by the period of militancy that followed: the recruitment of legions in Italy, the publication of *Tribune des Peuples*, and the Constantinople mission.

Is it right to idolize a poet, to put him on a pedestal and divest him of his thought merely because the people are in greater need of a monument than of a mind? The version of Mickiewicz just presented has long rested uneasily with scholars—as evidenced by their recourse to such circumlocutions as "the enigma of Mickiewicz"—but who nonetheless found it expedient not to voice their qualms.

When a forty- or fifty-year-old poet evaluates his work and that of others, when he makes statements about religion and history, it is hard to affect ignorance. Mickiewicz traced a definite continuity in his work, running from his early poems to the mature vision of the later period. In a conversation with Aleksander Chodźko, held in 1847, he is quoted as saying: "Zaleski is the greatest among living poets of the old school. What makes me different is that I went my own way, from the start. And the later poetry has its germ in 'The Romantic': 'faith and love.' I was searching, like that girl in the poem; I saw something, and I never strayed from my course; *Wallenrod* and *Pan Tadeusz* were mere diversions."

Only one book to my knowledge, Andrzej Niemojewski's *Mickiewicz and Tradition*, today a rare and neglected work, published in Warsaw immediately after the First World War, has ever posed explicitly the problem that is of paramount concern to me here. Niemojewski was a man of remarkable curiosity, which took him into hitherto unexplored regions, even though a lack of formal training lent an amateurish quality to his anthropological-religious theories. One of the book's chapters, "Mickiewicz's Philosophy," written in 1910, has retained its relevance and acuity of insight. Much of its argument is explainable in terms of Niemojewski's Positivist background. If the Positivists were uncomfortable with a vatic bard whose work abounded in the supernatural, they were at pains to demonstrate that poets will be poets and so were to be indulged their world of "make-believe" phantoms. Although a militant freethinker, Niemojewski nonetheless disagrees with Chmielowski when he defends Mickiewicz from those who would make him a believer in "nocturnal spirits, ghosts, and wizardry." Chmielowski: "All that can be ascertained is that Mickiewicz, Romantic poet that he was, was infatuated with the mysterious side of natural phenomena and the human soul, and that without ceasing to give reason its due he strongly emphasized the elements of feeling and fantasy." On the contrary, argued Niemojewski. It was precisely because of his disrespect for reason, because of his belief in nocturnal spirits that his philosophy needs to be critically reevaluated. The chief fallacy of all interpretations thus far, according to Niemojewski, has been that their authors have stressed, each according to his bias, one facet at the expense of others; if ideas were found to be objectionable, it was said that, after all, Mickiewicz was a "child of the age"—which, claimed Niemojewski, was "blatantly false."

The nineteenth century, argued Niemojewski, marked the end of all traditional, religiously based civilizations. The final victory went to the eye and the lens, as a consequence of which "we are all evolutionists today." Yet, lamented Niemojewski, scientific progress is often bought at the price of transferring new perceptions to the past, with a distorting effect on historical truth. He writes:

> Our position is the more difficult and anomalous because, while evolutionism has established itself as an intellectual category, it has yet to take hold in the emotional realm. It has not yet been extended to art and poetry, nor has it exerted the slightest influence on our moral behavior. Our life still contains many vestiges of the past, and it will not soon be rid of them; they are enshrined in our legislation. Everywhere we are witnesses to the struggle for influence being waged between

the theologian and the naturalist. In this sense we are not the end-product but rather the first and perhaps imperfect draft of a new human formation, the first generation of evolutionists, transitional types, intermediaries between today and tomorrow.

A progressive with a traditional cast of mind is always a moving figure. Still, if scrupulously read, Niemojewski must be credited with the same insight as that deduced many years later by the geneticist Jacques Monod (in his *Chance and Necessity*)—namely, that the conflict between the "animistic tradition" and "objective truth" (science) is truly immense in its consequences. Niemojewski seems to posit a collective subconscious state defiant of "the new man." Further, that it was this antiquated consciousness which produced, at the juncture of two historical epochs, Mickiewicz's work of genius, above all *Forefathers' Eve*, which constituted "the last and most powerful manifestation of ancient philosophy, the swan song of a great and vanishing age. A work in which whole millennia—the 'ages' muted antiphony,' in the words of the bard—were to have their final say, before passing into history and making way for the modern."

Mickiewicz sprang from a hinterland untouched by the skepticism of the Age of Reason. The Warsaw of Stanisław Augustus Poniatowski stood planets apart from life in a Lithuanian village. At the university, he was exposed to the influence of the *philosophes*, though their influence proved ephemeral. Indeed, Mickiewicz's imagination never divested itself of pre-scientific cosmologies. "It is highly improbable," writes Niemojewski, "that the Copernican system was widely known in the Wilno of Mickiewicz's day. If it was taught at all at the university, then it entered those young minds by rote. Copernicus impressed Mickiewicz as a brilliant thinker, without ever altering the poet's eye or soul."

For Niemojewski, only a poet with a pre-scientific imagination (the Earth capped by a celestial dome) could write of a bird "pinned by its wing to the sky." In times of national and personal crisis, Mickiewicz would draw on beliefs that were the antithesis of modernity. So, too, *Forefathers' Eve*, Part III, is only ostensibly a political drama. Its real theme is neither freedom nor equality nor fraternity nor national sovereignty. It is a drama of the Apocalypse. The forces of light do battle with the Beast (Russian tsardom), which will be vanquished by the "viceroy" prophesied in the Vision of Father Peter. For Niemojewski, all apocalypses are political, and so Mickiewicz, a lifelong reader of the Bible (thus breaking with the traditional practice of Polish Catholicism), was easily able to transpose the Beast of antiquity (the Roman Empire) into a modern one, all the more so as the machinery of the foreign state was doubly pernicious in his eyes: both as a state (in the absence of any to call his own) and as Russia.

By defining Mickiewicz's sensibility as decidedly un-Polish, Niemojewski is a partisan of the then fairly widespread theory juxtaposing Poland and Lithuania. By this theory, the rationalism of the Śniadecki brothers, of the Enlightenment, corresponded to the natural (tribal?) proclivities of the Poles, which was corroborated by the subsequent evolution of Polish philosophy (the Lvov school, the Warsaw school, and the Polish school of mathematical logic). Everything in Mickiewicz was appropriated except his mysticism, because "the Polish people, patterned mainly on the Mazovian and Małopolski types, were organically unequipped to receive such a gift." While

Mickiewicz "roused the nation with the patriotism of *Forefathers' Eve*," insists Niemojewski, "his religious philosophy, superficially understood in terms of religious practice, was substantially ignored."

One final, tantalizing quote: "Lithuania is a land thoroughly imbued with mysticism; Poland not at all. Mickiewicz was an exemplary Catholic and Catholic philosopher just because Polish Catholicism can survive only so long as it is not usurped by a liberal-minded education. When that happens, mystics and non-mystics will engage in a decisive battle, in which the mystics stand to lose the ground of support lent them by Christianity. Such prophecies are naturally unwelcome. Neo-mysticism is already on the rise"—the allusion is to Lutosławski, I suspect—"and a revival of Catholicism, thanks to some brilliant minds, may also be imminent. But, in today's democratization, simpler ideas are favored over more complex ones. Philosophical materialism is more accessible to the masses hungering for illumination than is neo-mysticism. Renanism proved more accessible than Symbolism, which succeeded it, and therefore won for itself many minds, not excluding many of the clergy."

The theory of a rational Poland versus a mystical Lithuania seems to have been expressly invoked to deal with the Mickiewicz phenomenon. He was plainly too much for Polish literature, his presence too great a burden, which is why that literature—beginning with Słowacki and ending with Gombrowicz—would become, in the main, a succession of revolts against Mickiewicz. By citing Lithuania's backwardness, Niemojewski might have dispensed with any additional theories, since from his point of view it was only appropriate that the "swan song" of religious millennia should have been heard in one of the most backwater regions of Europe, with its mixture of pagan and Christian beliefs.

Is Niemojewski eccentric in his interpretation of Mickiewicz? If he appears so, it is only because militant freethinkers have been rare in Poland. Freethinking might be practiced in private but not displayed publicly, lest it be deemed unpatriotic. If not for self-censorship, the Niemojewskian approach would not be such a rarity. It has the virtue of restoring continuity to a career traditionally viewed as erratic, inconsistent. Mickiewicz's "silence" achieves now a new eloquence. For one thing, his "Lausanne lyrics" and *Apothegms and Sayings*, with their renunciation of ornament, their stripping of language to the elementary, and their freedom from the obsessions of authorship and originality, stand as Mickiewicz's supreme achievement as a religious poet (note how the *Apothegms and Sayings* have been neglected by Polish scholars!). For another, Mickiewicz never resorted to aggressive tactics by carrying the contest to the enemy, as Blake and Goethe both tried to do. Rather, he protected himself from the "learned," who were now being cast as the satanic masters of laboratories (as in Mary Shelley's *Frankenstein, or the Modern Prometheus*, published in 1818), with "faith and love." Yet, as the adversary broadened his domain, European poetry was more and more seeking salvation in irony, until it would become the last refuge. But Mickiewicz— here Niemojewski's thesis is very helpful—was not of the age of irony. True, he had translated Byron, but then he had also translated Voltaire. He was not a Byronist (compared to Mickiewicz, Byron is all gush) and had little sympathy for the sneering sufferers of *mal du siècle* or *mirovaja skorb'*. And how could he have written ironic poetry—in the style, let us say, of Baudelaire's *Fleurs du*

Mal—after the sheer nakedness of *Apothegms and Sayings?* Similarly, Mickiewicz's initiation into the Towiański cult, that dementia of the spirit banished by a civilization of pedants and merchants, now becomes intelligible. It contributed almost nothing to his vision that was not already contained in *Forefathers' Eve*, at most reinforcing certain aspects. Even after he parted company with Towiański, Mickiewicz remained loyal to his convictions from the time of the Circle, something he kept stressing in private till the end of his life.

Parochial: just how much so becomes evident when we survey the literary names that were gaining prominence in the last decade of Mickiewicz's life. It was a decade that saw Baudelaire engaged as a poet and art critic, which saw the publication of Dostoevsky's *The Double*, Flaubert at work on *Madame Bovary*, and Kierkegaard publishing his principal works. The "disinherited mind," in other words, was seeking new modes and styles. And the attitude toward Mickiewicz of a modern like Gombrowicz, nurtured on various modes of irony and sarcasm, is essentially the attitude of the professional freethinker Niemojewski—if decidedly less magnanimous. For Gombrowicz, Mickiewicz was flawed by his philosophy—the "philosophy of a superstitious child." For Niemojewski, on the other hand, he stood as "the son of millennia," in the sense that years could be spent in mining the submerged layers of Mickiewicz's thought, so rich and symbolically suggestive were its premises, both Christian and pre-Christian—in a way, Niemojewski anticipated the Jungian school. He bemoaned the lack of religious scholarship on the part of Polish commentators, and predicted that competent studies of Mickiewicz would have to await the future.

23

IF YOU DO NOT UNDERSTAND something, it is better to admit as much. For me the relation between Mickiewicz the thinker and his work, above all *Forefathers' Eve*, is beyond comprehension. I am equally baffled by the presence of ghosts and specters in a literary work. Nor do I expect the "enigma of Mickiewicz" ever to be solved, at best reinterpreted. The sixteenth volume of Mickiewicz's *Collected Works*, devoted to conversations with his contemporaries, is all the more bewildering when we cease to indulge poets as uncontrollable instruments in the service of "fantasies" and "visions." Here was a man of strong faith, persuaded that Christianity was founded on prophecy, and who, in a conversation with Aleksander Chodźko, expressed the view that "Jakob Boehme was a divine prophet and seer of today's Christianity no less than Isaiah was for the Hebrews." Swedenborg was another, though—says Mickiewicz—"he was not as strictly or as thoroughly initiated into the world of the spirit. A man of occasionally profound but more often ordinary visions." That is, Mickiewicz revered as prophets two highly unorthodox Lutherans. Not to mention one Catholic of dubious orthodoxy: "Saint-Martin understood Boehme well; he lived among skeptics— Voltaire, Rousseau—in what was a hard time for believers, and he is the third prophet."

A prophet foresees the future. Were Christian prophets born only to foretell the end of Christianity, indeed, of all religion? Not so. They bear witness to the decline, the decadence, the breakdown, and herald the beginning of a new era. Common to all three of Mickiewicz's prophets is a perception of the crisis of the age provoked by the alternative elected by science. Boehme springs directly from Renaissance alchemy. The eighteenth-century opposition to post-Cartesian science is illustrated by the biography of Swedenborg, one of its most brilliant votaries, who suffered an internal crisis and abandoned science for theurgy. Claude de Saint-Martin, on the other hand, rebelled against science's ally: the philosophy of the Enlightenment. By paying them tribute, Mickiewicz could not help but regard the anguish of "the disinherited mind" as the consequence of mankind's deviation from the correct path, and it is not hard to guess why he dismissed the "new literature." The problem he confronted was the dynastic succession of prophets, the question of who is a prophet in his own time. In more modern terms, the problem might be posed as the great antinomy between contingency (*contingentia*) and necessity. In this context, the terms denote the following proposition: either a man lives because he lives, with no necessity for having been born this very man, or each individual existence is necessary because preordained in the divine scheme. If one were to try to capture in a few sentences the essence of our modern anxieties and grievances, such a formulation might well suffice. He who accepts the arbitrariness, the fortuity of his life, elects the atheistic solution at its most painful, at its least abstract. The man of religion must contend with other worries. Assign as he may a providential role to some—to sages, saints, prophets—he is much harder put to decide his own destiny: there is always the risk of self-delusion through pride and egoism. Prophets, on the other hand, all share an inner and inviolable certitude as to their exceptional mission. This was the case with Mickiewicz's three prophets. Boehme was mercilessly persecuted by his fellow Lutherans, yet persevered with the publication of his books aimed at bequeathing his teaching to posterity. Swedenborg openly declared that the one prophesied by the Gospel, St. John Parakletos (the "Comforter"), had arrived; that he had appointed Swedenborg as his instrument; and that the New Church, the most radical departure since the Holy Spirit descended on the Apostles and the faithful in Jerusalem, began with him. Claude de Saint-Martin, known to his contemporaries as "Le Philosophe Inconnu," was seized with fervor and dedication out of a conviction that he alone had been called, at a critical historical moment, to refute the errors of the Encyclopedists. It was this belief in a preordained destiny and mission that would pose such an obstacle to modern existentialism, at least in its atheistic version. Man is free just because his life is devoid of any "mission"; whatever sense it has is conferred by him alone. Sartre accordingly bestowed the epithet *les salauds* on all who would assign a metaphysical significance to the fact of their birth.

The epithet might also be applied to Mickiewicz. The dialectic of pride and humility allowed him, on the one hand, to cast himself as prophet and, on the other, to submit to the Master, Andrzej Towiański. A skeptic, more apt to accuse prophets of self-delusion, might ascertain from Mickiewicz's example the rashness of such accusations. The "man of dread," the "viceroy," the "one named forty-four," may not have saved the peoples of Europe, much less converted the Poles to his religion, but he did embalm the nation with a messianic nationalism strong enough to consume all who would resist it—horse, armor, and all. Prophets may not always reap the consequences of their actions, but the sense they possess of their own power is no self-delusion.

If Mickiewicz's nationalism was thus appropriated, his religiosity was handled with suspicion. Whether that religiosity is deserving of the name Roman Catholic is another matter. But that it forms the true poetic substance of *Forefathers' Eve* is indisputable. Its exposition, as recorded in a conversation with Seweryn Goszczyński in 1844, may seem a parody alongside Mickiewicz's poetry, but it nonetheless conveys, in another language, what is already anticipated in the drama:

What I'm telling you is not something I dreamed up, not some doctrine or other; I have seen that world, I have been there, touched it with the naked soul.

The other world is no different from this one; believe me, it's the same there as it is here. When a man dies, he does not change his place of habitation but abides in those places to which he was bound in spirit; there's your mystery of the souls in Purgatory. There you live among the same spirits as you did here; there you accomplish what, on earth, in the flesh, you were meant to accomplish, but didn't. But it's awfully hard work without a body; you have to act on earth but without any earthly devices. It can take up to five hundred years of waiting and wailing.

It is a great joy for the world of spirits when a man in the flesh can stir it. It feels then the way we would feel to hear a dog speak; for them, it's a miracle. That's why Christ descended into Hell in the flesh.

The master treads the earth with his feet but he lives and works in the world of spirits, he is always there; all his labors start and end there.

This is not strictly Catholicism. The priests must have been sorely vexed with Mickiewicz, since they could neither affirm nor deny such a vision. At most, they might have remonstrated that it was unbecoming of a Christian to indulge in idle discourse about what went on in the other world, on which point they would have been loyal to tradition. That same tradition implies several propositions. Among them the belief that form and content are indivisible in religion, that everything in it is a text—the text of Holy Writ, the text of exegesis, the text of the liturgy—which is inevitable, given man's rough and approximate knowledge of the divine, a knowledge commensurate with his nature and hence circumscribed by the possibilities of language. Mickiewicz would seem to be professing a doctrine congenial to Catholicism (and to the Eastern Rite): the Communion of Saints, the doctrine of the one Church uniting the living and the dead—the Church Militant (those here on earth), the Church Suffering (the souls in Purgatory), and the Church Triumphant (the saved). But in the Catholic version, that eternal society, existing both in time and beyond time, lives through prayer, through pleas for the intercession of the dead on behalf of the living and of the living on behalf of the dead—pleas described by a certain ritual. Who would set forth into the world of spirits in order "to work"? No saint would be so inclined. Folk religion, on the other hand, with its phantoms soliciting a paternoster for "the souls burning in Purgatory," is even more inclined to ritual, incantation, and metaphor.

When we come to Mickiewicz's belief in metempsychosis, we can only shrug in dismay. To invoke St. Paul, as Mickiewicz did in conversation with Aleksander Chodźko in 1848, requires no little mental acrobatics: "Much was intuited by Pythagoras and Plato. But it was St. Paul's letters which revealed the doctrine of metempsychosis. Clothing the soul with a body, in particular with a human body, is a great heavenly blessing, the soul's most salutary hour, marking its rebirth and return to its original state of perfection. Such a labor is more time-consuming and arduous in the invisible world."

From a variety of sources dating from different periods, there can be no doubt that Mickiewicz accepted the transmigration of souls, as opposed to eternal perdition, which he could not accept. In the conversation just cited, Chodźko records a remark which impresses us today as a statement of either lunacy or presumptuousness: "Human life is a page inside a book: not until the preceding pages are known can it be understood. It is all a matter of breaching the cradle. Of discovering our past lives." Here, by the way, we are already in the poet's post-Towiańskian phase. And to Armand Lévy, in 1854, at the very end of his life, Mickiewicz would remark: "After the soul has left the body, before the moment of reincarnation, it lingers in places where it once lived, where its body still is, and binds itself to objects close to it. We always deposit something of our souls in the things we touch."

As an admirer of the poet Mickiewicz, as one vaguely embarrassed by his involvement in the Towiański sect, indeed, by the full range of his publicistic-proselytizing activities, I have always felt a certain unease when reading the scholarship on him: something was missing, the quick of it. Mickiewicz's proclamations were treated with the honor due the flights and visionary transports of a seer, and with a critical abstemiousness all too eager to attribute his sundry eccentricities to the *Zeitgeist*. My research on Dostoevsky, on his journalistic writings, with their plethora of messianic and chauvinistic follies, and on his notebooks and drafts, has taught me that a noncommittal attitude toward "the poet's ideas" is inadequate. It is not so that everything transmitted by the past is of equal value and lends itself to a scholarly, "objective" treatment. A given civilization, or civilization in general, endures in its bodies of thought, forming crystal-like structures obedient to an internal logic. Whoever admits to proposition A must necessarily accede to B; conversely, whoever assents to B must accept A; that is, when we commit ourselves to something, we commit ourselves to more than what is directly apparent. Take the example of one of Europe's more critical periods, the Reformation. Martin Luther protested against the practice of trading in indulgences, and justifiably so, because it was a disgraceful practice. But consequently he had to discard the intercession of saints, abolish Purgatory, and purge Protestantism of the Communion of Saints—in other words, to condemn the individual to an isolation unfettered by past and future generations. Further examples are provided by the ideologies of our own time, which prescribe that given step 1, steps 2 and 3 must follow. The same holds for the case at hand, Mickiewicz's metempsychosis. I would even argue that it is the neurological nodal point where the disorder intrinsic to Romanticism, its insufficient corporeality, makes itself manifest.

To read a doctrine of metempsychosis into St. Paul is an unpardonable license. If anything, the opposite was true. As an allegory, as a Platonic myth, the migration of souls greatly appealed to the Hellenistic imagination; it was Christianity which sought to prevent the elevation of poetic myth into doctrine, a tendency prevalent among various cults. Abhorrence for the world, despair, boredom, and disaffection must have been no less acute then than in the second half of the twentieth century—just how acute is illustrated by the popular image of the corporeal as the soul's prison (an image favored both by the Gnostics and by their adversary, Plotinus). The Christians, in the belief that man had only one life on earth, were in effect defending the dignity of the world given to our senses; by professing the resurrection of bodies, St. Paul erected a perpetual barrier between Christianity and those religions coming directly or indirectly out of India. The conflicting attitudes can be expressed in terms of a polarity: the more we incline to the hope that man will be saved in his entirety, that his body will be restored and "transfigured," the more disinclined we are to visions of astral spirits migrating from one bodily form to another. When we read such "resurrectionist" works as Słowacki's *Samuel Zborowski*, we become suspicious: the invention of astral spirits seems too facile, their ethereality too obviously the penalty of a revolt against matter—whether conceived of as a prison or, as in Słowacki's case, as clay fashioned by the Spirit. And this ethereality is characteristic of Romanticism as a whole, a movement proliferating in works of "mist and ink," with the result that dreams are often confused with acts of the imagination and all sense of humor sacrificed, as when Mickiewicz declared to Armand Lévy that Richelieu, believing he would be a horse in the next life, ate hay on his deathbed.

If the sources of Mickiewicz's metempsychosis have been profusely researched, the results have been inconclusive, insofar as by themselves literary influences reveal little. Nowhere, for example, do we find it in Swedenborg. True, Pigoń cites a number of French and German writers from the turn of the nineteenth century who professed a belief in metempsychosis, yet he neglects to add that the reigning sensibility—an amalgam of skepticism, fascination with the marvelous, and a fondness for mysterious rites (the "Egyptian lodges")—could accommodate just about anything. Mickiewicz's case is the more mystifying in that metempsychosis appears early in his work, in the Wilno–Kovno installment of *Forefathers' Eve*, where we find an atoning usurer cast as a beetle and former officials as moths.

·115·

These images are invested with too much emotionality to be of literary provenance. One suspects something of more native origin, the vestiges of a pagan symbolism still preserved in Lithuania, or of folklore, also of local origin.

The Encyclopedia Judaica assumes, perhaps rashly so, that Mickiewicz's mother was of Jewish ancestry. Among the arguments advanced (compiled by Samuel Scheps in his book *Adam Mickiewicz: Ses affinités juives*, 1964), two are of crucial importance: first, the reference in *Forefathers' Eve* to a redeemer "born of a foreign mother," and to his name "forty-four," the numerical equivalent of the Hebrew letters forming the word Adam—assuming, of course, the poet had himself in mind;* second, the testimony of Ksawery Branicki, to whom the poet is alleged to have said: "My father was a Mazovian, my mother a late convert. That makes me half Lechite† and half Israelite, an ancestry of which I am proud."‡

The mother's low social status—her father was a land steward—argues against a Frankist origin. The Frankists were usually of the nobility and therefore socially superior to the common gentry. By whatever route Mickiewicz was exposed to Jewish influences, whether directly or indirectly (even very indirectly, via the disciples of Martinez Pasqualis, founder of the "mystical lodges" in France and a Portuguese Jew by origin), an intriguing dimension is offered by Gershom G. Scholem in his book *On the Kab-*

---

* Adam, in fact, equals 45. Possible solutions, through a reduction of the letter A, are listed by Abraham G. Duker in his "Some Cabbalistic and Frankist Elements in Mickiewicz's 'Dziady'," *Studies in Polish Civilization*, ed. by Damian S. Wandycz (New York, 1971).

† Lechite is a synonym for Pole.—Trans.

‡ The German memoirist Karl Varnhagen von Ense cites a conversation with Karolina Jaenisch-Pavlova, held after Mickiewicz's death, in which she is quoted as saying: "Mickiewicz was a Jew."

balah and Its Symbolism (a translation from the German), 1965. I quote:

> But the exile of the body in outward history has its parallel in the exile of the soul in its migrations from embodiment to embodiment, from one form of being to another. The doctrine of metempsychosis as the exile of the soul acquired unprecedented popularity among the Jewish masses of the generations following the Lurianic period.

The sufferings of the Jews in the diaspora (in the realm of "external history"), especially in Spain, promoted, according to Scholem, a curious transposition of fate: from that of a people in exile surrounded by foreigners, to that of exiled souls surrounded by a foreign substance—a transposition typical of cabalistic folklore after the sixteenth century, the time of the great cabalist, Isaac Luria.

Possibly the metempsychosis of Mickiewicz, Towiański, and Słowacki, regardless of any conjectured borrowings from Jewish folk religion, was a response to the condition of exile and isolation, not only in the political but in the intellectual-artistic sense. As a young man Mickiewicz had rebelled against "the eye and the lenses" of the Śniadeckis, yet the savants—"their minds honed on their books" (i.e., scientists and philosophers)—would gain steadily in authority during the poet's lifetime, so that by the time of his death, Europe was already traveling by railroad, erecting factories, and reading realistic romances. Its heart pulsed in the modern city, in Baudelaire's *cité infernale*, or in Dostoevsky's Babylon, the name he bestowed on London after his trip there in 1862. Mickiewicz's gradual articulation of the doctrine of metempsychosis, from its shy

beginnings in the Wilno–Kovno installment of *Forefathers'
Eve* to its final codification in the Towiański Circle, illustrates the stages by which he, and the Polish Romantics in
general, parted company with the *Zeitgeist.*

In ancient, pre-Christian symbolism, the difference between a repentant spirit and a night bird, a moth, or an
insect was blurred, the one being synonymous with the
other, just as it is blurred in the early Mickiewicz, to the
glory of his poetry. These same spirits may later take on a
gelatinous solidity and commence to lead a life of their
own. So, too, one's native land. At first it is a visible,
palpable Lithuania: native landscapes, relatives, friends,
body and soul coalesced. Later the soul abandons the body,
to become an Idea, a presence, until it is finally raised to
the mythical. It will be recalled that in the end all three
—Mickiewicz, Towiański, and, following their example,
Słowacki—came to believe that the "woman clothed with
the Sun" in St. John's Revelation symbolized Poland.

Today it is presumably known, though not eagerly
acknowledged, that the Polish–Lithuanian Commonwealth
of the seventeenth and eighteenth centuries had within its
territory the largest concentration of Jews in the world,
among whom the most extraordinary religious movements
were propagated. In the second half of the seventeenth
century, news of the arrival of the Messiah in Asia Minor
saw thousands of Jews selling their possessions and migrating southward. The Messiah, Sabbatai Zevi, a native of
Smyrna, had begun as an adept of Lurianic cabalistics. Nor
should the Commonwealth's common border and continual traffic with Turkey be ignored: the next Messiah,
Jacob Frank, in a way Sabbatai Zevi's eighteenth-century
successor, grew up in Saloniki, before a vision instructed
him to embark on a trip to Poland, the Promised Land.

In Poland the Frankist practice of mass baptism and ennoblement—after their expulsion from the synagogue—dates from 1759, and the year of Frank's death, 1791, falls within a decade of Mickiewicz's birth. For several generations the Frankists married exclusively among themselves and secretly professed their doctrine of the Great Crisis. That Mickiewicz's wife was a Frankist is well known. Another, more important movement, that of Hasidism, founded by Ba'al Shem-Tov from Czarnohora, was also born on Commonwealth territory. And where else, in what other pocket of Europe, could another messianism of a suffering and chosen nation have arisen? Poland (and all that the concept connoted) was to be the new Israel. Mickiewicz was not to be deterred by contradictions. Just as little as metempsychosis was consistent with Christianity, the idea of a "chosen nation" was incompatible with the New Testament; the New Dispensation announced that the covenant between God and Israel was to be succeeded by another, this one between God and Ecclesia. The Christians would put one another to the sword in defense of what they took to be the true Church, the New Israel; yet Christianity has never tolerated the concept of a "chosen nation." To portray a nation as a collective Christ, as Mickiewicz did, is not only a contradiction but a blasphemy, not much better than the one Konrad was on the verge of committing by calling God a tsar.

The following pronouncements by Mickiewicz, as recorded by Chodźko in 1847, are awesome, full of grandeur, but they reek of brimstone:

For the first three centuries, Christians were martyred for *eating a man's body and drinking his blood.* We know it as the mystery of the Eucharist, which many

Christians refused to deny. But the pagans took it literally, missing the mystical significance, and thought they were doing right by killing the cannibals.

Something like that is happening today. Russia fears nothing so much as the "Polish idea." But no Pole in Russian bondage, not even the basest, most outwardly servile and slavish, not even those who torture their own compatriots, is allied heart and soul with the Muscovite. But Poles of today are not uplifting it—the Polish idea—and are to the Russians what the Jews before Christ were to the Romans.

The "Polish idea" would seem to correspond perfectly to the "Russian idea," only its end is exactly the reverse. As expounded at least in Dostoevsky's essays, the "Russian idea" might be translated as follows: the time will come when a godless, communist Europe, headed by "a barefoot Pope," will be challenged by a God-fearing nation, Russia, who will deliver its Christ on the points of bayonets.

24

YOU AMONG THE VULTURES—you, a Polish poet who has said that your every line of verse was indebted to Mickiewicz and that among the moderns, whether Polish, French, English, or German, there was not one to rival his simplicity and power of the word? Here I wish to avert a misunderstanding. A literary work is not a vestment for the author's "philosophy," a cocoon form spun to house its matter. Mickiewicz's work and his philosophy inhabit two different realms; criticism of the latter in no way impugns the former. No more than Dostoevsky's achievement is diminished by condemnation of the national bias informing his essays, insofar as Dostoevsky the novelist is distinguishable from Dostoevsky the essayist.

Distinguishable? Not altogether so. If an author's work and his intellectual persuasions are bound together, intricately, inextricably, then those persuasions merit scrutiny, in the hope that they will facilitate our comprehension of the work. Here an analogy drawn from nature comes to mind. In surveying a snowy mountain landscape, one alive with skiers, children building snowmen, icicles glistening under eave troughs, one could argue that such winter scenes are simply water in a composite state, that it is all a matter of the temperature. Which would be both valid and invalid. The analogy limps to the extent that the author's world-view (an infelicitous expression) is not necessarily embodied in his work; other layers of consciousness may assert themselves, and an author may even contradict what he professes publicly. Even so, that world-view ought not to be neglected, though in the case of Mickiewicz it has been effectively evaded by recourse to the term "mysticism," which has a negative connotation in Polish, implying something "otherworldly." The use of such a term is a sign of either extreme literal-mindedness or sheer laziness; it assumes that "mysticism," the attempt to grasp the ungraspable, can only bring frustration, and so is better left alone.

The name Dostoevsky keeps issuing from my pen. That is so because life is short, and I am attracted less and less to a literature which is self-consciously literary. The degree to which a work is of extraliterary importance is determined by the power of a given author's philosophy, that is, by the passion with which it is engaged with ultimate things, resulting in an extreme tension between the art and the thought. For my purpose, a few names will suffice to represent a tradition in European literature that began when the mind first entered the land of the disinherited—Blake's Ulro; a land where man is reduced to a supererogatory number, worse, where he becomes as much for himself, in his own eyes, in his own mind. Blake, and at least to some extent Goethe, were two who bravely joined the battle, choosing to attack rather than defend. Mickiewicz was sheltered, for a time, by his provincial Muse, Lithuania. Despite appearances, despite even the author's own conscious intent, *Pan Tadeusz* is at heart a metaphysical poem, its subject being one seldom perceived in quotidian reality: *the world of existence as an image of pure Being.* Herein lies the secret of this "last epos in European literature," for *Pan Tadeusz* is not merely a product of a patriarchal social order. It could only have been written by a poet who—in 1849, let us note—once said: "A man's most important books are the calendar and the breviary"; a poet, in other words, in whom the old time-ritualizing ways were vestigially rooted in the agrarian year and in the liturgical year, respectively. Ultimately, only a time measured by sacral standards, and not mechanical clock-time, can sanction a belief in the reality of things. A sunrise or sunset, such mundane acts as making coffee or mushroom hunting are both what the reader knows them to be and a surface bespeaking a sublime acceptance, one to animate and sustain the imaging. This same acceptance, even more than fidelity to detail and color harmony, is what distinguishes the paintings of some of the Dutch masters. If the poetic movement known as Symbolism had not prejudiced our understanding of the term "symbol," we might declare the cucumbers and watermelons of the Soplica garden to be eminently worthy of the designation—as things that are both themselves, in the fullness of being, and not themselves. Mickiewicz, who after *Pan Tadeusz* swore never again "to waste the pen on frivolities," who even dimissed the work as a "diversion," would no doubt dissent from our interpretation, yet two circumstances should be cited in its defense. First, *Pan Tadeusz* belongs to the same body of metaphysical and religious poetry as his "Roman lyrics" and *Forefathers' Eve*, Part III, and the "enigma of Mickiewicz" would indeed be unsolvable if, instead of persistently mining the same vein in a variety of forms and genres, as artists are accustomed to working, the poet had been capable of shutting off one tap and turning on another. Second, professors of the literature, despite exertions as pathetic as they are desperate, have never been able to explain "why we should love *Pan Tadeusz*"; indeed, as long as we remain on the surface, this banally plotted tale à la Walter Scott is hardly deserving of adoration; and since its hidden message is lost in translation, foreigners are justified in treating with suspicion the claims of greatness advanced for it. And not only foreigners. The resistance of Polish readers to the work's earthiness has promoted a search for "profundity" in the work of Słowacki, Krasiński and, more recently, of Norwid, even though not one of these can stand comparison with Mickiewicz as a poet.

Dostoevsky belongs to another era, and his intellectual *raisonneur*-heroes are deprived of that felicitous earth-garden which in *Pan Tadeusz* steps forth in all its loveliness. Like their predecessors—Pushkin's Onegin and Lermontov's Pechorin—they are inhabitants of the Infernal City, the land of the disinherited, in which all are reduced to specters, to phantoms of the abstracted intellect. The Man from the Underground, Raskolnikov, Ippolit Terentiev, Stavrogin, Kirilov, and Ivan Karamazov are blood of blood, bone of bone of their creator; and

Dostoevsky, internally riven, corrupted by the "scientific world-view," wages a desperate war, whence comes his extraliterary literature that, sad to say, is well adapted to the aberrations of our time.

Forefathers' Eve is predicated on a communion of the living and the dead, on a belief in intercession. The dead implore the help of the living (the rite of Forefathers' Eve); the living save the living through prayer (Eve, Father Peter); the dead protect the living ("your mother's earthly merits"). The hierarchy is triadic: on one side, Heaven, the Church Triumphant, Good; on the other, Hell, the damned, Evil; and in the center, closely allied, Purgatory, the Church Suffering, and Earth, the Church Militant, Good and Evil. The contest between Good and Evil is uneven; even if a man is occasionally saved from perdition with the help of the good spirits, Evil is strong, Good weak —if ultimately triumphant.

The reasons for the play's jolting effect, whether read in private or seen in performance, must be sought through introspection. Its paramount theme, man in the face of misfortune, is one that compels a personal response. Nearly everyone reacts to misfortune with shock, as something that though forbidden to happen has happened. It seems a violation of that unwritten pact with life. We believe in the pact, by which we are to be saved, however much we may suffer. But if the pact be violated, then let there be a higher court capable of punishing the violator (who?); and it is the absence of that court which is deemed a perfidy. We scream—for how long is a matter of individual sensibility, temperament. Most of us experience it at least once in our lives—with the loss of a loved one, an incurable illness, a professional disappointment. But if, as has become all too habitual in our century, one is presented with the spectacle of foreign tanks entering the streets of one's hometown, then one has known another, more public misfortune. In the end, every form of collective misfortune amounts to the same thing—an invasion, real or anticipated, from within or without; a conquest of defenseless human beings by institutionalized force. The higher court to which we would appeal then becomes "the world," other nations, other countries. One final touch: "the world," either overtly or covertly, takes the side of the conqueror, because he who surrenders gives proof of his weakness and is therefore undeserving of solicitude.

Gustav-Konrad has suffered a double misfortune, both personal and public, the latter in the form of a foreign invasion. In antiquity, wars of conquest were accepted as a natural consequence of military hegemony, yet even today, at the close of our savage century, we read with unease of the massacres inflicted by the Romans wherever they met with resistance, whether in Gaul or in Palestine. By the eighteenth century, wars of conquest were obsolete in Europe; the partitions of Poland, the Praga massacre, the dealing in countries at the Congress of Vienna were a novel departure prefiguring events of a much later date.

To subsume everything political in *Forefathers' Eve* under the term "patriotism" is to curtail analysis of certain aspects that are the play's substance. The despair provoked by foreign invasion is only partially nurtured by the opposition "native" versus "foreign." Anyone who remembers reading as a child, with fists clenched, of the noble redskins divested of their native land knows that it concerns, rather, a moral injustice, one demanding that the evildoers be punished; when the guilty not only go unpunished but appear to be in connivance with the laws of this world, we regard it as a moral outrage. For reasons difficult to define, Polish culture is marked by an optimistic faith in a preordained, divinely sanctioned order, which may be violated but not for long. I quote Brzozowski: "Is not Polish history premised on the near certitude that the world is in appearance a sorrow and in reality a joy, in appearance a debacle and in reality a triumph?" And: "Through the impetuosity of that nation there glimmers a luminous profundity." And just because the rights of the Prince of Darkness are not acknowledged, a foreign invasion becomes a jolting experience, literally a bolt out of the blue, a misfortune of moral proportions.

Mickiewicz, in many respects old-fashioned, was also very modern. Konrad's indictment of God shares in that tradition begun by the French philosophers, who indicted God for the enormity of suffering endured by ordinary mortals. The accusation bore mainly on individual suffering, occasionally on mass suffering of the sort caused by natural calamities. An event which figured prominently in the philosophical debate of the time was the great Lisbon earthquake of 1755, which took the lives of tens of thousands. Konrad, on the other hand, adduces the argument of foreign invasions and captive nations. To accuse God of being not the world's father but its tsar may seem an act of childish impudence or, at the very least, a *lèse majesté*. In fact, a great deal more is at stake, just how much more becomes apparent when we turn to Dostoevsky's heroes burdened by the same problem.

That uncongenial but brilliant young man, Ivan Karamazov, is no mere atheist, atheism being much too crude for him. He would invalidate God on purely moral grounds. For him, the order of creation is morally untenable. To quote Nikolai Berdyaev:

At the root of Ivan Karamazov's problem is a false Russian sensitivity and sentimentality [*kakaja-to lozhnaja russkaja chustvitel'nost' i santimental'nost'*], a spurious sympathy for men manifested as a hatred of God and of the divine scheme of worldly existence. Russians are sometimes moved to become nihilist-rebels from a bogus morality. A Russian will indict God for a child's solitary tear, return his ticket, reject all values and all things sacred; will not tolerate suffering or victims. Yet, instead of doing anything to reduce the number of tears shed, he will multiply them; he will start a revolution sustained by countless tears and sufferings.

That Ivan Karamazov is the author of the *Legend of the Grand Inquisitor* is not accidental. The moment God has been "invalidated," the distinction between good and evil, truth and falsehood, has become groundless, and Nature, obedient to its own laws, becomes supreme. Thrice Jesus was tempted, and thrice he refused to break those laws; consequently, the Grand Inquisitor, who would grant mankind happiness (thereby "correcting" Jesus), decides to act sensibly, i.e., in compliance with the laws both of Nature and of human nature. But the latter are the domain of the dreaded Spirit of Non-Being. Accordingly, the Grand Inquisitor (here read Ivan Karamazov, the lover of children) must regard those whom he governs as both children and slaves.

If Konrad had called God a tsar, he would have had to grant a self-sustaining universe destitute of divine mercy; in other words, he would have had to repeat the same argument advanced by Ivan Karamazov. In the balance, then, hangs the universe: either it is absurd or it is ordered. Konrad, true to the Polish tradition, to a tradition intrinsically inimical to pessimism, chooses the latter, a choice made possible through the prayerful intercession of others. Mickiewicz's next work, the narrative poem *Pan*

Tadeusz, becomes in a way the logical consequence of that choice: a work bodying forth its own kind of theodicy, a vindication of the Creator—creator of the Earth-garden.

Coming at Mickiewicz by way of Dostoevsky allows us to dispense with all sorts of scholarly trivia. A Russian has even remarked a similarity between Konrad's sensation of power (in the monologue "The Great Improvisation"), and the pre-epileptic stages experienced by some of Dostoevsky's heroes: that second, says Myshkin, when time stops, and the epileptic Mahomet has time to behold the throne of Allah before the overturned water pitcher has emptied. Konrad's climactic moments are disproportionate to the length of the monologue as a whole, which is minutes long in duration. It is also noteworthy that Konrad, at the height of his visionary trance, like Kirilov in *The Possessed,* sees himself as a Man-god.

Forefathers' Eve would be a great Christian drama, if it were not for its intruding heresy, which is the same heresy that taints Dostoevsky's journalism and even certain chapters of his novels. It is a heresy which would erase the distinction between religion and "the national idea." Declares Shatov in *The Possessed*: "I believe in Russia, in Russian Orthodoxy . . . I believe in the body of Christ . . . I believe the next coming will take place in Russia . . ." But asked if he believes in God, he replies: "I . . . I will believe in God." Not "I do," but "I will." Still, Shatov is spared by Dostoevsky by reason of a somewhat strained syllogism: he who loves the Russian people is blessed with *caritas,* and that alone makes him capable of brotherly love and humane forgiveness—as illustrated by the way in which Shatov forgives his wife. A similar argument can be traced through Mickiewicz's text, culminating in the Vision of Father Peter. Yet, even if the tragic experience of an invasion can easily provoke a momentary aberration, our respect for someone's justifiable anger does not exempt us from critical objectivity. A collective body crucified in atonement of the sins of mankind? And who is this person whose love for the nation exalts him to a "national redeemer," a "viceroy," a figure "above peoples and potentates"? Admittedly, Słowacki's aim was satirical in the Prologue to *Kordian*. But he interpreted the Vision of Father Peter in the only way it could have been interpreted: as a travesty of St. John's Revelation, in which Mickiewicz is cast, no more and no less, as the Son of Man, the alpha and the omega, the Logos ("A robe of sumptuous fold/ draping to my feet, my loins girt with gold,/ My head wool-mantled, snowy-white;/ My eye ablaze with diamond fire").

A Christian drama of victory thus becomes a drama of defeat. Expelled from Konrad by the exorcisms of Father Peter, the devil, not one to be outwitted, enters the exorcist and dictates his vision—an irony unfortunately lost on the poet himself. Konrad aspired to be a Man-god but, assisted by the prayers of loved ones, retreated in time. But who rescues the self-appointed Man-god prophesied in Father Peter's vision?

As a vision of theatrical space, *Forefathers' Eve* is unprecedented. It is a powerful act of the imagination, but one that would not be possible without the play's constant evocation of the supernatural. Here we must contend with certain impediments, previously either ignored or only dimly foreseen. The drama's spirits, devils and angels, are full-bodied characters, and nothing can justify such acts of license as rendering these otherworldly figures by loudspeaker voices, a practice initiated by Leon Schiller. The play's "magic," which is so to Mickiewicz's purpose, is very tactile and serves as a means of enlarging space. Not only is the box stage abandoned in favor of a succession of *tableaux vivants* in multiple settings (a cemetery, a chapel, a prison cell, the salons of Wilno and Warsaw); not only is horizontal movement on the earthly level combined with vertical movement (during the ancestors' rite, spirits descend from above and circle " 'neath the chapel ceiling"), but the intruders from the beyond expand space by creating the illusion of that other, "make-believe" space whence they have come.

Do Mickiewicz's spirits exist? Here is where we run into difficulties. The reader or viewer, on unbiased reflection, will answer: yes, for us they do exist in the drama *Forefathers' Eve*, in the same way that Gustav-Konrad, Novosiltsov, the Doctor, etc., may be said to exist. But how can one equate people with fictional creations? And is not Gustav-Konrad himself a fictional creation? Was there ever a Longinus Podbipięta except on the pages of Sienkiewicz's *Trilogy*—even if loyal readers paid to have Masses said for the repose of his soul? Or a Wokulski apart from Prus's *The Doll*, even if the house in which he "lived" has been mounted with a commemorative plaque? Then, too, would anyone casually dismiss a Don Quixote or Hamlet as being nothing more than a fictional creation?

Elsewhere I have written how in this respect Dante's *Inferno* is a disturbing work. A poem written in an Age of Faith might be presumed to desist from "fictionalizing" otherworldly figures. Yet Dante teems with figures borrowed from mythology and the literature of antiquity, so that a reader seeking genuine communion with a "medieval mind" soon realizes that he has been duped: figures whose reality a medieval poet would find credible are joined with others that, from a Christian point of view, are patently fictional. Dante's *Inferno* suggests, finally, that we really do not know what it is "to believe" or "not to believe" in someone or something, that the human mind eludes a facile division into "the real" and "the imaginary," "the literal" and "the figurative." Why else did the Middle Ages indulge in *les diableries*, in those profanations staged at Shrovetide by throngs of horned, long-tailed devils? And Mickiewicz, let us not forget, was also the author of "Darczanka," the story of a monk decapitated by a knight as he is about to ravish St. Joan of Arc, and who, after landing directly in Hell, meets the founder of his order, St. Dominic, in the company of many other saints and popes. And what of Mickiewicz the balladeer, of Mephisto's grotesque emissary in "Tukaj," for example, or the devil's pact in "Twardowski's Wife"? And why, if the beyond is deserving of seriousness, do the devils in *Forefathers' Eve* squeal, kick, and speak a mixture of tongues, predominantly French, during the exorcism scene? In Mickiewicz's drama, the comic devil of folklore obviously serves to reveal the work's central optimistic truth. The evil spirit, traditionally the wise and powerful one, is in fact a fool; the more he plays the spoiler, the corruptor, and the desecrator, the more it is to his own detriment. When Adam, on his way out of Paradise, ignores the kernels of grain placed in his path by a pitying God, Satan suspects they contain some hidden asset: "He furrowed with his horn and sowed the grain/ Spat, raked with his hoof, and made firm the terrain."

All right, the frustrated reader will say. Suppose Mickiewicz's spirits can claim equality with his other characters. The people onstage are nonetheless impersonations of people offstage. Can the same really be said of the spirits? A fair question. In Mickiewicz's youth, literature—whether poetry, drama, or the Gothic novel—reveled in phantoms, werewolves, and spirits both extraterrestrial and terrestrial (e.g., water nymphs, ondines). Their existence, similar in kind to the Voltairian Hell in "Darczanka," was assured by convention. Yet *Forefathers' Eve* attempts a unique coupling: spirits extend theatrical space and share in the Communion of Saints, which in turn transcends time and space, to become a communion of generations in history. Such a combustible fusion of elements, of the supernatural and the historical, the one enhancing the other, is unknown in world literature. For Mickiewicz (see his Lecture XVI at the Collège de France) such a fusion was the hallmark of the future Slavic drama.

Since Polish drama in its Romantic and Neo-Romantic phase would pursue the line begun by Mickiewicz's *Forefathers' Eve*, the question of the reality versus unreality of his spirits might be clarified through comparison with the fate of Polish drama in general. A dramatist who figures as one of the final links in the chain is Wyspiański. If in Wyspiański the concepts of an open space and a communion of generations are preserved, then the metaphysical dimension, in its traditional Christian interpretation, is wholly absent. Wyspiański's deity is entirely national; it is Poland. His other gods and specters are either allegories, inspired by the author's classical studies at the Cracow Gymnasium, or "things of the soul's own staging"; so that in a play like *The Wedding*, for example, it matters little whether they figure as hallucinations or as wedding guests. Obviously, if a modern author makes use of such mythological figures as Pallas Athene, Ares, or Apollo, they are intended as tropes, whereas, thanks to centuries of Christianity, emissaries from Heaven, Purgatory, and Hell have maintained their evocative power, as shown by the vitality of such figures in urban folklore and among humorists. But what is the provenance of Stańczyk and Szela? Clearly, the lore of national history. The comparison, then, not to mention experience itself, teaches that *Forefathers' Eve* and the dramas of Wyspiański are works made of a different substance. "And the people believe reverently." Mickiewicz was also a believer, and that is why *Forefathers' Eve* is a mystery play conceived on a grand scale.

25

AT THE TIME MICKIEWICZ WROTE "The Romantic," only a small minority had ever heard of a magnifying lens. Not only had life in the villages of Lithuania and Byelorussia been materially unaltered by Western European inventions, but whole civilizations—those of Asia, Africa, and, to a large extent, America—had been left altogether untouched. Since 1821 the civilization of the "lens" has subjected the entire Earth to the rule of technology—not excluding itself. To quote a Renaissance poem on the ruins of Rome, translated from Latin into various European languages, including Polish (from which the following version by Sęp-Szarzyński is taken): "That city in conquering the world conquered itself too,/ As nothing could escape its conquest." To the extent that a New Rome, the global state, with all its internal atrophy, no longer lies beyond the realm of possibility, the lines quoted above are still timely. Libraries have been written of our increasingly dark prospects—and suddenly, even comically, we are back to the age-old pattern: parental authority warns, unruly child disobeys at its own peril. (Witness the many maxims and proverbs in different languages, e.g., "As you make your bed, so you must lie on it," or the Gospels' "By their fruits ye shall know them.") Nor can one complain of a lack of prophetic warnings as to the consequences of the choice made by eighteenth-century science and philosophy. Regrettably these warnings took mostly the form of reactionary diatribes against the "laws of progress," and so were easily susceptible to ridicule. In Mickiewicz's time, the quarrel between the two reigning sensibilities was seen by Hoene-Wroński (who, *nota bene*, could not abide the "rhymester" and his "mystical mob") as a clash between the principles of *Être* and *Savoir*, a clash roughly corresponding to the split between the partisans of hereditary monarchy and republicanism, or between the Slavophiles and Westernizers in Russia. Mickiewicz's political radicalism cannot alter the fact that his philosophy is entirely in the service of *Être*. "On the occasion of God's funeral/ The savants savored the cups of their conceit"— the poet wrote in 1830. And a few years later: "When the godless go in for learning,/ Beware: cutthroats are searching for a weapon." Such words must have been music to the ears of the conservatives, those opponents of the middle class pressing everywhere in Western Europe for more freedoms and more power for their parliaments.

Mickiewicz's equating of bookish abstraction with the workings of the evil spirit—in his "Roman lyrics," in *Forefathers' Eve*, in *Apothegms and Sayings*—is scarcely deserving of ridicule, just as little as Dostoevsky's demonology in *The Possessed* can be taken lightly. Not that these chapters on Mickiewicz should be read as a dirge on behalf of a lost innocence, as a desire to return to an imaginary idyllic state predating the scientific-technological revolution. The Romantic strategy—faith as opposed to reason, subjectivity as a refuge against the press of "objective" necessity and of movement governed by it—failed, both in its earlier version as exemplified by "The Romantic" and in later variants with their recourse to sarcasm, irony, and "polyphony" in the novel. A possible deliverance is offered by the imagination: not in any accusations brought against science, as if *it* were to blame for the great desolation, but in its construction of a vision of man and the world vastly different from that adduced by eighteenth-century science and its modern descendants—a vision such as was entertained by Goethe in waging his "Thirty Years' War against Newton."

26

TO SPEAK OF SWEDENBORG is to violate a Polish taboo that prohibits writers from taking a serious interest in religion. The penalty is already preordained in the form of the parroted cliché: "He succumbed to mysticism." Naturally you were always free to declare yourself a Catholic writer, but only at the risk of being classified as "lowbrow," on a level with outdoor or juvenile literature—with a literature, moreover, politically allied with the Right. As I scan the terrain of twentieth-century Polish literature, I fail to find any poets or prose writers who escaped the label, with a few possible exceptions. This is not to say that quasi-religious persuasions did not enjoy popularity, especially among the modernists of Young Poland and their descendants. But anyone read in Christian theology and philosophy must reprove their intellectual and verbal laxity. One exception was the poet, Bolesław Leśmian, who, as a "disinherited mind" outside the Judeo-Christian orbit, only confirms my thesis.

If not for my readings of the French Catholic philosophers, I might have remained insensitive to this neglect in

Polish letters. And if not for my interest in the work of Oscar Milosz, I would be largely uninformed about Swedenborg. Nor, I hasten to add, are the French, despite what Balzac and Baudelaire may have borrowed from Swedenborg, the best informed, either. Oscar Milosz read Swedenborg in English; so, too, my years spent in America, where Swedenborg readers and admirers outnumber those in other countries, have given me easier access to the Royal Counselor's work and to the secondary literature on him.

Let me explain in advance why Swedenborg merits scrutiny. It is a fact that the greatest poets and prose writers have borrowed liberally from him. The list is long: first Blake, as his direct spiritual descendant; then Goethe, a fervent reader of Swedenborg (as was Kant!); followed by Edgar Allan Poe, Baudelaire, Balzac, Mickiewicz, Słowacki, Emerson (who placed him between Plato and Napoleon in his temple of the great), and Dostoevsky, in whose work we find resonances of Swedenborg in the character of Svidrigailov and in the sermons of Father Zosima. Such obvious fascination must have its reasons. Nor are the reasons unrelated to the peculiarities of the age in which Swedenborg exerted an influence through his work. That work has attracted others through the mysterious power of an imagination capable of summoning it to life. As I hope the following will show, it occupies a special place, one which I would classify as "borderline disinherited."

Swedenborg was read widely throughout the late eighteenth and early nineteenth centuries. Today Swedenborg's coffin in the Uppsala cathedral probably says little to tourists, other than as a tangible sign of tribute paid one of Sweden's great sons. If his work is read by scholars and men of letters, then it is from a sense of professional duty —in conjunction with their research on Blake, for example. Circumstances (i.e., Oscar Milosz) have made me an exception, though I sense a Swedenborg revival currently in the making, not necessarily for reasons of which he would have approved: the Swedenborg phenomenon, in effect, belongs to those enigmas which, if ever solved, would shed light on the laws of the human imagination in general.

Emanuel Swedenborg (1688–1772) was a prominent scientist whose works on geology, astronomy, and physiology purportedly contain a wealth of brilliant discoveries. This immediately poses an obstacle, as it would take a historian of science to properly assess his achievement. No less an obstacle is posed by the later work dating from his illumination, at which time he began work on a new interpretation of Christianity, a multi-volumed work running into thousands of pages, and all composed in a pedantic Latin. To read it whole (so far, I have explored only a fraction of it) is to wander through a hall of mirrors arousing a range of conflicting emotions: mockery abruptly turns to awe, rejection to assent and vice versa, curiosity to strenuous boredom, and acceptance to categorical rejection. One thing is certain. Any suspicion of quackery is refuted by the man's exemplary life, by the conscientious way in which he discharged his civic and professional duties (as a member of the Royal Mining Commission), by his meticulous work habits, by his veracity and amiability. Emerson, unstinting in his praise of Swedenborg, alludes to mental illness as the price paid for transgressing the bounds permitted us, as if to remind us that there is no genius without a flaw. The twentieth century, as I said, has been neglectful of Swedenborg. Karl Jaspers devoted a chapter to him in his work on schizophrenia, along with chapters on Hölderlin, Van Gogh, and Strindberg; yet he is cautious in his diagnosis because Swedenborg's pathological symptoms became manifest only during the years of his crisis, 1743–45, after which he led a tranquil life, free of any strife or discord—unlike Hölderlin, for example.

Certain commonplaces about Swedenborg, to which he himself gave rise, are unavoidable, and I shall begin with these. By his own testimony, he received from God the power to transport himself to the extramundane world, and daily inhabited both realms for the duration of some thirty years. As a record of his otherworldly journey, as a vision of a triadic world in the beyond, his work stands, after *The Divine Comedy*, as the second such enterprise in Western civilization. Although Swedenborg, the son of a Swedish clergyman (to whom he owed the name Emanuel, meaning "God is with us"), was equally critical of both Lutheran and Catholic theology, he was sufficiently Protestant to omit Purgatory. His three realms are Heaven, Hell, and midway between the two the "spirit world," the place to which all go after death, and where gradually, themselves unaware, their will's true "intention" (their love) is revealed, whereby a person either ascends to Heaven or descends to Hell. Stylistically, Swedenborg's realism evokes comparison with the early English novel, e.g., Defoe's *Robinson Crusoe*, which, considering the work's subject matter, now and then has its comic effects; to quote Emerson, Swedenborg's otherworldly inhabitants often remind us more of elves and gnomes. The strictly reportorial passages, what the author called *Memorabilia*, lend validity to the question posed by Oscar Milosz, a careful Swedenborg reader, in the margin of his copy of *The True Christian Religion* (the English translation of *Vera Christiana Religio*), preserved in his private library: "The work is composed of two parts: the one revealed in the *spiritual world*, the other constructed in the form of a theological-philosophical system in the *natural world*. Which came first? Did the memorabilia come before or after the system?

Was the work born of a vision or an idea? Because these 'memorabilia' have the look of inventions designed as an *allegorical proof*."

A question that goes straight to the heart of the matter, but one which defies a definitive answer. As a writer, Swedenborg was susceptible to eighteenth-century conventions, among others to the authenticating device of the pseudo-memoir or pseudo-diary, the "manuscript found in the tree trunk," etc. In other words, the role of convention in Swedenborg's artistic rendering of theological material cannot be neglected, particularly as the meticulous documenting of theological disputes in the other world serves an expressly utilitarian aim: the losers in these debates correspond to the author's earthly adversaries. On the other hand, the imaging of ideas antedates the actual process of writing. The crisis of 1743–45, profuse in visions and conversations with the dead, occurred in the absence of any system, which had yet to be elaborated; later the visions kept pace with the painstakingly composed volumes that followed in succession. That crisis might well be attributed to the fierce pressures exerted on a scientific mind suddenly caught in its own trap. Only after his previous intellectual framework had been demolished by dreams and visions did Swedenborg free himself from that trap.

Like the girl in Mickiewicz's "The Romantic," he suddenly had a vision of the extrasensory world; but the savants with their "eyes and lenses" had more trouble with Swedenborg, who was after all one of their own fraternity, than with a village maid. If the girl of the poem could become so crazed by the loss of her Johnny as to converse with the dead, Swedenborg's visions were born of horror at a loss so immense as to affect all men. The illiterate and even the semi-illiterate, only dimly conscious of the incipient intellectual crisis, were unresponsive to Swedenborg's forebodings. But as a member of Europe's scientific elite, Swedenborg was well aware that Nature, perceived as a system of mathematical relations, had begun to usurp God in the minds of the educated. The universe was construed as an infinity of absolute, void, Newtonian space (even the Cartesian vision of a space filled with "vortices" had been rejected), whose rotating planets and planetary systems overwhelmed the mind by their infinite profusion: thus was man's dethronement, a process begun with the death of the geocentric theory, made complete. Yet the Christian religion had posited an Earth-centered, man-centered universe. Religious faith was now professed not with the heart but with the lips only; whereas Swedenborg, and here he remained loyal to the Age of Reason, held that a man could not assent to anything which was contrary to reason. Christianity, in his opinion, was entering its final phase. And it was given to him, Swedenborg, at this critical moment for the human race, to see and bear witness to the truth. He had been anointed, no more and no less, as a Messiah announcing a new era.

Swedenborg's private diary dating from the years of his crisis purportedly testifies to the strongly erotic character of his dreams and visions. The author, it is argued, being a pious and abstemious man, yet possessed of a powerful sensuality, became perturbed through habitual self-denial, as many ascetics have been known to do. Admittedly, Swedenborg's images are tinged with eroticism; granted that at the center of his doctrine is an "angelic sexuality." But such fashionable explanations fail to do the work justice, for his theological works specifically address those matters with which he was genuinely, dramatically engaged and against which he wrote.

"Against": that is the key. After the revelation of his

mission, Swedenborg began issuing one volume after another, publishing them under his own imprint. Among men of science, especially in the smaller countries like Sweden, Latin was still in common use; Swedenborg's contemporary, the naturalist Linnaeus, wrote in Latin. But a reading public of enlightened, philosophically minded ladies and salon wits, either ignorant of Latin or deficient in it, now had to be addressed in the new international language of French. Swedenborg strove neither for immediate effects nor for public acclamation. Destined to close one era and open another, he was content to record his message in print, in the belief that his books would eventually triumph over the ideas of the age.

His ambition was nothing less than a major defense of Christianity, and it was addressed to atheists and Deists as much as to the theologians. A hundred years before him, the mathematician Blaise Pascal, accurately intuiting the course which the European mind would take, set himself a similar task. A brief life cut short his apologia; the notes that have survived are known today as *Les pensées*. Pascal's reflections were centered on man as understood by humanists reared on the ancient philosophers. If, as the humanists argued, man was indeed such a rational creature, such an integral part of the cosmic scheme, then mankind could dispense with Revelation and Biblical religion was rendered superfluous. By contrast, Pascal showed that man, that "thinking reed," because of the strange pairing of opposites inherent in him, was distinct from every other living creature and alien to the galactic wastes; that he alone was endowed with consciousness and yet, because of the natural, animal part resident in him, lacking in self-governance and self-sufficiency. There is in Pascal a kind of Manichaean distrust of nature and the things of "this world" which has made him a hero in the eyes of the pessimists, of those who later, in an era proclaiming the intrinsic good of the "noble savage," responded with a mordant irony. Pascal's defense of Christianity is thus waged in anthropocentric terms, asserting the "anti-naturalness" of that unique phenomenon called consciousness.

Swedenborg proceeds in like fashion. But a common strategy should not impel us to search for a shared style or sensibility. Tainted though he was by Jansenism, Pascal remained at heart a Catholic, whereas Swedenborg was manifestly rooted in a traditional Protestantism. Swedenborg, moreover, to a far greater extent than is implied by the term "mystic," was a true son of the Enlightenment (N. Aksakov, Swedenborg's nineteenth-century Russian translator, wrote a book entitled *Swedenborg's Rationalism*; similarly, in his book on Swedenborg, William James, Sr., father of William James, the author of *The Varieties of Religious Experience*, and of the novelist Henry James, underscores the rationalist bias of his doctrine). A love of symmetry, poise, and balanced constructions is one of the marvels of Swedenborgian syntax, from which it might be said that he embodies the "spirit of geometry" much more than the mathematician Pascal.

Swedenborg focused on man's exclusive property: the Written Word, both as it refers to the word revealed, Holy Writ, and to language generally. He applied himself to the decoding of words found in Scripture, distinguishing between three Biblical layers: the literal, the spiritual, and the celestial. This search for meanings was for him a means of enriching human language, in the broadest sense, because it was a manifestation of man's foremost power: the imagination.

The universe was created exclusively for man, for human use. Not only Earth but myriads of planets are populated by humans. But the visible world is merely a reflection of the spiritual world, everything perceived on Earth by the five senses is a "correspondence," an equivalent of a given state in the spiritual realm. I deliberately avoid such commonplaces as "allegory" or "symbol," whose field of reference is not always commensurate with that which Swedenborg assigned to the word *correspondentia*. That some flowers, beasts, trees, landscapes, human faces are beautiful and others ugly derives from the fact that they are spiritual values; shapes, colors, and smells, by supplying the stuff of human speech, fulfill a function analogous to that of words. Here Swedenborg is heir to the medieval, Platonic-inspired axiom "as above, so below," which held that the whole of creation was one of the two languages in which God spoke to man—the other was Holy Writ. This would explain why Swedenborg felt so drawn to the artistic sensibility. In effect, his system constitutes a kind of "meta-aesthetics," to borrow a term coined by Oscar Milosz apropos of Swedenborg.

But that is not all. Swedenborg appeared at a time when the entire spatial order had been challenged, first by the debunking of the geocentric theory, later by theories expanding the interplanetary void to infinity. The Christian vision had traditionally relied on a Heaven and Hell endowed with space. As far back as the fourth century, St. Gregory of Nyssa traced the vision of Hell of his contemporaries to pagan sources and deplored the belief in a Hades type of hell as unworthy of a Christian. Yet for centuries the Hades image persisted, and Dante's *Inferno* shows to what extent such images were contingent on a belief in Earth's primacy and the existence of subterranean realms.

Swedenborg restored that space. But how? To treat his immaterial world as spatial, to take every verb of motion literally ("he ascended," "he went," "he landed," etc.) would be to make of him an ordinary lunatic. The truth is immensely more complex. Those caves; those miasmic barrens; those slums where the damned assail each other with knives in the streets; those subterranean concentration camps where the condemned slave day in and day out for their niggardly portion; those celestial houses with their luscious gardens, summer cottages, and arbors nestled among trees: whatever the landscape portrayed, it is always of the same physical texture as that visited by the diminutive heroine of *Alice in Wonderland*. A man's internal condition, determined by the intention of his will (his love), assumes a form corresponding to his sensuous experiences on earth; an afterlife, in the objective sense, does not exist, only the good or evil in man. "You are what you see": if nature is composed of signs, those signs now become liberated to form an alphabet of joy or anguish. Swedenborg's space is *internal*. The reports of his otherworldly odyssey figure rather as illustrations within the totality of the Swedenborgian oeuvre. But our imagination is continually locating things through juxtaposition, relative to something else, as evidenced in painting and poetry, or even in music, where the sequence of sounds in time bears a decidedly architectural, sculptural quality. In this sense, internal space is not an illusion; on the contrary, it is more real than the material one governed by time and space. If Swedenborg did not glorify art, he nonetheless effected a shift from object to *subject*, whereby the role of the artist became exalted, something readily seized upon by Blake. Blake's faith in the eternal life of the Imagination implied, after all, that the workings of the imagination (those infusions of Holy Spirit) were a prefiguring, a promise of the imagination freed of the corporeal and of Nature, by analogy with the creative process itself which was, in a very real sense, a "release from the body." Blake regarded Swedenborg's Heaven and Hell exactly as he did Dante's —as real *because* imagined.

If inner space is a purely subjective creation, it follows that the number of heavens and hells is legion. But since the moral order (defined as the will propelled either toward the Creator or to its *proprium*) is constant, all such spatial realms are relative to a centripetal Spiritual Sun (whose "correspondence" is the sun of our planetary system). How Swedenborg can deduce from these subjective states a map of the beyond is not altogether clear: if "you are what you see," on what does he base his topography? Would not each realm be possessed of its own? Not necessarily. True, the damned see everything in distorted perspective, but he who dwells in truth, as Swedenborg did, charts with his infallible compass the land of visions where space is space only by analogy. That land, as implied by the words "sublime" and "base," is vertically structured. The closer the proximity to God, manifested as the Spiritual Sun, the higher the celestial realm occupied. Midway lies the "spirit world," which is so analogous to the terrestrial one that newcomers are hardly aware they have died. And Hell below. Swedenborg then reveals a remarkable secret—namely, that Heaven, the sum of myriads of personal heaven-projections, is Man-shaped. The universe was created that Heaven might be tenanted with spirits from countless planets and planetary civilizations (except for the saved and the damned, Swedenborg did not recognize angels or devils).

Here a serious misconception must be revised. Without enumerating what Towiański and the Polish Romantics borrowed from Swedenborg, such pronouncements as "All is fashioned by and for the Spirit, nothing serves a fleshly purpose"—this culled from Słowacki—read like a Swedenborgian maxim. Yet, despite certain surface similarities, Słowacki's is a vastly different sensibility. Odd as Swedenborg's vision may appear, his sentences are perfectly structured, and one has only to grasp the thread of his argument to arrive at a coherent whole. If our Polish taboo ("He succumbed to mysticism") was initially invoked by the Positivist intelligentsia in reaction to Słowacki's philosophical writings and to other works of a similar vein, it can be faulted only with a lack of discrimination. Słowacki's philosophical prose has a distinctly hallucinatory quality to it and, despite occasional moments of grandeur, is frankly unreadable. The Romantics (with the exception of Blake)—and not only Polish—misinterpreted Swedenborg's "spirituality," which is why Balzac's *Séraphita*, a work which purports to be an exposition of the Swedenborgian doctrine in fictive form, could become a perversion of it. But Słowacki went even further in his pursuit of the "spiritual." His retelling of the sin of Adam and Eve (conveyed in a letter to J. N. Rembowski), perhaps unique in the history of the treatment, is illustrative: as interpreted by Słowacki, Adam and Eve were so much of the spirit as to dispense with eating; by persuading Eve to eat the apple, the tempter bound them to the life of matter.

Far from being ethereal, Swedenborg, that loyal subject of his Royal Majesty engaged with the mundane affairs of his fellow citizens, construed brotherly love in an active sense, as utility (*usus*); that is, he exalted man's earthly duties toward society—its enrichment by tradesmen and merchants, its technological advancement by science, its defense by soldiers in times of peril. His Heaven, populated by communities bound by shared earthly dispositions, was a realm of unceasing "action" where love of the good was manifested solely as *usus*. Since "proximity" in analogous space is defined in terms of shared tastes, spirits congregate on the basis of their wills' deepest "intention." Swedenborg's more realistic passages derive from the axiom "as above, so below," which remains incomplete so long as it is not inverted—"as below, so above."

In school I was taught that in his mystical phase Słowacki combined the Lamarckian theory of evolution with the primacy of the soul—"bowed by the body's travail"— that he "spiritualized" it, in effect, just as somewhat later he would season it with a belief in metempsychosis. His *Genesis from the Spirit*, which I read in those days, must certainly have had its effect on my intellectual growth, premised, like that of my contemporaries, on the tacitly assumed postulates of the natural sciences. Słowacki was like a foretaste of Teilhard de Chardin—read much later —whose muddleheadedness I cannot abide. Today I am of the opinion that Słowacki has nothing to offer the religiously minded person, that he has inflicted great harm by ensuring in Poland a disaffection with religious thought in general, for which even the Polish language would seem ill suited: under Słowacki's pen and those of other Messianists, the language turns flaccid, mushy.

The tension between Swedenborg's pedestrian style, stripped of poetic fancy, and the substance of his message conceals a richness difficult to name, before which we stand as before Escher's geometric drawings exploiting the paradoxes of three-dimensional space. Despite his cloying repetitiveness and manifold tautologies, Swedenborg makes profitable reading, even if one is in no way moved to become a Swedenborgian. I share Oscar Milosz's antipathy for Polish messianism, preeminently that of Słowacki, which he characterized by such epithets as *fadasse* (sickly) and *désossé* (boneless). I can well understand, too, why he respected Swedenborg, whereby he would not lack for company—even if he was greatly ahead of his time.

27

FOR THE THEOLOGIAN SWEDENBORG, the prophecy contained in the Apocalypse had come to pass in his own time. Of the Christian Church all that was left was "the abomination of desolation." The decline of religion—the mouthing of words in which the heart no longer believed—was, in his opinion, facilitated by two doctrines. The first, the doctrine of the Trinity, adopted by the Council of Nicaea in 325 as a weapon against the heresy of Arius, constituted an enigma resolved only by the mind's imposition of three gods instead of one. Christianity, in effect, became polytheistic, the consequences of which would not become apparent until centuries later. Although a rationalist, Swedenborg refused to concede the Arian argument that Christ was a man only. On the contrary, there was no other God but the God-man, Creator of heaven and earth, who was born of a virgin, died, and was resurrected. Christ, in other words, was not *consubstantialis* (the term proposed at the Council by Emperor Constantine) with the Father but was himself Father; hence that "Divine Human" signifying the Creator of the universe. This was the great secret revealed to Swedenborg: our heavenly Father is a man, Heaven has a human shape. The second fatal doctrine was the act of Redemption by which Christ obtained God's forgiveness for the sins of mankind. From Mary, Christ received a human, that is, sinful nature, and His life was a succession of temptations overcome, thanks to which human nature became divinized. Here Swedenborg was challenging the Catholics, for whom Christ's human nature was without sin, and the Lutherans, who professed that man was saved by faith alone, that salvation was made possible through Christ's bloody atonement. The fallacy of both doctrines, it would appear, lay in the way in which they interfered with a decidedly anthropocentric vision of Godmanhood (the God-man and human nature divinized).

Human will is free. But man is unmitigatedly evil and by himself can effect only evil. Whatever good he does is a result of divine "influx" (Swedenborg avoids the term "grace"), which he is free to accept or reject. Swedenborg's cosmology and ethics are built around two correspondences: Fire equals Love, Light equals Truth. Christ-God is a trinity in the sense that Fire and Light, which are correlative, are expressed in action. Man is saved when he concedes that by himself he is incapable of love and truth; doomed when he ascribes that ability to his own *proprium*. Of particular note is Swedenborg's pessimistic critique of human nature in combination with his defense of free will. Being quintessentially a man of the eighteenth century, he rejects the will-impairing effects of original sin. In his allegorical reading of the Book of Genesis, Adam and Eve are symbolic not of our first parents (primordial man lived in a state of ignorance) but of the first Church (or civilization). There have been four such Churches, as foretold in the Biblical prophecy of Daniel and as symbolized in the Greek legend of the four ages—golden, silver, bronze, and iron. Each Church had its Revelation: God revealed in human form, God as the "angel of Jehovah," as voice, and as fire. The fall of the first civilization, when man ascribed to himself the power to do good, broke the bond between God and man, thus ending the Golden Age, which rupture signaled the first of Hell's victories and wreaked the flood. The next civilization—or Church—also had its Revelation, to which the Bible makes allusion (in the "Books of Yasher"). The third was that of Israel. The human race grew in wickedness and the powers of Hell became so powerful as to threaten Heaven. Swedenborg's afterlife, as I said, is "action," movement in analogous space. No one is condemned by God to Hell, each dwells in the company and setting of his choice, according to his will's intention. The damned, when surrounded by the saved, suffer revulsion and anguish. (A similar Hell is painted by Father Zosima in *The Brothers Karamazov*, and the following words, attributed to Zosima, bespeak familiarity with Swedenborg: "On earth, indeed, we are as it were astray, and if it were not for the precious image of Christ before us, we should be undone and altogether lost, as was the human race before the flood. Much on earth is hidden from us, but to make up for that we have been given a precious mystic sense of our living bond with the other world, with the higher heavenly world, and the roots of our thoughts and feelings are not here but in other worlds" [translated by Constance Garnett].) Swedenborg believed the "higher" world to be so threatened that, if not for Christ-God's descent to earth, mankind would have suffered annihilation. Of all the planetary civilizations, only Earth was deemed worthy of the Incarnation, making it a privileged planet. To the fourth, the Christian Church, was announced the Second Advent and those events prophesied by St. John. Swedenborg posited the year 1757 as the year of the Last Judgment, assigning a strictly allegorical meaning to the Apocalypse. The Judgment took place in the other world; neither Earth nor mankind would come to an end, because the higher world could exist without mankind as little as mankind could exist without the higher world. The Second Advent had also come to pass, not literally but as the truth incarnated in Swedenborg's writings, which became the foundation of a Fifth Church, the New Jerusalem. Swedenborg thus transposed the Biblical story of Creation and "the final things" to a purely spiritual plane. His theology admits neither to the resurrection of bodies, with the exception of Christ, nor to the other extreme, that of metempsychosis. Only through a misinterpretation, therefore, could he have been invoked by the Polish Romantics.

Swedenborg's theology, as just outlined, betrays its heretical allusions. The historian of religion will easily recognize certain centuries-old motifs. The Creator's manlike divinity evokes the Gnostic and Manichaean image of a Primordial Man in Heaven, conceived by the King of Light, and the Adam Kadmon of the Jewish cabalists. The four ages are resonant of the ubiquitous myth of Paradise, fusing a cyclical view of history with a strongly chiliastic bias.

Here I question the value of such a summary and wonder whether it is not a mere waste of time. Swedenborg's theological system, however important to its author, fails to explain why Oscar Milosz called him a second Faust, a Faust without a personal tragedy. By summarizing it, perhaps I am intent on doing justice to its most implausible ideas, which, given the large number of prominent figures who confided in their own messianic destiny, need not astonish. Swedenborg's importance lies not in his theology so much as in his effort to decode the Bible, to build a "verbal space," as Osip Mandelstam once said of Dante. Though non-poetic in style, Swedenborg's work, no less than *The Divine Comedy*, is a vast honeycomb built by the bees of the imagination and obeying a certain imperative. A man must abide somewhere, a physical roof over his head is not enough; his mind needs its bearings, its points of reference, vertically as well as horizontally. Do we not speak of *edifying* readings?

Moreover, if the Last Judgment meant that in the "spirit world" there was to be a strict distinction—hitherto increasingly effaced—between salvation and damnation, then we should have no quarrel with the year 1757. For it coincides with the rise of the Industrial Revolution, along with its concomitant, that of spiritual disinheritance. In his rescue operation, Swedenborg drew on certain religious attitudes from an earlier phase of civilization, one not without analogy to our own: the Hellenized part of the Roman Empire in the first centuries after Christ. In his study of Gnosticism,* Hans Jonas attributes the success of gnosis—the attainment of salvation through secret knowledge—to, among other factors, the disintegration of the *polis* and the atomization of the masses under imperial rule; to the decline of a religion and philosophy which perceived the world as an order, a *kosmos*; to an inchoate vision, in other words, of man's alienation from the universe. A God responsible for such an evil world was either not good or not omnipotent; the Gnostics chose the good God, who was now transformed into the Other God, the Unknown God, while the Jehovah of the Old Testament received the title of a lower demiurge. Earlier figures had sought a covenant between man and the Other God, a pre-cosmic covenant against the world ruled by the Archon of Darkness. The concept of a Primordial Man, found in the second-century Gnostic, Valentinus of Alexandria, and

---

* English tr.: *The Gnostic Religion*, 1958; German ed.: *Gnosis und spätantiker Geist*, 1934–54.

later taken up by the religion of Mani in the third century, was essentially aimed at humanizing the very premise of existence. I quote:

> To the Gnostics the existence of a pre-cosmic god "Man" expressed one of the major secrets of their Knowledge, and some sects even went so far as to call the highest godhead himself "Man": "This [according to one branch of the Valentinians] is the great and hidden secret, that the name of the power that is above all things, the fore-beginning of everything, is Man."
> —*The Gnostic Religion*, p. 217

In Gnostic and Manichaean speculation, Christ is sometimes cast as the suffering and pre-cosmic Man. Swedenborg's Christ is God the Father-Man incarnate, a vision that nonetheless betrays nothing of Docetism, the doctrine which held that Christ only appeared to be born, to lead a corporeal life, to die and be resurrected.

The eighteenth-century cosmos: myriads of planets spinning around in an infinite and absolute space. Easily said; but let us try to imagine, to locate our home in that infinity. Swedenborg understood that the only refuge lay in assigning a central place to the Divine Human. And what distinguished the human if not the mind and imagination —the *inner* life of a subject, in other words—whence that other world, the subjective, which was not only parallel to the objective world but was its reason and purpose. Here we have a vague foreglimpse of Hegel and the makings of an anti-Hegelian vaccine. It was, after all, the rational premise of existence, which in Hegel would obtain to the self-conscious element in man, that laid the foundation for an atheistic prometheanism. Dostoevsky (*"Vsyo v budushchem stoletii"*—"All depends on the next century") would be right in reducing the dilemma of the age, both his own and the succeeding one, to a choice between the God-man and the Man-god. Those in the "exact" sciences might reply, along with Jacques Monod, that religion, whether religion proper or such pseudo-religions as Hegelianism and Marxism, is a relic of the "animistic tradition," and that "objective truth" can assent to one as little as to the other of the two warring sides. Alas, on closer scrutiny, "scientific truth" is not what it once was, either.

A Swedenborgian concept that had great appeal for the Romantics was the *arcanum* of marriage, which referred as well to the marriage of spirits since, in Swedenborg's Heaven, angels were of both sexes. The literature of Romanticism has accustomed us to interpreting his "bonding of souls" in an asexual way, even though Swedenborg advocated rather a purified sexuality. For Swedenborg, earthly marriage was a "correspondence" central to Christianity, corresponding to the celestial marriage between love (*Amor*) and wisdom (*Sapientia*). Hence, too, the importance attached by him to a monogamous union, which, when it yields a harmony of the spiritual-carnal, is heaven on earth. This is the theme of Swedenborg's *Delitiae Sapientiae de Amore Conjugali* (*The Delights of Wisdom Concerning Conjugial Love*), which expounds a fundamental interpretation of the Adam and Eve relationship, in particular of those aspects illuminating the spiritual differences between man and woman. I shall return to this later, because Swedenborg's *arcanum* of marriage provides a key to some of Oscar Milosz's work.

28

I WAS A STUDENT OF Polish literature at the University of Wilno for two weeks before I transferred to law (though I remained active in the Literary Circle, in its Creative Writing Section, throughout my law studies). I have often wondered about the reason for my disaffection. Was it the musty effluvia of pedantic endeavors, the constriction of vision peculiar to the literary discipline? In deserting Polish literature for law, I was guided by an urge for what later would be called "relevance," though I was acting partly to my own detriment because, as time would show, I was possessed of certain pedagogic abilities, a definite asset in a scholarly career. In the end, I did become a professor of literature, if a somewhat unorthodox one, who wished to spare his students the same sneering disaffection I had once displayed. Among the English majors who take my courses—on Dostoevsky, on Manichaeanism, on Polish drama—some seem as bored with English literature as I had been with Polish.

What were my interests in those days? Not nineteenth-century Polish novels, not the symbolism of Słowacki's *Lilla Weneda*, and not the grammar of Old Church Slavonic. I was interested in the twentieth century, and I might have remained in the Faculty of Humanities if they had taught Apollinaire, Max Jacob, Thomas Mann, or a work such as *Companionate Marriage*, our version of the sexual manifesto by a since forgotten author (Lindsey was his name). A passion for avant-garde poetry, painting, film, politics, the latest manners and mores—in short, for the contemporary—was to deliver me to various forms of snobbery and affectation, though without it you were hardly considered fit for the poet's guild. In my case, that passion could not quiet a certain distrust, no less dangerous in a way, which at times made me susceptible to flagrantly totalitarian, moralistic-terroristic impulses. Nonetheless, I take that nascent distrust for the literature and art of my century as a measure of my internal progress.

When I browse through the books and articles published in Poland, primarily those of the younger generation, I am awed by their thorough and manifest familiarity with contemporary world literature. The range of their knowledge exceeds anything found in America among those of a comparable background. At times their interest seems convulsed, rooted in an acute claustrophobia, in an exorbitant fear of "losing touch." Ninety percent of the names and titles flaunted by them would be unknown to their Berkeley contemporaries, though one wonders whether they are any the poorer for it. A hermetic artistic-literary culture is a cage dedicated to the chasing of one's tail. This is because the intellectual baggage of artists, regardless of nationality, is more or less the same everywhere: all are "children of the age" and, consciously or unconsciously, all pay homage to the nihilistic canon of the day. Those who seek release from that cage, from the magic circle, by going outside the mainstream are disappointed in their hopes. The "leading" role played by belles-lettres is of relatively recent date, and we should not be surprised to see its authority duly diminished. Not that a "literary literature" will cease irrevocably, only that the search for things of substance will be conducted elsewhere.

The difference between vigor and decadence is difficult to define. Difficult, but not impossible. In auspicious times, literature aspires to problems fundamental to man; in inauspicious times it forfeits that ability, as if oblivious of their existence. In the course of the past two hundred years there has been no problem more fundamental to man than the acceptance or rejection of that body of assumptions which is called "scientific truth." In the nineteenth century that "scientific truth" was not yet found to be compelling (as in Mickiewicz's "The Romantic"), or else it was contemplated in terms of the consequences for man when he is forced to assent. If its impact was that of a mighty boulder hitting the water, then art and literaure would constitute the waves and ripples, spreading to those realms seemingly untouched by the scientific revolution, such as the scornful aestheticism of a Flaubert. The tremors were recorded in an accelerated collapse of artistic forms and genres, and the more acutely the impending nihilism— which was winning the contest by default—was perceived, the more extreme the breakup. In the literature of the mid- and late twentieth century, no one would presume to challenge the laws of physics, biology, psychology, sociology, and so on; they are flatly taken for granted. But if as a result of continual reduction man was no longer king but some subspecies of anthropoidal ape; if he was stripped of Eden, of Heaven and Hell, of good and evil, now defined as the product of social determinants, then was he not ripe for the ultimate reduction, for his metamorphosis into a planetary society of two-legged insects?

I shall not play preacher, the illness resides in me, too; I am analyzing it in myself, as I have done before, whence comes my skepticism and my regret that I could not be born in an age when I might have aspired to be a truly great poet. But better to be aware of the rodent inside and of his daily devastation. Granted, literature serves not only as a tool of cognition; but to surrender one's awareness in advance, to regard the disease as not a disease, is to assent to one's own decadence.

One of the warning signs is boredom. Why read novelists

and poets when I know what I shall find: another treatise on the insignificance of man, of that creature in whom all is illusory except for physical pleasure and pain. "A little writing, a little wenching"—as a Polish writer, now deceased, modestly summarized our brief sojourn under the sun. The rodent in me is of the same opinion, which is why I avoid that author's novels: too modest in scale.

Let the above stand as a commentary on my extra-literary explorations in search—if we speak of books only —of a countervailing argument, one that nonetheless holds some promise. For the most part it is found in works that rise above neat distinctions of genre to carve out new riverbeds. To these works belongs that body of poems called *Prophetic Books*, in which their author, William Blake, engaged the "scientific world-view" in a fundamental dialogue.

Blake was born in 1757—the year of the Last Judgment, according to Swedenborg—and the significance of his birth date was not lost on him. In his lifetime, and even for a half century after his death (in 1827), Blake was practically unknown; not until the first decades of this century was his reputation firmly established. And how, if I am writing in Polish, am I to deal with the body of Blakean criticism? It would be pointless to summarize the commentaries of others—to play the specialist, in other words. Efforts to paraphrase Blake through direct quotation are seldom successful, either; nor does it seem possible to do him justice in Polish. Therefore, I shall select only those things that bear directly on my theme.

First, I must try to correct a certain habit of thinking imposed on us by the "scholars," be they Polish, British, or American: Blake is a figure of the distant past, a "phenomenon" to be studied in the context of a given era, against the political and social disturbances of his time (the

American Revolution, the French Revolution, the Napoleonic Wars); against the classical movement in the arts, Romanticism in poetry, and so on. Useful as such considerations may be, they do not get to the heart of the matter. A comparison with Füssli (or Fuseli, as he is also known), a Swiss artist living in London, illustrates just how superficial and deceptive are the resemblances between Blake and his contemporaries; it only shows to what extent Blake transcended the stylistic vagaries of the day. If Blake himself numbered among the prophets of the Old Testament anyone well practiced in "Divine Works of the Imagination," why should he be chronologically restricted? In this way I escape the humiliating practice of Polish writers who, whenever they speak of a foreign poet, behave like bees in a clover field, collecting their harvest for the national beehive. In the past, I too was guilty of the practice, but I swear that I am not now trying to convert anyone to Blake—still less when I foresee how he would be travestied in translation. I insist on the freedom, on my right to browse at will among the basic texts that are the inheritance of centuries—be they those of St. Augustine, Pascal, or Blake.

Literarily, with respect to literary technique, I have borrowed little from Blake—not one to be easily imitated, by the way—just as little as I have from Oscar Milosz. That Blake and Swedenborg figure importantly in my intellectual life does not imply any radical reversal of previous attachments. On the contrary, only now do I discern the thread joining the various phases of, and influences on, my mind's progress: Catholicism, Stanisław Brzozowski, Oscar Milosz, Hegelianism (in the person of my friend Tadeusz Juliusz Kroński), Swedenborg, Simone Weil, Shestov, Blake. That thread is my anthropocentrism and my bias against Nature. The succession of influences forms a pattern that begins with my interest in Manichaeanism, first stirred by my readings in Church history, and ends with my course on Manichaeanism at Berkeley. Perhaps the sum of these experiences has given me readier access—compared to Anglo-Saxons—to Blake, because in him I found a coalescence of what had been privately appropriated.

Blake did not approve of Nature. At a time when conservationists are fighting to protect the "natural environment," this might be misconstrued. Blake disliked Nature in the same way Nature dislikes itself, as expressed in the words of St. Paul: "For we know that the whole creation [*ktisis*] groaneth and travaileth in pain together until now" (Romans 8:22). As a prominent American Blakean once said to me: "Blake was at heart a Valentinian Gnostic"—an opinion not ventured in any of that same scholar's books. In an age when the Deists revered Nature as an ingenious machine, when Rousseau prescribed it as the cure for a corrupted civilization, when the sentimental novel and early Romantic poetry were hymning the exaltation of souls in communion with a Nature viewed pantheistically, Blake strenuously opposed all such fashionable cults, waiting, along with St. Paul, for "the manifestation of the sons of God"—for the transfigured man destined to save Nature from suffering and death.

I said that Swedenborg, by humanizing God, supplied the makings of an anti-Hegelian vaccine. To pronounce the name of Hegel is to immediately assume the philosopher's gown; I therefore hasten to confess that I do not understand Hegel, even though I have felt his influence, albeit indirectly, more intensely than the majority of my contemporaries. If Swedenborg's excursion into the interior of language borders at times on madness, to the extent that Jaspers could diagnose him as a classic schizophrenic, then Hegel's reduction of the universe to the logical manipulations of human language may be a more sinister madness for posing behind an impeccable reasoning—as rational madmen will do in their iron-clad, foolproof systems. Nothing compels me to "take a stance" on Hegel, for, as I have always insisted, I am not a philosopher. I am fighting for the right to exercise my mind outside accepted disciplines. Here, at least, as a professor, I can always hold forth under what is known as "intellectual history."

I return now, after this brief digression, to the Swedenborg vaccine. In comparison, Blake is an even better antidote to Hegel, all the more because of his seeming compatibility with the German idealist. Blake's God-man —the recognition of Christ as the only God—is from Swedenborg; but those who would declare Blake a lay humanist, who would persuade us that his marriage of the Divine and the human signifies a faith in man only, are mistaken. Blake was deeply indebted to Swedenborg, so much so that one can hardly read the former without the latter. Yet Blake differs from his teacher in one important respect: while extolling energy and constant movement, he makes them conditional on a collision of opposites.

The purpose of my endeavor, here and elsewhere, is highly ambitious, verging perhaps on the impossible: to present what are often recondite but to me intensely personal ideas, and to do that in a readable language. Tadeusz Kroński, one of the few in Poland to experience intellectual matters in a deeply personal manner, is winking at me from the beyond. I also feel, as I write these words, the presence of his wife, Irena, whose love for him was great and abiding, and who, though she survived him by many years and died a practicing Catholic, never doubted that he was a man saved by virtue of his intensity. For a long time, beginning in 1943 and ending in 1951, Kroński exerted on me—in that conflict between the Universal Idea and Poland's national interest—a positively demonic influence. In my present obsession with Blake I recognize certain *mouvements* of my soul, recurrent, persistent, that once attracted me to the Hegelian Kroński.

Against Nature. Implicit here, of course, is not only a defiance of that external thing that bends us to a blind determinism but a defiance of what we ourselves are, both as members of a given species of animal and as discrete physiological beings, as collections of genes. I shall not elaborate on the reasons for Blake's attacks on "natural religion," on why he bestowed the term "atheist" on all who would praise or sanction Nature. My own antipathy is rooted in a morbid sense of guilt, in a horror of the "shadow" in me, for which I have never had any remedy except the self-therapy of writing.

If Blake had grieved over the fate of the human soul as a divine spark fallen into matter and hungering for an otherworldly home in the Kingdom of Light, he would merely be a Manichaean, or possibly a Neoplatonist. Indeed, attempts have been made (e.g., by the noted British Blakean commentator, Kathleen Raine) to claim him for Neoplatonism; but, as usually happens with Blake, just when the case seems closed, we have only to open a volume of his work to discover a wealth of counterargument. He is, after all, the author of *The Book of Thel*, a fable about the human soul before its incarnation: Thel, in her desire to be released from her vague and ethereal state, is willing to assume the burden of suffering creation, that of birth, sex, and death. But at the last moment she loses her courage; barren, useless purity will be her punishment. Some years later (*The Book of Thel* was written in 1789), the poet Mickiewicz would put it this way:

> For hear and weigh well
> That according to the divine order
> He who has never tasted bitterness
> Will never taste sweetness in heaven.

A revolt against Nature does not, in Blake, imply a yearning for an ideal realm or, if you prefer, a heaven of ideas. On the contrary, his Garden of Eden is earth; his source of heavenly pleasure, the five senses; his salvation, the eternal *now* and not some tomorrow beyond the sunset of life. For no one can understand Blake who ignores that war of opposites—the "no" rendered every "yes," and vice versa—raised by him to the level of axiom. Nonetheless, Blake is adamant in distinguishing opposition from negation, which he condemns. Nor does he subscribe to any dialectical triad—of a thesis, an antithesis, and a synthesis —and its procession in time. Antinomies exist for their own sake, for their mutual enhancement through *conjunctio oppositorum*, and that is why Blake's heaven, while no less dedicated to action than Swedenborg's, is founded on a collision of opposites—but opposites liberated from the egoistic will: to be saved is to participate, both in the now and in the eternal, in the "Intellectual War" and "Intellectual Hunts."

Therein lies the secret of my unison with Blake. As a person of pronounced Manichaean tendencies (today one speaks not of Manichaeanism in the strict sense but of a tendency of varying degrees of intensity), I was always an ecstatic pessimist. I was too enthralled by the earth to see in it a reflection of pure, unattainable Good, as Simone Weil did, who, despite my having translated her and written about her, was much too Neoplatonic and Manichaean and intellectual for my coarse Eastern European skin. As a romantic nature lover who in the Ponary Mountains collected specimens for a herbarium and who hunted with Józef Maruszewski on the outskirts of the Rudnicki Wilderness—aware, almost simultaneously, that I was only swelling my head with dreams, embellishing with poetry the great machinery of birth and murder—I discovered in Blake a similar belief (only intuited by me at the time) in our dualistic possession of the world. And I am not to blame if the literature of my age failed to venture into such vast and fathomless waters.

29

BLAKE'S THOUGHT IS ROOTED in the Fall. His interpretation of the Bible, if as allegorical as Swedenborg's, acquires a new dimension: if the Swedish visionary was a practitioner of the imagination, Blake was both theorist and practitioner, in the sense that the Imagination (capitalized) was for him the animating and redemptive power of the Human Form Divine, an emanation of the Holy Spirit. In Blake religion and poetry merge, art becomes prophecy, just as religion, before it became debased, was once prophecy—the writings of the prophets of the Old Testament and the Gospels stood for him as perfect models of inspired speech. Blake's poet is a vatic figure, a seer. But because Blake resorts to language neither as a vehicle of pure subjectivity nor as a tool of discourse, he is not a patron of what would come to be known as Symbolism or of linguistic experiments in the post-Modernist phase, just as little as he would have approved of efforts to rehabilitate a "rational" syntax on behalf of some ideology. Proper use of the poet-seer's language is made when Imagination allows him, the poet, to surmount the fallen state in which our species resides. That is why Blake's own poetry defies translation into the language of philosophy, itself a product of the Fall. Through the consistency of its correspondences (not to be confused with symbols, randomly and capriciously bestrewn), his poetry, like the books of Scripture, both demands and escapes such a transposition.

For Blake, as much as for Swedenborg, man's fall results not from the violation of any interdiction but—if I may be allowed to simplify—from the victory of the *proprium*, of the ego. We shall sidestep the complex issue of Blake's successive Churches, or civilizations, as we shall the Blakean enigma: the placing of an equal sign between the Human Form Divine and the cosmos, in consequence of which any disruption of order in man is tantamount to a cosmic disruption. In reading Blake we are never quite certain whether the Fall occurred before or after Creation, to which Blake would have replied that both are synonymous. The mythical figures introduced by him in the *Prophetic Books* symbolize those human faculties that were designed to work in concert but are divided, which is the cause of their travail. Although Blake's writings do not lack a past dimension, they compose above all an eschatological vision in which the eighteenth century is cast as the "abomination of desolation." Blake, one of the most open of poets to the pleasures of the senses, a poet given to the same childlike eroticism as the Sienese painters, is also a poet of fury. Embattled with the age, he attacks and indicts where others might bemoan: a Christianity become an instrument of control in the hands of the powerful, a system of rules and punishments; the tyranny of kings who wage bloody wars; the human misery wreaked by the Industrial Revolution, then under way in England; the plight of slaves and Indians, of women and children; the puritanical hypocrisy of sexual prohibitions; prostitution. Above all, his fury was directed at that which sustained, facilitated, and sanctioned such an order, which became in a way its code, the language of the Fall: at the science and philosophy founded by Francis Bacon.

The number 4 was crucial in Swedenborg (four ages of mankind, four seasons of the year, four points of the compass, four stages of life). So, too, in Blake four mythical figures join in man to make a family; from their cleavage came calamity. The spatial relationship between these figures—as in Swedenborg's "other space"—is of particular note: (1) *Tharmas*, or the body. Its orientation: West. Its element: water (the ocean of Time and Space). Its location: the loins. Its sense: touch. Its art: painting. (2) *Urthona*, or the individual creative Imagination (Christ is the all-encompassing Imagination). Its orientation: North. Its element: earth. Its metal: iron. Its trade: blacksmith. Its location: the subconscious. Its sense: hearing. Its art: poetry. (3) *Luvah*, or the emotions (love and hatred). Its orientation: East. Its element: fire. Its metal: silver. Its trade: weaver. Its location: the heart. Its art: music. And finally (4) *Urizen*, or Reason (the Lawgiver). Its orientation: South. Its element: air. Its metal: gold. Its trade: plowman, master builder. Its location: the head. Its sense: vision. Its art: architecture. Tharmas, Urthona, and Luvah may personify the Holy Trinity in man (the human body as an image of the Father, love as an image of the Son, the imagination as an image of the Spirit), in which case Urizen, as some commentators have suggested, would be the fallen aspect of the Godhead, or Satan.

I would be the loser if the reader were to indulge these mythic personifications as literary-historical *curiosa*. In contesting the age in which he lived, Blake could not adopt its language without disarming himself. Behind the naïve lyricism of his early poems lies a scathing irony, making the young Blake a precursor of a much later generation of European poets. Not content with irony, he later invented a whole menagerie of fantastic creatures to serve as agents. A similar strategy was later used by the poet Leśmian, with the difference that his creatures are confined to a single poem. *Nota bene*, Blake's heroes, like those of Leśmian, bear names derived from native etymologies (rarely from Greek), and in general Blake is a poet strongly rooted in the native poetic tradition, which may explain his near-inaccessibility beyond the pale of English, as witnessed by his reception in France, bordering on the nonexistent.

In its age-old, metaphysical origin, the evil combatted by Blake, that self-appointed heir to the Biblical prophets, was entirely consistent with the age. Throughout Christianity the *mysterium iniquitatis* had pertained only to human fate, guilt, suffering, while man himself, as king of nature, had been released from nature, placed above it. When science introduced the concept of nature's laws, a new dimension was revealed: man's kinship in pain with all things living. Swedenborg's reticence on this point was a cause for Blake's disaffection with the master: Swedenborg was too "angelic." Yet, in his general resolution of the problem, Blake was his successor, making his allegiance to the Gnostic and Manichaean tradition all the more plausible. Christ is God. Was it God who created a universe that "dwells in evil"? No, this state arose from a cataclysm in the Primordial Man, from a violation of the harmony once prevailing among the four elements of his psyche, one of which, Urizen, became architect of the universe, Blake's version of Satan. Urizen is present in the Book of Genesis, where he bears the name of Elohim. It was he who brought negation and drew distinctions where none were meant to be and where none would remain after the restoration of the Human Form Divine: the distinction between man and woman (the Primordial Man was both man and woman); good and evil (the temptation of the Tree of Knowledge); Heaven and Hell; body and soul (caused by death); the confusion of tongues (the Tower of Babel).

Blake's cosmology is not a retelling of Creation meant to compete with the Book of Genesis or with any scientific hypotheses. Rather, it is a poetic—read prophetic, religious—myth; its intent is to present the creation of the world, not "factually" but as evoked by the Imagination when it abides in truth, that is, when it acknowledges God as energy and love rather than as a land surveyor, a mathematician, and a guardian of the law.

Urizen, or Reason, fell through pride and broke away from Tharmas, Luvah, and Urthona, leaving him incorporeal, passionless and, most significantly, barred from the source of all workings of the Imagination: the subconscious. Urizen is thus endowed with those attributes traditionally ascribed to Satan: solitude and distance; power of the intellect and a fanatic ability to wield abstraction; despair and envy of any creature capable of reconciling the four elements—of man, in other words. He is none other than the evil spirit served by Mickiewicz's "learned," by those who drained the "cup of their conceit" at God's funeral.

In the course of his otherworldly travels, Swedenborg was told that the Last Judgment had come to pass in 1757, a date by no means arbitrarily chosen. That earthly mortals were unaware was incidental. Blake interpreted the Last Judgment as a manifestation of the lie, which first had to achieve a state of perfection before it could be exposed. To himself, born in the year of the Judgment, he assigned a providential mission, that of a knight who, armed with pen, graving tool, and brush, would deal the dragon a mortal wound. The perfection of the lie had been achieved in his time: Urizen was venerated as the true God, both by the Christian churches and by the philosophers who, dispensing with Jesus, clung to the idea of the Creator as a Clockmaker.

A heretical Christian, Blake was non-religious (his membership in a Swedenborgian congregation in London was of short duration). A non-worshipper, in his poems he cast the Anglican churches as places dedicated to a satanic cult. (Let us note that in its sermons the clergy of Blake's time reveled in terrorizing the faithful with the punishments of Hell.) Religion was reduced to a set of prohibitions, above all sexual, where its role as guardian of the established order was most nakedly manifested. The God of that religion was Urizen, a sovereign who ruled by repression and demanded self-repression of his subjects; who was continually frustrating that energy which seeks ways of realizing itself. Cold and aloof, from his throne he surveyed the city along the "chartered Thames." If ever a phantom-city had its own history, a city of street lamps in the fog, of sobs in the dark, of slinking, wraith-like prostitutes, of drunkards, of people reeling from hunger—then the London of Blake's poetry has pride of place, ahead of Dickens's (and Norwid's) London, ahead of Balzac's and Baudelaire's Paris, of Gogol's and Dostoevsky's St. Petersburg. Only those subjects living in falsehood could revere the protective deity, whose antithesis was Blake's God-man, Christ. In place of the prohibitions of law, Jesus had brought freedom; instead of the punishments of Hell, forgiveness; instead of repression, the ecstatic release of energy. And what was this thing they called Hell? For Jesus said: "I am the resurrection, and the life: he that believeth in me, though he were dead, yet shall he live" (John 11:25–26). For Jesus said: "All manner of sin and blasphemy shall be forgiven unto men: but the blasphemy against the Holy Ghost shall not be forgiven unto men. And whosoever speaketh a word against the Son of man, it shall be forgiven him: but whosoever speaketh against the Holy Ghost, it shall not be forgiven him, neither in this world, neither in the world to come" (Matthew 12:31–32). Only one sin, then, is truly unforgivable: the sin against the Holy Ghost. But if Swedenborg conceived of Hell as a state freely willed, Blake held that not man but his sinful states were cast into eternal fire, and he accused his master of having indirectly espoused a belief in predestination. To blaspheme against the Man-Son was a serious sin, yet Blake believed that even Voltaire, guilty though he was of such a sin, was saved through his labors in the service of Imagination, something his enemies never understood. In Blake's eschatological vision, even Urizen would be saved when the Human-Divine Family was restored, that is, on the day of the great Restitution (*apokatastasis*)—just as in St. Gregory of Nyssa's vision Satan is spared eternal torment.

Sexual freedom was a revolutionary catchword arising from a philosophy advocating a return to the "natural man," and the passion with which Blake defended it is somewhat surprising for a poet of the Fall. It is indicative of his whole search for a union of opposites, not for the sake of their resolution (in which case how could there be a Heaven of "Intellectual Hunts"?) but of their transfer to a higher plane; his was not "naturalness" per se, but a "naturalness" transfigured—recalling Swedenborg's "angelic sexuality."

The guiding exemplars of science and philosophy were the three villains: Bacon, Locke, and Newton. Yet all were of a piece with the theologians of a bogus Christianity: all genuflected before Urizen, the god of this world. Blake, in other words, drew a definite analogy between the vision of a mechanistic universe and religion conceived of as a moral code. Both proclaimed the universal at the expense of the particular, be it a particular moment in time, singular and irreducible, the shape and color of a particular plant, or the life of a particular man. Urizen, in effect, is the god of reduction who reduces everything to quantitative terms.

Hence Blake's attack on the very foundations of the "scientific world-view." How that attack was pressed is not within my power to document. The task is made the more arduous because it would take us, as I said, outside the purely literary realm. A literary critic engaged with any of the Romantic poets hardly runs the risk of antagonizing the scientific community. The fact is that today Blake still manages to provoke and antagonize; I know of an instance in the United States where a Blakean was denied a professorship because of opposition mounted by the physics faculty, who were protective not of their theorems so much as of the language of their formulation. Here I only allude to the Blakean attack, referring the interested reader to the major studies: Northrop Frye's *Fearful Symmetry* (1947), Ronald L. Grimes's *The Divine Imagination: William Blake's Major Prophetic Visions* (1972), and Donald Ault's *Visionary Physics: Blake's Response to Newton* (1974). The material contained in these works, like the Blakean oeuvre itself, would provide enough food for thought to last the next couple of decades. It is enough for me to signal a war mounted by a poet who was endowed, according to the experts, with an intuitive grasp of the most complicated problems of physics. The difficulty, even for his English commentators, is that a "translation" of his symbols into discursive language is unavoidable, even though such a "translation" must significantly diminish the richness of his symbols.

It is now time to introduce the figure of Los (a probable anagram of *Sol*, or Sun). Man, exiled from his homeland, strives to regain that homeland—or Eden, eternal Paradise, the eternal Golden Age—while the poet-prophet foretells and hastens that return. Of the four eternal elements of human nature, whose dissension was precipitated by the Fall, only one, Urthona (Imagination), can serve as guide for the return voyage. She is represented in time and space by Los (time) and his wedded spouse Enitharmon (space). The Manichaean doctrine held that the creation of the world was an "act of grace," that without it the pre-cosmic Fall could not be redeemed. So it is with Blake. Los, time, has a redemptive function; it is not absolute but man-related, humanizing time, just as Enitharmon is not absolute, Newtonian space. I am inclined to see Los as rhythm, born of the heart's pulsation; as a cosmic poet who saves, by embodying in rhythm, the most infinitesimal moment and object from irrevocable loss, who forges them into incorruptible shapes. Says Los:

> . . . for not one Moment
> Of Time is lost, nor one Event of Space unpermanent,
> But all remain: every fabric of Six Thousand Years
> Remains permanent, tho' on Earth where Satan
> Fell and was cut off, all things vanish & are seen no more,

They vanish not from me & mine, we guard them
first and last.
The generations of men run on in the tide of Time,
But leave their destin'd lineaments permanent for
ever and ever.

—Milton, Book I, plate 22

And in the following passage:

But others of the Sons of Los build Moments & Minutes
& Hours
And Days & Months & Ages & Periods, wondrous buildings;
And every Moment has a Couch of gold for soft repose,
(A moment equals a pulsation of the artery),
And between every two Moments stands a Daughter of
Beulah
To feed the Sleepers on their Couches with maternal care.
And every Minute has an azure Tent with silken Veils:
And every Hour has a bright golden Gate carved with skill:
And every Day and Night has Walls of Grass & Gates
of adamant
Shining like precious Stones & ornamented with
appropriate signs:
And every Month a silver paved Terrace builded high:
And every Year invulnerable Barriers with high Towers:
And every Age is Moated deep with Bridges of silver &
gold:
And every Seven Ages is Incircled with a Flaming Fire.
Now Seven Ages is amounting to Two Hundred Years.
Each has its Guard, each Moment, Minute, Hour, Day,
Month & Year.
All are the work of Fairy hands of the Four Elements:
Every Time less than a pulsation of the artery
Is equal in its period & value to Six Thousand Years,
For in this Period the Poet's Work is Done, and all the
Great

Events of Time start forth and are conceiv'd in such a
    Period,
Within a Moment, a Pulsation of the artery.

              —*Milton,* Book I, plate 28

To quote Blake is to explain little; every few lines re-
quire commentary. I would only append a footnote: in
Blake's cosmology, Beulah stands for the nocturnal realm,
poetic inspiration, the subconscious, and the erotic.
Beulah's daughters are the Muses of inspired poetry, as
opposed to the classical Muses, which are the daughters of
Mnemosyne, or memory.

Los is active as time shaped by man. Man can be a computer—to adopt our modern vocabulary—and atomize the
world only at the expense of his own humanity. Fallen
man, the worshipper of Urizen, conceives of the eternal as
time without end. Eternity, measurable in clock seconds,
trails endlessly into oblivion and reaches indefinitely into
the future; it forms a chain of causes and effects reaching
back to the First Cause, the false god of the Deists. It defies
the imagination: an eternity of mathematical relations and
laws, a spatial dimension purged of time. Infinity will then
be perceived as pure duration, as time without space. The
scientific mind beholden to such notions will always deduce the same product: the indefinite.

To repeat the Swedenborgian maxim: "You see as you
are." Blake placed man at the center, and just as the artist
bodies forth his work from the essential thing in him, so
God, in fashioning man, gives proof of His essence: His
divine humanity. God (Jesus) beholds Nature through
human eyes, but not through the eyes of fallen man. Blake's
Jesus was not the bearer of lofty moral precepts but the
whole man; by emulating Him, we exchange our flawed

physical perception of the world for a whole one. A scientist of the Baconian, Lockian, or Newtonian school suffers the illusion that knowledge is something impersonal, disembodied—that, in other words, only one faculty, the rational, suffices. The image of the world adduced by this science is a false one. To be free of its coercive power is to refute that false eternity (an endless succession of moments lapsing into nothingness) and false infinity (of illusory space, indefinite duration), and to know true eternity and infinity as the eternal Now. This is the message of the Blakean maxim:

> The desire of Man being Infinite, the possession is Infinite & himself Infinite.
> *Application.* He who sees the Infinite in all things, sees God. He who sees the Ratio only, sees himself only.
> Therefore God becomes as we are, that we may be as he is.

There is no such thing as a neutral science: its vision of the world can be benign or destructive. Both the scientists and their allies, the theologians, meet with the same opprobrium:

> He never can be a Friend to the Human Race who is the Preacher of Natural Morality or Natural Religion; he is a flatterer who means to betray, to perpetuate Tyrant Pride & the Laws of that Babylon which he foresees shall shortly be destroyed, with the Spiritual and not the Natural Sword . [...]
> You, O Deists, profess yourselves the Enemies of Christianity, and you are so: you are also the Enemies of the Human Race & of Universal Nature. Man is born a Spectre or Satan & is altogether an Evil, & requires a New Selfhood continually, & must continually be changed

into his direct Contrary. But your Greek Philosophy (which is a remnant of Druidism) teaches that Man is Righteous in his Vegetated Spectre: an Opinion of fatal & accursed consequence to Man, as the Ancients saw plainly by Revelation, to the intire abrogation of Experimental Theory; and many believed what they saw and Prophecied of Jesus.

Man must & will have Some Religion: if he has not the religion of Jesus, he will have the religion of Satan & will erect the Synagogue of Satan, calling the Prince of this World, God, and destroying all who do not worship Satan under the Name of God. Will any one say, 'Where are those who worship Satan under the Name of God?' Where are they? Listen! Every religion that Preaches Vengeance for Sin is the Religion of the Enemy & Avenger and not of the Forgiver of Sin, and their God is Satan, Named by the Divine Name. Your religion, O Deists! Deism, is the Worship of the God of this World by the means of what you call Natural Religion and Natural Philosophy, and of Natural Morality or Self-Righteousness, the Selfish Virtues of the Natural Heart. This was the religion of the Pharisees who murder'd Jesus. Deism is the same & ends in the same . [. . .]

[. . .] Voltaire! Rousseau! You cannot escape my charge that you are Pharisees & Hypocrites, for you are constantly talking of the Virtues of the Human Heart and particularly of your own, that you may accuse others, & especially the Religious, whose errors you, by this display of pretended Virtue, chiefly design to expose. Rousseau thought Men Good by Nature: he found them Evil & found no friend. Friendship cannot exist without Forgiveness of Sins continually. The Book written by Rousseau call'd his Confessions, is an apology & cloke for his sin & not a confession.

—*Jerusalem,* plate 52

The modern scientist, particularly one given to the extremism of the geneticist Jacques Monod, would shrug at such an obvious blurring of two distinct categories, of "objective truth" and ethics. Yet he could hardly deny an exact correlation between eighteenth-century science and Deism. And, to be consistent, he would keep to his own domain and not encroach (as he does) on that territory designated by Blake as "natural philosophy" and "natural morality." Blake's pairing of these categories is not exactly clear from my paraphrase, hence some further elaboration.

Blake was not an advocate of Mystery as something inaccessible to reason, as something circumscribing the narrow circle of our knowledge. The word "Mystery" has a negative connotation in his vocabulary: it is a terrorizing of the mind through the religion and philosophy of Urizen. The world around us is real, not illusory; neither can it be divided into that which has been discovered and that which awaits discovery by the human mind, but only into the true, or that which is contained by the Imagination, and the false, the "vegetative mirror" that is a parody of the former. The first is for man a living heaven, the second a hell, the Land of Ulro. I quote Northrop Frye:

> There are two poles in human thought, the conception of life as eternal existence in one divine Man, and the conception of life as an unending series of cycles in nature. Most of us spend our mental lives vacillating somewhere between these two, without being fully conscious of either, certainly without any great impulse to accept either. But the rise of Deism has increased our awareness of the extent to which we are attracted by the latter. Between the beginning of life in our world and ourselves, a long interval of time may have elapsed, and a great development have taken place; but the beginning

of our world cannot have been, from a natural point of view, anything more than an accident in the revolving stars in the sky. As soon as our idea of a beginning of time or creation disappears into the "starry wheels," we have attained the complete fallen vision of the world [. . .] the wheel of death [. . .] Such an idea, Blake insists, is a mental cancer: man is not capable of accepting it purely as an objective fact; its moral and emotional implications must accompany it into the mind, and breed there into cynical indifference, a short-range vision, selfish pursuit of expediency, and all the other diseases of the Selfhood, ending in horror and despair. But we cannot shut our eyes and deny its reality; we must see its reality as a reflected image of the eternal mental life of God and Man, the wheel of life, the automotive energy of the risen body.

—*Fearful Symmetry,* pp. 383–84

Frye comes close to paraphrasing Blake in conventional terms, in terms of recognizable concepts, though he succeeds only partially. Crucial in the passage above is the mind's inability to accede to "objective facts" as being truly "objective." The tree of knowledge of good and evil, or the tree of contradictions, is the tree of scientific cognition, based on the principle of consistency. Whoever tastes of that tree is immediately beset by a series of paired negations, casting the mind into the role of an arbiter, which in the moral realm is synonymous with the triumph of arrogance (Swedenborg's *proprium,* Blake's Selfhood). In the Wheel of Death, in Ulro, man reduces other men to vacant shadows, to creatures of chance quickly consigned to oblivion; unable to believe in their reality, he becomes a captive of ego, of the "Spectre":

The Negation in the Spectre, the Reasoning Power in
    Man:
This is a false Body, in Incrustation over my Immortal
Spirit, a Selfhood which must be put off & annihilated
    alway.
To cleanse the Face of my Spirit by Self-examination,
To bathe in the Waters of Life, to wash off the Not
    Human,
I come in Self-annihilation & the grandeur of Inspiration,
To cast off Rational Demonstration by Faith in the Saviour,
To cast off the rotten rags of Memory by Inspiration,
To cast off Bacon, Locke & Newton from Albion's covering,
To take off his filthy garments & clothe him with
    Imagination . . .

—*Milton*, Book II, plate 40

If man in the Age of Reason lived with the vision of
"Starry Wheels," how much more susceptible to such a
vision are we who have seen our Earth photographed from
the Moon in the shape of a sphere? Such a vision, Blake
insisted, was wrong: Earth is flat, circumscribed by the
horizon and the celestial dome. This, his heresy, was not
propounded by him as a "scientific fact." If I understand
him correctly, he treated both images as constructively
antithetical, in the sense of issuing from the power of the
intellect, whereas man's spiritual needs are better satisfied
by the "naïve" imagination. Blake wanted man to inhabit
an Earth-garden (*dichterisch*, as Hölderlin said), the same
as that embodied in Mickiewicz's *Pan Tadeusz*, written
several years after Blake's death:

The Sky is an immortal Tent built by the Sons of Los:
And every space that a Man views around his
    dwelling-place

Standing on his own roof or in his garden on a mount
Of twenty-five cubits in height, such space is his Universe:
And on its verge the Sun rises & sets, the Clouds bow
To meet the flat Earth & the Sea in such an order'd Space:
The Starry heavens reach no further, but here bend and set
On all sides, & the two Poles turn on their valves of gold;
And if he moves his dwelling-place, his heavens also move
Where'er he goes, & all his neighborhood bewail his loss.
Such are the Spaces called Earth & such its dimension.
As to that false appearance which appears to the reasoner
As of a Globe rolling thro' Voidness, it is a delusion of Ulro.
The Microscope knows not of this nor the Telescope: they
    alter
The ratio of the Spectator's Organs, but leave Objects
    untouch'd.
For every Space larger than a red Globule of Man's blood
Is visionary, and is created by the Hammer of Los:
And every Space smaller than a Globule of Man's blood
    opens
Into Eternity of which this vegetable Earth is but a
    shadow.

—*Milton*, Book I, plate 29

Swedenborg's Last Judgment took place outside what
Blake called the vegetative world. Blake's major poems, on
the other hand, are an anticipation of the Harvest of
Wrath, of the consummation of time—the "end of that
age" when the "dream of Albion" (mankind) is over and
the four conflicting elements of human nature are restored
to harmony. Blake's eschatological expectations are no less
fervid than those of the Polish Messianists, though their
Age of the Spirit seems more a historical "third stage" than
does his Jerusalem, the title he gave to the last of his
Prophetic Books. His symbolic holy city, Jesus' betrothed,
lies beyond history. The whole power of his cranky and

extravagant style (for a long time he was considered a schizophrenic) derives from such a vision, even though, we should hasten to add, the future was for him not only "tomorrow" but a dimension of the present, now and forever. Poetry and religion, as I have stated, are synonymous, provided they be authentic, i.e., eschatological. The only language recognized by Blake was the language of prophecy, the language of "the final things." As examples he cited the Gospel symbolism of fruition: the harvest, grape gathering, the nuptial ceremony. Bread from the harvest is changed into the body of Christ and wine into His blood, an event foretold by the miraculous changing of water into wine at the wedding feast at Cana.

Even a theologically trained Christian must puzzle over the Gospel references to the future Kingdom of God. For how are the words "My Kingdom is not of this world" to be reconciled with the repeated and emphatic promise that it will come to pass here on earth, at the end of this eon? The Gospels have been invoked both by millenarists of every persuasion and by pessimistically inclined Christians, for whom the earth will always be a valley of tears. Here again, rather than attempt to paraphrase Blake, I would rely on a quotation from Northrop Frye. Paraphrasing is laborious work; if this task has already been performed for us, there is no reason why we should not make use of it.

> [. . .] In the resurrection of the body the physical universe would take the form in which it would be perceived by the risen body, and the risen body would perceive it in the form of Paradise.
>
> The complete conquest of nature implied by the words "resurrection" and "apocalypse" is a mystery bound up with the end of time, but not with death. When the Selfhood is asked what it wants to do, it can only answer,

with the Sibyl in Petronius, that it wants to die, and it thinks of death as a resolution. To the imagination physical death isolates the part that lives in the spiritual world; but as that world is the real here and the real now, we do not have to wait to die to live in it. "Whenever any Individual Rejects Error & Embraces Truth, a Last Judgment passes upon that Individual." Similarly, the apocalypse could occur at any time in history if men wanted it badly enough to stop playing their silly game of hide-and-seek with nature. Visionaries, artists, prophets and martyrs all live as though an apocalypse were around the corner, and without this sense of a potentially imminent crisis imagination loses most of its driving power. The expectation of a Last Judgment does not mean that the Christians of that time were victims of a mass delusion, or that they were hypnotizing themselves in order to nerve themselves for martyrdom, but that they saw the physical universe as precariously balanced on the mental cowardice of man. And when Blake and Milton elaborate theories of history suggesting that time is reaching its final crisis during their own lives, they are only doing what Jesus did before them.

—*Fearful Symmetry*, p. 195

This may indeed be the glad tidings which Blake brings us: for the Imagination it is unreasonable and unjustified to assent to this world, while to anticipate its end is both justified and reasonable. And because the final reaping was continually being accomplished in the here and now, the seventy-year-old Blake, in no way disillusioned by its deferment in time, could die with a hymn to Jesus on his lips.

30

I INHABITED THE Land of Ulro long before Blake taught me its proper name, though it was not a place in which I was comfortable residing. Like others, I surrendered to the ideas and visions of my century, even enlisted them actively in my writing, recognizing at the same time that it was a betrayal portending a disaster. To what extent that surrender was a conscious one and to what extent dictated by unknown forces, I cannot say. My book of poems, *Three Winters*, appeared in 1936, at a time so distant and in a country so extinct as to make the Romantic era seem closer. In retrospect I believe I was sufficiently cognizant, in myself, of Ulro's abominations. My curse was always the Specter—an ego strong enough to keep me a prisoner of Urizen's domain, where only the general, the collective, the statistical, etc., have any claim to validity. My poor Urthona, or Imagination, tried to release me from that imprisonment; finding all exits barred, she began tunneling an escape route, occasionally—as in *Three Winters*—succeeding. If I were to bow to fashion and adopt a more Jungian terminology, I would say that my female anima was hard put to make me acknowledge her as my own. And had I not been raised in the Roman Catholic rite, mine would have been a pitiable fate. For that rite liberates the feminine in us, a passivity which makes us receptive to Christ or poetic inspiration—Blake would have said "that is" instead of "or." And though I am still hounded by my ego, I stand now fully on the side of Imagination, of Urthona, of anima. I feel a profound gratitude that there is *Una Sancta Catholica Ecclesia*—note that grammatically the word is of feminine gender. I feel an equally profound gratitude for my Lithuanian childhood. Whether Jung was right in making the subconscious dependent on geographical and therefore telluric conditions, this based on correspondences which he discovered between the dreams of American Indians and those of the white settlers, I cannot judge. If correct, it would lend credence to the Positivist thesis of a "mystical Lithuania." Whether or not we assent to that thesis, my religious experience was other than it might have been if I had been Warsaw-bred.

Blake's bestiary is by no means lunatic; his symbolic creatures are descended from a centuries-old tradition, figuring both as Gnostic and alchemistic archetypes. Since reference has been made to Jung, I would here render, in passing, my own assessment of him. If I am not a philosopher but a poet and a historian of ideas, even less do I claim anything but a layman's knowledge of psychiatry. While I do not agree with Jung when he strays from psychology into the metaphysical realm (as he does, for example, in his interpretation of the Book of Job), I would grant that many have profited from his work. An empiricist who passionately defended the empirical method, Jung, on the basis of his numerous clinical studies, adduced formulations more or less identical to those of the great laborers of the Imagination. Ignoring the question of whether the phenomenon of religion was a remnant of the "animistic tradition," he took the religious impulse to be as primary to man as hunger or the sexual urge. At the same time, he observed the gradual fading of Christian symbols in the Western imagination, along with the disorders traceable to that disappearance, and the vicarious role played by various "isms," which emerged merely as the cruel gods resurrected. Jung's writings are a vindication of what I said a moment ago by way of paraphrasing Blake. Some passages read almost like a verbatim transposition, which suggests not so much a plagiarism as a corroboration of his theory of archetypes. Of singular importance to both is the role of the Tetrad. Just as Urizen signified the satanic element among Blake's four "Eternals," so Jung, in treating the Father, Son, and Holy Ghost as symbolic of the personality, expanded the Trinity to include evil, or Satan, arguing that the full personality was expressed in dreams, art, and literature, not as a triad but as a tetrad. Parenthetically I would add that that most extraordinary philosophical novel in world literature, *The Brothers Karamazov*, has a rich symbolic texture, consciously but also, one suspects, unconsciously devised. The four Karamazovs correspond exactly to the Blakean Tetrad. The father, Fyodor, represents the burden of carnality, Tharmas. Dmitri is the embodiment of blind passion, be it love or hatred—or Luvah. Ivan is Urizen, or the suffering Luciferian element. Finally, Alyosha personifies Urthona, Imagination, a vulnerability to the inspiration of the Holy Ghost—it is he, for example, who dreams of Cana of Galilee. There is also Smerdyakov, the shadow and Specter of Ivan–Urizen: negation made manifest. The crime (i.e., parricide or, symbolically, regicide, the murder of Christian Russia) is committed not because one of the Karamazov sons is unmitigatedly evil, since all three are culpable through default. In Blake, as in Jung, a full human personality is possible only when none of the four elements is denied, when all are bound together in *conjunctio oppositorum*. No one, to my knowledge, has deduced the tetradic symbolism in *The Brothers Karamazov*. When applied to the novel as a whole, it can charge, as though electrically, many hitherto dormant energies into something vibrant and volatile.

Ivan–Urizen fashions a God in his own image—his God-Creator is the Urizen of the Deists—then tries him morally and pronounces him guilty. But since Urizen is really Satan worshipped as God, Dostoevsky juxtaposes him with Christ. *The Brothers Karamazov* can thus be read as a more modern version of that same defense strategy seen earlier in Swedenborg and Blake, a strategy based on Godman-hood, on the cosmic dimension of the Primordial Adam. The Great Clockmaker who sets the infernal, inhuman machine in motion is succeeded by the Divine-Human, which admittedly verges on the Manichaean solution, on that version which holds that the Great Clockmaker, Urizen, the Prince of this World, can be a legislator of matter only by the grace of the true God.

Such a strategy suggests that Church theology, whether Catholic, Protestant, or Orthodox (assuming the latter was not already dormant), had suffered a setback as early as the eighteenth century, from which it has never really re-covered, while an unorthodox, even heretical religiosity has enjoyed a great vitality by appealing to the imagina-tion. While a liberal Protestantism was ceding one posi-tion after another and Catholicism withdrawing more and more into its fortress, such minds as Swedenborg, Blake, Mickiewicz, Towiański, and Dostoevsky were stationing themselves beyond the front erected by the theologians. Mickiewicz, it may be recalled, invoked not St. Thomas Aquinas or St. Augustine but those prophets standing out-side the Church—Boehme, Swedenborg, and Saint-Martin.

The California of Far Eastern and satanic cults is an illustration of what happens when Christianity "abstains." I have devoted much thought to Thomism, the most closed and rationally compelling of theological systems, and I can state from experience that it defies the imagination— that is, it defies that translation into images without which no reading can be efficacious. Ideas were of course re-fashioned as images, not only in Aquinas's time but in later periods. If, even as they pay homage to Aquinas, the inhabitants of Ulro can profit little from him, still less are they persuaded by those theologians who, horrified of being accused of backwardness, practice a kind of Christian-social journalism. But the void must be filled, and so it is: with a syncretic mush, with a religious offal indiscriminately and nonsensically selected, as foretold by Vladimir Solovyov in his novel *Three Conversations* (1899) about the coming of the Antichrist in the twenty-first century.

I suppose that in the present literary enterprise I am guided, partially at least, by a perverse ambition: can I, by citing an unorthodox tradition, say something about matters I regard as urgent, in a language at once intellectually lucid and evocative, so as to leave an impress on the mind and in that way help to break down the gates of Ulro?

31

In 1924 A SMALL BOOK by Oscar Milosz was published in Paris under the Latin title *Ars Magna*. It consisted of five chapters or, as he called them, "metaphysical poems," the first of which was written in 1916. *Les Arcanes*, written in 1926 and published in 1927, is both a sequel to and an expanded version of the first book. It contains only one "metaphysical poem," but is appended with a voluminous commentary. I came into possession of these books as a young man of twenty, and both, I can say without exaggeration, decided my intellectual career. Or, more precisely, the questions inspired by them—and which I would put to myself unremittingly—decided my career. Both make fiercely difficult reading, exasperating in the way their author deliberately frustrates the reader's progress by mixing Cartesian discourse with poetic ambuscade. Among the French admirers of Milosz's verse few have ventured into that inhospitable region demanding unstinting dedication, which, or so it is claimed, lies so at the periphery as to be incidental to an appreciation of the poetry. Some fifty years later the "metaphysical poems" would become the subject of a doctoral dissertation assigning them a central place in the Milosz oeuvre.*

Even in those days I debated whether these works were translatable into Polish—assuming the translator could make sense of them, which was far from being so in my case. After playing around with a few sentences, I decided that the text, demanding as it was intellectually, would prove inaccessible. Besides, there was hardly a Polish reader who, because of unavoidable associations with a taboo Romantic and Modernist vocabulary, would not have bridled at such works. Yet my translator's ambition must have entrenched itself, as the project was eventually realized, albeit much later, indeed as recently as a few years ago. I have now translated both works, not into Polish but into English. Why now? No doubt because it coincided with an urge to bind together, clasp-like, the earlier intuitions with the later insights; it was a way of closing the circle. But the time it consumed! Time devoted just to a careful reading of sentences so intractable as to gain in clarity only when vetted in another language. The English version, as a consequence, is probably a shade more trans-

---

* Defended by Jean Bellemin-Noël at the Sorbonne, in 1975. I should add, however, that I find his interpretation, based on a Laconian Freudianism, untenable.

parent than the French original, and this opinion is not mine alone. I worked on it, in other words, principally for myself, though not without the thought that I was acquitting myself of an obligation by acting as an intermediary between Milosz and a small coterie of American readers. Quite hypothetical readers, by the way, and this because of the deceptive similarity these works bear to other works belonging to the genres of occultism, theosophy, and Eastern esoterica. There are those who are so repulsed by this genre as to shun anything even faintly resembling it. Others, though attracted, might feel cheated on opening a Milosz work—Oscar Milosz was quite blunt in declaring himself against spiritual imports from the East. Only one group, it would appear, finds his "metaphysical poems" neither abstruse nor unreadable—the Blakeans. There is nothing to suggest that Oscar Milosz knew Blake. Yet the similarities are pronounced.

Even though today the boundary between poetry and prose has become sufficiently blurred, the terms still preserve at least a practical utility. Although styled "metaphysical poems" by their author, the works themselves elude either rubric. Rather, they form a distinct category of their own, grounded in a specific human situation embracing both the author and the reader. Before describing that situation, a few prefatory remarks about the history of our modern, "obscure" poetry. The climax of the artistic revolution in Europe coincided with the time of my childhood and adolescence, that is, with the second and third decades of our century. But my lifetime has also witnessed a corresponding disenthrallment, not because the various "isms" foundered but because they triumphed, and in so doing revealed the emptiness of their promises. Occasionally a genuine poet might profit from the tolerance forced on the man on the street by a rowdy avant-garde, but the conquest proved to be another prank staged by that mistress of irony, History, because, thanks to it, an "obscure" poetry became mainstream: a situation of "all-talk-and-no-listening," of "all-writing-and-no-reading." Milosz, though he lived in avant-garde Paris, was lukewarm to the "isms" of his time. If some avant-gardists were driven by unconscious motives to court a clientele through obfuscation, through mystery, thereby acting as the true heirs to that theory proclaiming the "priesthood of art," Milosz was a man decidedly in search of something else—a way to cloister his work in a specific language inaccessible to all but the chosen. Solitude and a wounded pride made him regard any concessions as a compromise beneath his dignity. An abhorrence for the ugliness of the age, which he judged to be criminal and vulgar, disposed him to resistance through an insurgent form. The title of his 1910 novel, *L'Amoureuse Initiation*, is telling, initiation being the way by which in the past a few attained to alchemy and the study of the Cabala, two versions of the science of mystery held by him in high regard. In bolting the door to his domain he has been quite successful. *Ars Magna* and *Les Arcanes* take the form of prophetic letters, addressed neither to the author's nor the following generation but to the author's great-grandson, in the firm belief that he would inhabit a happier age, one more receptive to truths unknown to his forebears, with the exception of the author himself. Other formal consequences follow: since the man of the future will grasp intuitively the author's message, no further elaboration is needed, hence the author's extremely hermetic style.

The situation of the intended reader is no less worthy of consideration. If the message of these works is addressed to later generations, then their publication is strictly a protective measure; their aim is preservation in the future, not approbation in the present. Who, then, is this sufficiently enlightened reader? Almost certainly a citizen of the future, at the very least a one-eyed man among the blind, which is very gratifying to the ego and therefore insidious. By giving the author his due, the reader must count himself among the privileged, one of the few on the face of the planet to be afforded a glimpse beyond the curtain of tomorrow. But since few can imagine themselves to be so gifted, the works lose in credibility. Let us assume that the author was entirely misguided, deluding both himself and others; that he was not altogether in his right mind. Even granting this were so, the reader not only cannot breathe a sigh but risks falling victim of an even worse dilemma. If the pages before him are more mesmerizing than beautiful, then he must sense the impropriety of applying purely literary criteria. The most fitting adjective for such works would seem to be the word "sublime." That this category exists can no more be documented than the taste of bread can or even needs to be verified. It impresses itself on us whenever the intensity native to it makes any work devoid of it seem bland and jejune by comparison. If sublimity is merely the power of militant faith, of apostolic fervor, why should it imbue these works and not the confessions of countless cranks and fanatics? What makes one work sublime and not another? Unfortunately, it seems always to be accompanied by a lack of decorum. Blake's *Prophetic Books* belong to the category of the sublime, but the inscrutability of their code militated against their publication. Blake engraved them in copper, accompanying them with illustrations, thereby creating a poetic-graphic whole, and printed them in limited editions for collectors of his art. It is not even certain whether his closest collaborator, Catherine Blake, understood anything of her husband's philosophy.

The sublime nature of Milosz's "metaphysical poems" is not of this century, which suggests that sublimity is no longer within our power, or so I have always imagined. As we travel in search of his spiritual homeland, we all but pass over the Positivist half of the nineteenth century and find ourselves in the company of Goethe and a handful of poets whom he repeatedly invoked by name: Hölderlin, Lamartine, Byron, Heine, Edgar Allan Poe. These "elective affinities," in combination with numerous personal statements, allow us to retrace his persuasions back to the Middle Ages, to the Renaissance, and to the dawn of the modern era. He saw himself in a certain tradition, convinced that a hermetic science going back to the Pythagoreans had been transmitted through the ages, and that the legend of the Templars was not a fabrication. Milosz was greatly indebted to his contemporary, the French scholar René Guénon, in whose study *L'Esotérisme de Dante* he discovered a thesis postulating Dante's membership in the Order of the Templars. And it was Dante who, along with Goethe, embodied for Milosz the most sublime poetry since the New Testament. The hermetic line that persisted during the Renaissance (in the form of alchemy and a Christian Cabala) labored to sustain the unity of religion and science, a unity that was subsequently undone. It was to this second, clandestine Renaissance that Milosz paid the most tribute, because only it contained the promise of future reconciliation, not only of religion and science but of religion, art, and philosophy—the future that he addressed was hailed by him as the "new Jerusalem." The hermetic tradition was continued by three who stand at the very threshold of the modern: Paracelsus, or Theophrastus Bombastus von Hohenheim (1493–1541); the Polish alchemist Sendigovius, or Michał Sędziwoj (1556–1636); and Jakob Boehme (1575–1624). Despite the traditional date given for the breakup of religion and science, Descartes is cast by Milosz not as the father of rationalism but as an intuitionist, a "man parading in a mask," and a Rosicrucian. If Descartes was distorted by his successors, Milosz, who described himself as "a son of Descartes," was not one of them. The science and philosophy of the Age of Reason were to blame for the tragedy of modern man: spiritual vacancy, isolation of the individual, the minatory character of civilization as a whole. But the underground tradition endured, thanks to Martinez Pasqualis, Saint-Martin, and Swedenborg. If Milosz could speak of Goethe as his "spiritual master," then he would claim Swedenborg as his "celestial master," based on the triadic division of the earthly, the spiritual, and the celestial.

A topography not exactly unknown to us. With some modifications, it stands as the topography of all the Romantics, testifying to their awareness of the disinheritance and to the defense mechanisms adopted by the alienated man. The past as the refuge of a genuine homeland, a lost homeland. The present as exile. The future as both a radical renewal and a restitution of the past. The Polish Romantics, in this sense, were the quintessential Romantics: for them the three time boundaries were set off by political events, and theirs was a homeland literally lost. This literalness, at the same time, shifted the problem to the international realm and deadened—it was not the time to weep over the roses—all sensitivity to the internal predicament of the "disinherited mind." Milosz, an exile, a foreigner in the fullest sense of the word, was a Romantic by reason of his nostalgia alone; in his private mythology, the lost land of childhood grows imperceptibly to become the ideal realm of a yet to be reborn mankind. He differs from the Romantics, both Polish and Western, in his fixing on the causes and effects of the scientific-technological revolution, recalling both Blake and Goethe in this regard. If for both of these Newton symbolized the scientific method of the "lens," then all the more so did he for Milosz, who with recourse to physics practiced a meta-physics.

Even if we assent to the Brzozowskian thesis of our age as a continuation of Romanticism, of the Romantic schism, there is little to be gained by labeling as a "Romantic" a man nurtured around the turn of the century and whose literary maturity dates from around 1914. Moreover, *Ars Magna* and *Les Arcanes* were written during the most intense phase of the author's diplomatic and political career, bearing witness to his newly acquired expertise in economics and the social sciences. During the First World War, as the bearer of a Russian passport, he was assigned to the Press Office of the French Ministry of Foreign Affairs (he was fluent in Russian, English, and German); after 1918, he represented independent Lithuania, organized the Lithuanian legations in Paris and Brussels, and sat on commissions of the League of Nations. He was too sensitive to the interplay between the various sectors of human praxis to be suspected of having a purely "spiritual" vision of European history. The scientific-technological revolution had brought the working masses—"more alive, more receptive, and more anguished than ever"—into prominence; and it was the aim even of Milosz's most seemingly esoteric meditations, including the "metaphysical poems," to save the masses from the slaughters of war and the surrogate religions of ideology. Late in life he wrote: "Not the events themselves but their spiritual consequences cry out for men of inspiration. The Russian Revolution sought to manufacture its own bard. But the new social order, much less its poet, will not be summoned to life by the mechanical imposition of a materialist doctrine."

Both in his critique of the present, of bourgeois and proletarian society, and in his anticipation of a new age, Milosz was simultaneously a Romantic and a subversive, a stance that for me, shaped as I was by Polish Romanticism and Brzozowski, seemed entirely natural. The reader, by force of intellectual habit, may bridle at this pursuit of a link between a hermetic vision and revolutionary flux. Yet today's scholar will readily concede a bond between the Blakean oeuvre and the Industrial Revolution, just as Blake himself conceded it.

Milosz's early poetry—and not only the very early poetry but the work up to around 1911, or when he was already in his thirties—is usually classified, perhaps not inappropriately, as a late example of French Symbolism. The latter, in turn, is one of the postures assumed by the poet in Ulro, whether through the invention of a wholly imaginary universe, intended as an anti-world, or through irony, sarcasm, blasphemy, melancholy, or despair, all of which figure prominently in the work of Milosz and make him read at times like the tragic Jules Laforgue who died prematurely. Poems of a more sanguine tone are also in evidence, proof of how poetic movements roughly contemporaneous to one another, regardless of the country, tend to converge: around this same time, Polish poetry was moving from modernist melancholy to the buoyant optimism of a Leopold Staff. The subsequent shift in Polish poetry corresponding to the triumph of Cubism would yield its first experiments in the years prior to 1914. Oscar Milosz did not obey the trend. For him these formed merely the latest heroics of those condemned to Ulro, now performed with the help of masks, costumes, and a pseudo-blasé buffoonery. He sought not innovation in this sense, so much as release from Ulro, and for a long time he labored in ignorance as to the way. In France only Claudel,

thanks to his religious poetry, could claim to be an inno-
vator of a different kind. Milosz, meanwhile, had made his
decision, renouncing his melancholy Romantic patrons
in favor of a personal quest. Subsequently he would write
his "metaphysical poems," which stand as one of the curios-
ities of the age, plus a handful of poems recognized as his
finest. As a poet he is as much an anachronism as Leśmian
was in Poland. Which in the course of decades ceases to
have any bearing, one way or the other.

32

THE TITLE OF THE FIRST of the "metaphysical poems,"
Epître à Storge (*Epistle to Storge*), is illustrative of Milosz's
method of deliberate obscurity. What reader could be presumed to know the identity of Storge? At first it appears
as if the author is addressing a woman companion lying
beside him on an ocean beach. We soon discover that
Storge is androgynous and not to be taken as a living
person. A knowledge of Swedenborg would tell us that for
Milosz *storge*—Greek for parental love, maternal as well
as paternal—connoted a love of mankind, the guiding force
of his own mission and literary career. The notion of
humanitarian service would lead us back to Goethe of
Die Wanderjahre and the last part of Faust.

Before the occurrence of a certain incident in 1914,
about which more later, Milosz was ignorant of Swedenborg. He then passes through a period of intense reading,
maintaining a frequently critical but always reverential
attitude toward the Swedish theurgist. In this he recalls

Blake, hence the many consanguinities between Blake and Milosz, above all in their common attitude, inherited from Swedenborg, toward the "abomination of desolation" and the complicity of modern science. Even so, neither of them could be called "Swedenborgians" in the strict sense. Swedenborg, it should be stressed, is not to be judged on the basis of his reception by the French and Polish Romantics. What the latter took, Blake ignored, and vice versa. And Oscar Milosz, reading Swedenborg in the twentieth century, was even more biased in his selection.

I would not be exaggerating if I said that both *Les Arcanes* and *Ars Magna* are works centered on the problem of space. By that I do not mean in the sense of an abstract pursuit of scientific equations. Milosz was of the belief that certain cosmological conceptions had a distorting, maiming effect on the human imagination. The vision of space as a boundless vessel, tantamount to a void of "Starry Wheels," was not the exclusive province of the eighteenth century. It merely gave expression to those inclinations of the human mind originating in the Fall, the sin of Adam being his conversion to a cosmology conceived of pride (just as for Blake the Newtonian system embodied the Urizenian vision of the universe). In presenting Milosz's argument in its barest outline, I wish to avoid two misunderstandings. First, the Romantic renunciation of the claims of Reason should not be generalized, lest the most diverse strategies be reduced to a stereotype. The early-Romantic stance is marked by escape into the "paradisiacal realm of illusion," the late-Romantic by a belief that, despite our grieving subjectivity, truth was vested in science. When Dostoevsky said that he would have chosen Christ even if he accepted the argument refuting Christ's divinity, he was stating incisively both the late-Romantic and our modern dilemma, because the truth of which he spoke bears on the scientifically discovered and "inviolable" laws of Nature, of the sort that would impugn a miracle (e.g., the Resurrection). A further elaboration of this dilemma is to be found in the massive attack mounted by Dostoevsky's disciple, Lev Shestov, against every brand of philosophy that would invalidate the Particular on behalf of the General. Such strategies are to be distinguished from direct incursions into the realm of science, from those propositions aimed at erecting a new science, one to wed the mind and Imagination, such as were made by poets like Goethe and Blake. The reaction of scientists to these poetic visions has been so militant as to arouse suspicion that a nerve has indeed been touched.

Secondly, considering that ours is an age of pseudo-religious and pseudo-mystical cults, I lay myself open to nasty imputations by alluding to alchemy or to the Swedenborg doctrine. I hereby proclaim my distaste for occultism and declare that I have always been eminently defiant of the temptations of a craze that in America has inflicted on thousands of misguided souls a cellophane-wrapped Buddhism, be it the quackery of a Gurdjieff or of other such gurus. I owe that defiance to a Roman Catholic (i.e., Thomistic) education, but also, in large part, to my allegiance to Oscar Milosz, who stressed the Mediterranean-born as opposed to Far Eastern religions, and above all recommended exploration of our own Judeo-Christian tradition. Indeed, his "metaphysical poems" can be appreciated as a powerful feat of the imagination only by those desirous of pursuing this one tradition, and not by those who would desert it for some Eastern obfuscations.

Ars Magna and *Les Arcanes*, both of them formidable works, gain in transparency when the reader begins with their fundamental postulate; if, while remaining seated, he extends his arm and reflects on the meaning of human movement. According to Milosz, the primal experience, the one underlying all thought and feeling, is the perception of space:

> To the man who sees, space is revealed by the movement of light; to the blind man, by that of his arm, of any limb or of his whole body; to the blind man and to the man who sees, and also to the paralytic stricken with blindness, by the very notion of movement, their basic thought, point of departure of the most abstract operations, in short, *a spiritual principle linked in an indissoluble manner to the very flow of their blood.*
>
> —*Les Arcanes,* commentary to verset 1

The way in which a man visualizes space, situates himself in his imagination in relation to other things, is synonymous with his way of thinking; it is at the very source of the thought process:

> In truth, we do not bring either space or time into nature, but just the movement of our body and knowledge, or rather awareness and love of that movement, awareness and love which we call Thought and which is at the origin of our first and fundamental ability to situate all things, beginning with ourselves. Space and time seem to have been prepared long in advance to receive us. Yet all our anxieties come from our need to situate this very space and time, and the mental operation we perform when, for lack of another imaginable place or containment, we assign to space and time a place in themselves, multiplying and dividing them without end, does not diminish these terrible anxieties in the least—these anxieties of love, Storge, which pursue us up to the confines of the Valley of the Shadow of Death.
>
> —*Epître à Storge*

The "son of Descartes," it is no exaggeration to say, set out to revise the maxim "I think, therefore I am," to read: "I move, therefore I am." He seeks proof of the first and finds it in a need to situate:

> It can be said of the compulsion to situate all things (including the space and time in which we situate everything) that it is the first among all mental manifestations of our life. There is certainly no thought and no emotion which come from any source other than this essential activity of being. The first movements of our mind when we become aware of the surrounding world are blindly submitted to it. Later we discover it again with the same domineering features in geometry and the natural sciences; its realm extends to the most extreme abstractions of philosophy, religion, morality and art; good, evil, love, conflicts of truth and falsehood, openness to the Revelation, forgetfulness, the state of innocence, inspiration— all our spiritual offspring demand their heritage of marvelous lands, and receive it; and the same ancient necessity to situate all things extends its power over delightful or dismal regions: the East of the Ancients, Hell, Saana, Armageddon, the Patmos of Boanerges, Lethe, Arcadia, Parnassus—and others, and still more, an infinite number of others.
>
> —*Epître à Storge*

The consequences, once we assent to the foregoing proposition, are enormous, for it acknowledges the imagination not as something incidental to sensory perception but as its prime condition. I shall not digress here on what would surely develop into a tedious discourse on, among other things, the reasons for Blake's contempt for the eighteenth-century theory of cognition. Such subjects are not for me to pursue, aware as I am of the terminological treacheries. Except to say that the universal nature of the primary impulse that compels us to situate all things—in this sense, the topography of the *Odyssey*, of Dante's *Hell*, *Purgatory*, and *Paradise*, the theory of evolution, and the second law of thermodynamics all spring from the same spatial imagination—implies that the various domains cultivated by the human mind are more conjoined, through the imagination, than anyone may have assumed. The images imposed on us by science are therefore not confined to any strictly scientific sphere, but pervade our entire thinking, even at its most "naïve."

We situate everything in space. Fine, but where is that space, in *what* is it situated? If it is infinitely expanded, then it cannot be located anywhere. If, as is sometimes speculated, there is a point beyond our solar system and the myriads of other systems where matter gives way to pure expansion, then it too is an infinite expansion, because the very notion of a boundary or of cessation is impossible. Thus are we compelled to multiply and divide space by space to infinity, so that expansion becomes infinitely great, on the one hand, and infinitely small, on the other.

The mind's nightmare, the very essence of what it means to be "disinherited," is embodied in the Newtonian proposition, which he posited as axiomatic:

> For times and spaces are, as it were, the Places as well of themselves as of all other things. All things are placed in Time as to order of Succession; and in Space as to order of Situation. It is from their essence or nature that they are Places; and that the primary places of things should be movable, is absurd.
>
> —NEWTON, *Principia*, II, 12, quoted in Ault,
> *Visionary Physics*

For Blake this proposition was blasphemy. Set against him was the whole of science, which proclaimed Newton's absolute space and absolute time. By contrast, Oscar Milosz, although he had not so much as heard the name Einstein in 1916, had found—as early as *Epître à Storge*—confirmation of his intuition of the general theory of relativity. His "metaphysical poems," in effect, castigate the mind which condemns itself to a homeless exile in a space factored and divided without end. Taken together, they lay out a kind of anti-Newtonian "visual physics." Space is reduced to the movement of body A relative to body B. Where there are no bodies, there is neither space nor time. From an infinitely expanded void of galactic clusters, inconceivable to the mind, the universe becomes a trinity of space-time-matter bound by universal Movement.

Human thought, what Milosz calls the "awareness and love of movement," is nothing more than the need to situate; it issues from a perception of space that inheres in the very structure of our organism, i.e., in our blood circulation. To put it another way, we think because our blood circulation binds us to the universal Movement.

Rhythm is therefore at the very heart of Milosz's metaphysics. "Rhythm is the highest earthly expression of what is called thought." We read in *Epître à Storge* of the "delicate tenderness" and "loving infallibility" with which man "assigns an appropriate place and time to a word and sound in a poem, to muscle and step in dance, to a tone and accent in speech, the main line of motion and life in sculpture, to the original as well as to the final vibration of color in painting, and in architecture, to stone and beam in a harmonious and logical distribution of effort." He alludes frequently to the role of sacred dances in various religions, as does the religious historian, René Guénon, whom I quote:

. . . from the "science of rhythm," so rich in application, stem all the means used to establish contact with higher states. This would explain the Islamic tradition which says that Adam spoke in verse while in Paradise, that is, spoke in a rhythmical language . . . It would also explain why the Scriptures are written in a rhythmical language, and, indeed, they are very far from being the simple "poems," in the purely secular sense, that the anti-traditionalists among modern "critics" would like them to be; besides, poetry, at its most primordial, was not the frivolous literature that it has become today . . .

—*La Langue des Oiseaux*, 1931

In paraphrasing the "metaphysical poems," I am purposely trying to proceed from the simple to the more complex. I do not know whether anyone will accompany me, but, then, most of human endeavor is a love's labor lost. It is relatively easy to imagine that "an appropriate place and time" assigned a given word or dance step, which is the secret of rhythm, answers to our need to situate. But if everything is relative to something else, if the movement of body A is relative to that of body B, the latter relative to that of body C, and so on, where is the place of places, the place to which all others are made relative? Let us now move from the general theory of relativity to its mystical version. The place of places for Milosz is that "Love which moves the sun and stars," indefinable in human language except in symbolic terms. Milosz assigned particular importance to the Song of Songs, into which he read several layers of meaning. To the extent that the love between a man and a woman is symbolic of the relationship between the Creator-as-Bridegroom and Creation-as-Bride, the *arcanum* of marriage goes to the very heart of being, which is erotic. Rhythm is unceasing quest, an unremitting drive for repose, for Place; but in a universe lacking any absolute reference point, man literally cannot find a place for himself—of which St. Augustine was well aware ("Restless is our heart until it finds rest in Thee"). It is also a truth known to every poet, who spends a lifetime writing a single, elusive, never to be fully realized poem. Oscar Milosz could find a place neither in Paris nor in Venice nor in London, and his wanderer's fate became for him a grand metaphor. Where there is only movement, devoid of any reference point, even such gestures as shifting from the table to the bookshelf are illusory when measured by the wall's immobility, which in turn must be made relative to the house, the house to the block, etc.—and the process is interminable in the absence of any fixity. In passing, it should be noted that among some Jewish cabalists one of the names for God is Place.

Movement minus any reference point is a great deception; only the passage from one state to another is real. If this sounds like Swedenborg, are we to infer that Oscar Milosz took refuge in a Swedenborgian Heaven bound to the material world by a web of "correspondences"? Here Milosz was most adamant: "I do not like the theory of the astral body of the adepts, nor the concept of spiritual worlds advanced by Swedenborg . . . Try as they may to tell us that their substantial worlds are alien to time and space, and that a place is only apparent, or even that all reality there is an instantaneous creation and correspondence of a mental state; nevertheless, one feels that as they are still constrained by the law of movement, they situate the immaterial construct in a place determined by its opposition to matter. So difficult it is to break completely our habit of situating A in relation to B . . ." (*Epître à Storge*).

And farther on:

Where nothing is situated, there is no passage from one place to another, Storge, only from one state—and that a state of love—to another. In the present state of our tenderness we endlessly multiply and divide, and we abandon ourselves to the furious torrent of rhythm, and nothing satisfies us. But we will die, Storge, and we will enter that blessed state where multiplication, division, and rhythm, constantly unsatisfied, find the supreme absolute number and the immutable, perfect ending of every poem. This is the second love, Storge, this is the Elysium of the Master Goethe, this is the Empyrean of the great Alighieri, this is the Adramandoni of the good Swedenborg, this is the Hesperia of the unlucky Hölderlin.

—*Epître à Storge*

"I move, therefore I am" thus becomes "I love, therefore I am," and this because the sensation of movement and love are identical in their quest for the place of places. At the center of Milosz's "metaphysical poems" is a philosophy of space. But it might also be said to be a philosophy of blood: "By the word 'blood' we understand living cosmic matter endowed with spontaneous movement."

33

I FACE A PROBLEM of no mean proportions. The doubt repeatedly expressed on these pages becomes exacerbated when I attempt the next-to-impossible task of rendering into Polish what is fairly unyielding even in the original. To what purpose, for whom this intellectual luxury? Granted, it may give heart to those who are writing dissertations on me; that is, my excursions into the exotic may explain why the books of my literary colleagues, so sensitive to the latest avant-garde fashions, impress me by and large as puerile. But to be read by doctoral students is meager consolation—is there anything they will not read? One would like to add to more than the volume of library dust. In all probability we are entering an age of wholesale trivialization, and it appears that Milosz was right not to expect anything of his contemporaries or of their sons. Even I, a figure of more modest stature, who would prefer to carve out some leisure for metaphysics rather than perform the duties of a Kraszewski or Sienkiewicz, have not been allowed to speak my mind, for what they heard in my voice was not always what I would have had them hear. After this brief tirade, again made under the duress of doubt, I return to Oscar Milosz, not raising my sights beyond the possible.

Milosz was the architect of his own system, but not in the sense of a philosophical system capable of being translated into discursive terms. In his case, there is always some residue of inscrutableness, so that the reader should not suffer any guilt for not comprehending; as every poetry critic knows, there are poetic systems whose resemblance to purely conceptual systems is only analogous. In trying to describe Milosz's thought, whether we call it a meta-physics or meta-poetics, we would more nearly approximate the truth by representing it as the meditation of a cabalist. The term "Cabala" has acquired a number of negative associations, to the point that it has become almost synonymous with magic, palmistry, incantations, exorcism—such as for centuries cabalism indeed was in the popular imagination.

In my chapters on Mickiewicz, I made reference to Gershom Scholem's work *On the Kabbalah and Its Symbolism*. Scholem, a historian, is also the author of another book, titled simply *Kabbalah* (English translation published in 1974). If Swedenborg is required reading for Blake and Milosz, then the Cabala is no less indispensable. What, then, is the Cabala—in the real sense, not in its vulgar, popular version? It is a meditation on the mysterious relationship between God and the universe; it seeks to answer the question of how the universe was created, to divine the intermediate stages between the inscrutable essence of the Deity and the material world. In this sense it is theosophy (*theo-sophia*) rather than theology. The Cabala enjoys an ancient tradition, and in its crowning achievements it belongs, I venture to say, to the great triumphs of the human imagination—in that civilization constituted of both Judaic and Hellenic elements. As Scholem observes, from its very inception the history of the Cabala was bound up with the history of late-Hellenic thought, and in the Middle Ages was almost inseparable from the intellectual history of Islam and Christianity. Says Scholem: "The Kabbalah, in its historical significance, can be defined as the product of the interpenetration of Jewish Gnosticism and Neoplatonism." That is why, if we bear in mind the presence of a Christian Cabala during the Renaissance, it is often difficult to say what in a given author—Milosz, for example—derives from the Jewish cabalists and what is the inheritance of a Platonic, Neoplatonic, and Gnostic tradition. As a student in Paris, Milosz learned Hebrew well enough to read the Bible in the original. Yet his knowledge of the Cabala is entirely indebted to the French commentaries. But influences count less than the elaboration of a system that transcends philosophy and theology, yet bears analogies to both, and that like the Cabala and many writings of the Christian hermetics stands as an instance of a high poetry.

In *Les Arcanes*, as in Milosz's poetry of the twenties, we find, in one form or another, motifs fundamental to the Cabala, above all that of a hierarchy of being, structured so that the unfathomable recesses of the Divine are manifested in stages, or "mirrors," the contemplation of which permits the human mind to form a certain image of God. These stages, or divine potencies, called *Sefirot* (they number ten), do not contain the full magnitude of God but emanate from Him; as He reveals Himself in them, His unity becomes a plurality and produces the world. Some versions of the Cabala, whose canonical work in the Middle Ages was called Zohar, compiled around 1300, commonly refer to four worlds of being (*Azilut, Beriah, Yezirah, Asiyyah*), which are also hierarchically arranged—from the highest, the pre-material, to the lowest, the terrestrial. In each of these realms, the *Sefirot* behave in a way that is commensurate with the level of being proper to that realm. The result is a complex of overlapping hierarchical structures. In this sense, the Cabala stands as the epitome of symbolic reasoning: whatever is above is reflected in the world below, which in turn is reflected in the world below it, and so on.

Oscar Milosz had recourse to the French terminology, derived no doubt from the Christian Cabala. One of the most remarkable features of the Cabala is the concept of the Primordial Man, the Adam Kadmon, often identified with the very essence of the Godhead (*Ein-Sof*). In the French text he bears the name of Macroprosope. His counterpart on the highest plane of Divine emanation is the Microprosope—the Logos, the Word Incarnate. Here Swedenborg and Blake, with their insistence on God's humanity, inevitably come to mind. Even Milosz is quoted as having told a friend: "God is a man. That is why the Bible has that passionate tone not found in other religions dominated by metaphysics. God does not practice metaphysics" (Théophile Briant, "Rencontre de Milosz," *Le Goéland*, June 1, 1939).

The following Milosz quote, though partially repetitious of passages already cited, introduces some new elements, namely the *correlativity* of the various strata of being:

> To think is first of all to situate and to compare: still, the two operations may be reduced to one, for the initial comparison is the relation of one place to another. Thus, to think is originally to situate oneself with respect to external objects, at first physically, then morally. Later on, it is to determine the position of our world with respect to that of surrounding worlds. To be is to be in a place, to cover a series of points which are themselves mobile; it is to move as a mind in a body endowed with motion and carried by a world gravitating around other gravitating worlds. Copernicus, Galileo, and Newton, long before they made their discoveries prompted by little mobile images coming from the external world, already carried all their knowledge in their latent memory. Intuitions are recollections. By reason of the basic universal law, that of *analogy* [italics mine], the essential operation of the mind extends to the moral sphere: to love and to hate is to obey a movement of attraction or of repulsion. In consequence, thought is only an awareness and *love* of movement, an aesthetic, a science of rhythm, for movement means determination of *place*, and place itself means determination of *being*.

> —*Les Arcanes*, commentary to verset 8

The law of analogy: here is the key to the "metaphysical poems," their guiding assumption. The law of analogy—

·209·

or "as above, so below"—is typical of medieval Christianity and the Cabala. It is also the basis of Swedenborg's theory of correspondence, which obviously did not materialize out of nowhere. Nor did Goethe wish to break with the medieval tradition when he tried to sustain a belief in the commensurability of the world and the human mind. And the poetry and art of William Blake, who aspired beyond a "vegetative" Nature to a true, "imaginary" Nature, was no less a conscious revival of the Middle Ages.

If Milosz says that "intuitions are recollections," it is not because he believed in the transmigration of souls—this aspect of the Cabala, unmistakable in Mickiewicz, is missing in Milosz. Proto-memory, or latent memory, is preserved in the blood, in that "living cosmic matter endowed with spontaneous movement": we remember because we are living beings. What do we remember? Another, higher reality, which is not unknowable because through intuition we are given access to the archetypal world. The language of religious cults and myths evokes in us such a strong response because we recognize in them what is known unconsciously. The entire movement of matter is analogous to the movement of incorporeal light which constitutes the universe—to be discussed in the next chapter. Here I would merely add that, according to Polynesian myths, God created man by fashioning him from clay and then dancing before him for three days to make him move.

The Middle Ages applied the law of analogy in philosophy (*analogia entis*), but this was in an age when analogies were perceived in every earthly thing, as evidenced by medieval art and architecture. The symbolic interpretation did not yet entail any clear distinction between a sign and the defined or undefined thing designated by it; it was a coalescence (*sym-bolein* means "to throw together").

Zwingli's more modern thesis, which stated that the body and blood of Christ are only symbolically present in the Eucharist, would have been unthinkable in the Middle Ages, which held the symbolic to be *preeminently* real (Erich Heller has written on the revolutionary aspects of Zwingli's thesis).

Milosz's inherent opposition to the twentieth century, an "age of jeering ugliness," was born of distress at the mind's diminished capacity to understand the law of analogy. Since the late eighteenth century, literature and art had been steadily forfeiting the ability to represent what I would call the "multi-layered object" (the phrase was not part of Milosz's vocabulary). Milosz was not an admirer of such poets as Wordsworth, whose images of Nature only seem to evoke real things. Nor was he an admirer of Shelley, though he did have praise for Byron as the first to render the diabolical mental anguish of the disinherited man.

Although he did not know Blake, Milosz with his indictment of the "natural muses" sounds close enough to be a paraphrase:

> In a truthful style, as well as in sound thought and genuine sensation, everything is phenomenon, nothing is image. The literary image is make-up to conceal the inexpressive face of the natural muses. The divine muse of the Bible does not pronounce a single word that does not correspond to an object or a fact of the three worlds, namely of the archetypal or celestial world, of the spiritual world of light, creator of the mathematical point, and of the natural world of physical light. All poets of modern times, except Dante, Goethe, and two or three others, are blind children of fallen natural muses.
>
> —*Les Arcanes*, commentary to verset 26

I shall return to those "three worlds" momentarily. Milosz envisioned the future of poetry as a transmutation both of the poet and of his art; hence the title *Ars Magna*, the Great Art—a synonym for alchemy in the Middle Ages. Now, alchemy, as we know, was premised, again by way of the law of analogy, on the simultaneous regeneration of the adept and of the matter being transmuted. But Milosz believed that in our century such a poetry was either impossible or if it presented itself it would not be understood. Yet poets keep searching desperately for that authentic speech, unconsciously remembered—for that language heeded, according to the Orpheic myth, by animals and stones.

34

NEITHER OUR COMMON SURNAME nor my longing for patriarchal authority would be enough to assure for Milosz's work the sort of influence it has had on me. Had I not known tragedy, both private and public, and if most of my life had not been a struggle at the scream's edge, I too would have found nothing there. Let us be honest: anyone raised in the Christian religion will find little help in this century before the unspeakable agonies such as are borne by the living creatures inhabiting this earth worked by a benign God. *Milosz, poète de l'amour*: yes, Milosz was a poet of love, but it was not a saccharine love, rather one of a higher degree, dearly come by. And his work, especially the metaphysical poetry, wrestles with the age-old question: how to assent to our existence on earth?

The Song of Songs and the conjugal *arcanum*: a metaphor of the love between God-the-Bridegroom and Creation-the-Bride . . . A peculiar love, some might say, and not without cause, given the nature of creation as we know it. But they forget—so adulterated has Christianity become even among Christians—that God not only created the world but took on a human form and willingly died the death of a tortured prisoner. And where there is no time, there can be no chronology, so that Golgotha is coincident in time with the act of Creation. This is the gist of Milosz's meditations.

Before moving on to his system, I shall try, on the basis of Gershom Scholem's work, to show how this problem was posed in the Cabala, particularly in Isaac Luria's sixteenth-century version. Here, then, are its cardinal points: (1) If we believe in God, the proposition that the world was created *ex nihilo* is inadmissible, inasmuch as God, being infinite, encompasses everything, and any space outside Him would be tantamount to a limitation of His infinity. Here Luria introduces the notion of *zimzum*, of God's voluntary withdrawal, sometimes compared to a contraction of breath. By contracting, God created a primordial space, the first "outward." (2) *Ein-Sof*, the innermost essence of the Godhead, emanated a ray of light into primordial space. The light of emanation assumes in primordial space certain configurations, the first being that of the Adam Kadmon. Scholem: "The *Adam Kadmon* serves as a kind of intermediary link between *Ein-Sof*, the light of whose substance continues to be active in him, and the hierarchy of worlds still to come. In comparison with the latter, indeed, the *Adam Kadmon* himself could well be, and sometimes was, called *Ein-Sof*." (3) In the primordial world, i.e., before the creation of the cosmos, a catastrophe occurred: the light emanating from the head of the Adam

Kadmon (the Word?) was so strong that the "vessels" (*Kelim*) meant to contain it broke, and this breaking of the vessels signaled the beginning of evil, the emergence of "the other side" (*sitra aḥra*). In the shards (*kelippot*) of the broken vessels lay the genesis of matter. (4) The creation of the world was an act of Divine goodness, because its aim was the ultimate redemption, or restoration (*tikkun*), of the world to its original state as conceived by the Creator. Scholem: "The Gnostic character of this cosmogony cannot be denied, though the detailed manner in which it is worked out is drawn entirely from internal Jewish sources. Typically Gnostic, for example, are the depiction of creation as a cosmic drama centered around a profoundly fateful crisis within the inner workings of the Godhead itself, and the search for a path of cosmic restoration, of a purging of the evil from the good, wherein man is assigned a central role." (5) The first people on earth, Adam and Eve, were endowed with spiritual bodies that became material bodies after their Fall. The Fall of man implicated the whole of Nature and repeated the first catastrophe ("as above, so below") of the breaking of vessels.

One can easily detect in these cabalistic doctrines certain assumptions that have guided the Christian imagination for centuries as it has had to contend with the world's cruelty and inhumanity. The Christian solutions have usually approximated those of the Gnostics, occasionally of the Manichaean variety. The rebellion of the angels, which begot the power of evil, was, in effect, a catastrophe affecting the whole of creation, even if it did not produce another, *equally powerful* extreme opposed to good. The first catastrophe is closely related to the second, the sin of our first parents. In Dante's *Divine Comedy* the earth's center is occupied by the fallen (literally, headlong from Heaven) angel, Satan. Milton's *Paradise Lost* treats the rebellion of angels as a cosmic catastrophe. William Blake, though poetically indebted to Milton, "corrects" him by exonerating Satan, because, said Blake, he rebelled against a false God, the autocratic Jehovah. For Blake, as I have said, the catastrophe occurred with the breakup of the unity of the human-divine family. It took place in an extracosmic dimension and "anticipated," as it were, the creation of the world, if anything can be "anticipated" in a timeless realm. Not even the Blakeans are in agreement as to Blake's interpretation of the act of creation. Some contend that he interpreted it as an "act of mercy"; others argue that he was less concerned with the act of creation than with our human conception of it.

The catastrophe in Christian art and poetry always performs the same function: it permits us to accept the world, not because of its order, which has been violated, but because it holds out the hope, as in the Cabala, that it will be followed by *tikkun*, a return to order.

The world's inhumanity, its indifference to the demands of men's hearts, is palliated when God is endowed with human features. Thus can He be dealt with—over and above the world, so to speak. In this sense, Christ—or the Word, Logos—figures as the supreme arbiter and ruler, the Pantocrator. The tendency of the cabalists to equate the inscrutable Divine essence, *Ein-Sof,* with the Adam Kadmon is extremely eloquent. Not by chance did Swedenborg, and later Blake, in that critical age that was the eighteenth century, found their religion on God's humanity.

In *Les Arcanes* Milosz expounds a cosmogony of fire and light, based on the Book of Genesis, where the divine command, *Fiat lux* ("Let there be light"), initiated the creation of the world (let us note that in the Slavic languages the words for "world" and "light"—*świat* and *światło* in Polish—are homonymous). God, the unnamable and inconceivable fire, created first the idea of the "Exterior." This was the "Nothing" (*le néant*), but not in the spatial sense, as neither void nor volume have any meaning here. Into the "Nothing" God projected His own spiritual light. Milosz cites the medieval schools of Chartres and Oxford, which ascribed the act of creation to the movement of light; this light, emitted by God, was then converted, through *transmutation*, into a physical light. So, too, in Milosz: the movement of spiritual light created the first mathematical point—was "transmuted," in other words. Physical light was then converted into electrical energy, which, as it expanded, brought forth the universe. Movement and human thought—which has its source in, and expresses itself through, movement—are analogous to the movement of the first, purely spiritual light.

But in Milosz the act of creation was a consequence of the catastrophe occurring within the divine "interior," prior to the creation of the "Exterior," of the "Nothing." Since reference has been made to the Cabala, the following quote should not come altogether as a surprise. In it we find a grafting of both Christian (the rebellion of angels) and cabalistic elements:

Insofar as God is an interior and is designated as aleph, God is the law, or, a being identical with its necessity, the inconceivable fire. For men of the archetypal world he was the place, in other words the immobility in which the metamorphosis of one state into another occurred, metamorphosis which was the idea-type of movement, of the future creator of space-time-matter. Those purely spiritual men lived in the divine fire of inner illumination and instantaneity. Inasmuch as the higher reality of all things present, past, and future of our material universe has for its place the archetypal world and the notion of an "interior," it was absolutely necessary that the first transgression prefiguring that of Adam should be committed by the angels according to the eternal concepts of resistance and of freedom. Then the Divine, in whom love of the first humanity had been subordinated to the law, resolved, through an initial sacrifice which typifies all others, to exalt this love above the law. To this end he had recourse to the Beth, to the idea of the exterior, of the nothing. In this exterior, this nothing, God, the inconceivable fire, shed his incorporeal light as later Our Lord shed his blood.

—*Les Arcanes*, commentary to verset 94

The creation of the universe as a sacrifice of supreme love: therein, according to Milosz, lay the most profound mystery of the Deity, ungraspable by the human intellect. In other words, the Creator's assent to a world of pain and to His own Incarnation remains unfathomably mysterious.

By the law of analogy, the first catastrophe is mirrored in the second, the Fall of Adam. The first sacrifice, the act of creation, is reflected, again by analogy, in the second, the death on the cross. The world of matter, as it left the hands of the Creator, was Edenic. Adam and Eve, being immortal, were only ostensibly endowed with physical bodies. Eden was the first Nature, whose fate rested entirely with the King (another name for Adam in the Cabala). Through Adam's sin, all of Nature was corrupted, that is, was transformed into a second Nature.

Like Blake, Milosz had little sympathy for the "natural fallen muses," because they operated on the level of a corrupted, counterfeit Nature. In 1938 he wrote in a letter to Gegenbach:

Nature (so beautiful in the eyes of most people), that nature in whose bosom we have been living for untold millennia, is somehow the epitome of ugliness and infamy. We tolerate it only because preserved in us is the memory of a first nature, which is divine and true. Everything in this second, surrounding nature is unspeakably evil. No beauty, no love, no true faith. Nothing good can come from man because man is a product of this second nature.

Which does not mean that man cannot be restored to the first Nature after regaining his divine Sonship.

In Blake, man has a cosmic function, in the sense that Nature, such as it is, is conditional on human vision. The Fall signaled the breakup of man's psychic faculties into four conflicting elements, of which that diabolical mathematician and surveyor, Urizen, became the preeminent one. Nature viewed in Urizenian terms is a dominion of death, Ulro; but Nature perceived as vision, Nature viewed as it ought to be viewed—in the Imagination, in the Holy Spirit, in Jesus—is paradise. In a way, the scientific revolution of the eighteenth century and for us, Blake's later readers, the reign of technology were both latent in the Fall.

So, too, in Milosz:

As the world, material in appearance, is nothing other than a spiritual vision of the Divine, its true nature is what man makes of it in his representation. Before the prevarication, beings and things were related to each other as they are today and looked exactly the same. But they were *pure* in the thought of the King, who did not yet situate them in their matter. Nature, conceived from the Holy Spirit in the incorporeal light, without seed and by transmutation, had received as its fundamental law a similarly spiritual procreation. In its higher, purely logical sense the word "natural" can only apply to the Immaculate Conception of the Virgin and to the birth of her divine Son.

—*Les Arcanes*, commentary to verset 93

In Milosz the Fall is connected with the conjugal *arcanum*, which is not astonishing when we recall the primacy which he assigned to man, on the pre-cosmic as well as the cosmic level. The breaking of the essential bond between man and woman (the Song of Songs, the miracle at Cana) is bound, therefore, to have cosmic implications. I had actually intended to explicate the love symbolism of "The Poem of the Arcana," but, as it is, I fear I may have overstepped the bounds of intelligibility. Very briefly, the lurking temptation that "you will be as gods" caused Adam and Eve to lose all memory of a divine origin, of the reciprocity between the various realms of being, and love was reduced to one dimension only, the material. This is what he means by "the material world situated in itself":

The absolute freedom of man who was the consciousness of the universe created by the sacrifice in this nothing, in this exterior, required that a possibility should be open to his intelligence and his will to overcome the temptation which promised him a road toward an absolute scientific possession of the universe in physical Nature, that is, in a universe of matter situated in itself.

—*Les Arcanes*, commentary to verset 102

In Milosz everything is contingent on the notion of space. Adam's "prevarication" is symbolically interpreted in the scene where he, the King, bearing memory in his blood, suddenly perceives that only what is measurable is real:

> Adam raised his head; an eagle was flying toward the sun. Space was there. Two clouds were gliding slowly as if to melt into one: there was an impatience in Adam; the light clouds were gliding in time. And under Adam's feet the stones were warm with a marvelous noon.
>
> —*Les Arcanes,* verset 104

In modern philosophical terms, this would mean that the world has ceased to be a world of divine vision and become a self-contained *en-soi* sustained through the force of inertia, leaving Adam no other choice but to become its master and god.

35

BY PARAPHRASING Milosz's system, I would not like to pose as one of those guides at a religious art exhibit who pays tribute to the works' aesthetic values in a purely secular sort of way. On the other hand, as I am interested in the substance, I cannot avoid a contradiction which for several millennia has inhered in the contemplation of godly matters. That contradiction has not been lost on the Jewish cabalists and Christian mystics. It arises from the very limitations of language. In realms that prohibit easy access, a person must rely on his own internal experiences; but the moment he tries to communicate his discoveries to others, what was once alive turns to stone. Speech, so circumscribed by the sequence of tenses as to be rendered incapable of capturing simultaneity, not to mention the atemporal, proves thoroughly deficient. Only the law of analogy offers any hope for the transmission of sacred truth. But when, as today, the law of analogy has ceased to compel belief, works such as Milosz's "metaphysical poems" will be acknowledged for their purely subjective value, at best as a final link in the long chain of the hermetic tradition.

Baptized a Roman Catholic, Milosz returned to religious practice in 1927, the same year that saw the publication of his *Les Arcanes*; until his death he remained a practicing Catholic, convinced that his work in no way deviated from Catholic teaching. His "metaphysical poems," I repeat, belong neither to philosophy nor to theology, and that is why there is no judging them by the standard of orthodoxy. No more than they can be disengaged from the fate of religion in the age in which they were written.

Swedenborg was right, it seems to me, when he said that man cannot believe what he cannot understand. At first this may seem an absurdity, inasmuch as Christians have always believed in doctrines not comprehensible to reason but which nonetheless are accepted as mysteries of faith. Yet, on closer consideration, one must admit that his words contain a sound intuition. Medieval man "understood" his religion ten times better than the man of the eighteenth century, let alone men of the next two centuries. This was so because the medieval religious vision and the sum of secular knowledge were not yet separated by that distance which, with the birth of the scientific method, was to widen decade by decade. With the new scientific method came attempts at a "new interpretation" of Christanity—

in Italian Platonism, in derivations of the Cabala, in hermeticism, doctrines that, initially, were so in harmony with the scientific revolution as to make the two currents of the Renaissance, the "official" and the "underground," indistinguishable. Swedenborg was not mistaken in supposing that for believers the chief obstacle was the mystifying doctrine of the Trinity, requiring as it does a belief in three gods. The rationalistically trained mind was forced either to reject the doctrine or to reinterpret it. If such investigations were of immediate concern only to very closed circles, the consequences would soon become more widely apparent.

In my investigations of sixteenth-century Poland and of the Italian provenance of the Polish Antitrinitarians known as Arians, I have met with imponderables beyond my power to solve. I would risk the proposition that the ferment among the intellectual elite of Italy and France in the years 1500–50 was more "prophetic" than the intellectual movements under way in those Northern European countries then going over to Protestantism. The Vicenza circle, which had revived the ancient Antitrinitarian heresy, was more than a marginal phenomenon; on the contrary, the controversy over Christ's divinity became the focal point of the prevailing movement toward a "new interpretation." But how was this group connected with the Platonists and the disciples of a Christian Cabala? Nor can the date 1492, marking the expulsion of the Jews from Spain and the migrations of the cabalists, be ignored. Indeed, it may have been the Cabala which, by introducing the figure of the Adam Kadmon, fostered a reinterpretation of the Trinity—but was it done in the spirit of the Arians, or was it to furnish arguments against their rationalism? And what became of those members of the

Vicenza group who fled to Turkey after their dispersion by the Inquisition? Did they find linkages to Palestine there? I do not know. Just as I know very little about the man whose name is known to all who have studied the literature on the Arians. Michael Servetus, the Spanish-French doctor burned at the stake by Calvin in Geneva in 1553, may have exercised far greater authority than has been traditionally conceded. An Antitrinitarian, yes—but were his arguments those of the Arians? Most likely not. Servetus was, in addition, one of the founders of the scientific method in medicine. Milosz, who took an interest in his career, argues in *Les Arcanes* that it was Servetus, and not Harvey, who first discovered blood circulation.

The clergy of Western Europe, Catholic as well as Protestant, was horrified by the specter of the Antitrinitarian heresy, by the "monster of Socinianism." Their fear was fully justified, as a refutation of the Trinity reduced Christ to a moralist-teacher and God to an impersonal Clockmaker (Blake's Urizen). Paradoxically, sixteenth-century Poland, through the Socinian presses in Raków, became the exporter of ideas conducive to the spread of the heresy—of what was, initially, a "rational Christianity." Among the contents of John Locke's library were a number of Raków publications, their margins richly annotated in the philosopher's own hand.

Swedenborg lived in the Age of Reason, so perhaps his use of the word "understands" should be purged of its eighteenth-century connotations. His intention is clear: if, as he claimed, a Christian cannot conceive of the Trinity while reciting the words of the Credo; if, on the contrary, he visualizes three distinct gods, it would imply that for Swedenborg the word "understands" is synonymous with "imagines." Swedenborg's system was aimed at *liberating* the imagination already fettered by "the scientific world-view." Since the Great Clockmaker had faded into an abstraction, Swedenborg shifted attention to Christ as the only God. And since Heaven and Hell, which were represented spatially in the medieval imagination, had lost their visually evocative power, Swedenborg proclaimed Heaven and Hell as a *subjective space.*

Whatever the differences among those exemplary of the "underground current" (only recently a subject of serious inquiry), the systems of such writers as Jakob Boehme, or that of the English metaphysical poet, Thomas Traherne, author of *Centuries,* or those of Swedenborg and Blake were encroaching on a domain shunned by Church theology. When Dante wrote his *Divine Comedy,* the reigning cosmology, astronomy, geography, and theology were mutually supportive of one another. But as the cumulative secular knowledge began to gravitate toward the scientific realm, theology, it would appear, expended all its energies on delaying tactics, unaware that the real danger was coming from another direction. For the battle was decided not by discourses or disquisitions, not by faith or heresy, but by visions of the universe increasingly shaped by "the scientific world-view." When a mind so fashioned tried to conceive of the basic tenets of Christianity—of Creation, Original Sin, the Incarnation, the Resurrection—it found nothing of nourishment in imaginative terms. The catechism was becoming more meager in substance, meatless, a testimony to the erosion of theological language.

In such circumstances, a kind of Christian gnosis, even though lacking in official support, answered to an express need. It formed a buffer or border zone, which organized religions historically have regarded with varying degrees of tolerance. The record of Christianity in this respect has differed from that of Judaism, which officially tolerated the Cabala even as it continually verged on unorthodoxy; yet here, too, limitations were imposed, e.g., the study of the Cabala was restricted to those of the age of forty or over. In the twentieth century the attitude of the Roman Church has been decidedly different from that of the Eastern Church. The latter has been far more permissive; I was quite amazed, for example, to find in the work of Sergei Bulgakov, a long-time professor at the Orthodox Theological Institute in Paris, some striking analogies with the Miloszian system. Bulgakov is regarded by the Orthodox faithful as an eminent authority, though not all Orthodox theologians share his views. At the heart of his system is the notion of an immanent *sofiinost'*—from *Sophia*, Divine Wisdom—while in Milosz the inherent femininity of Creation is rendered as *la Féminité de la Manifestation*.

The buffer zone—Christian gnosis—is imaginatively richer, more combustible than theology in the strict sense, yet even it has to contend with the claims of science. When the scientific notion of truth and error is applied indiscriminately, only the religious domain still preserves those diminishing enclaves where science must "abstain." That which distinguishes Milosz from his contemporaries is his surmise that the linear progress of science was confined to a few centuries, and that to extend this straight line through extrapolation would be to commit a fallacy. The conflict between science and religion was a historical phenomenon, peculiar to a certain phase in human history, lasting roughly from the sixteenth to the twentieth century, inclusive. The forthcoming revolution in science would remove that conflict. In his "metaphysical poems" Milosz bears witness to the beginning of this great revolution, precipitated, he believed, by the discoveries of modern physics, above all by the Einsteinian theory of relativity. In *Ars Magna* and *Les Arcanes* the progression of thought, from the relativity of spatial reference points to the "Place of places," to the Divine, is as difficult to follow as Blake's anti-Newtonian "visionary physics"; it is poetically, but not discursively, possible. Yet even I, a layman, can perceive the signs of a scientific crisis so awesome as to effect a rehabilitation of the hermetics and alchemists—of the symbolic vision, in other words. But whether physics will act as the catalytic agent, as Milosz would have it, is not for me to say. One thing is certain. Man's conception of the universe has been wrought by three revolutionary discoveries: (1) Copernicus's refutation of the geocentric theory; (2) Newton's absolutizing of space and time, whereby the universe became a void expanded to infinity; and (3) Einstein's relativizing of space and time, or the primacy of motion. The first two were seen as a diminishment of man and hostile to his purpose; hence the resistance mounted by the poets. The third was hailed by Milosz as a liberation—and his imagination was indeed liberated by it.

I must conclude this chapter with a fortuitous detail. A couple of days ago I had lunch at a restaurant whose walls were hung with photographs of this century's celebrities: Groucho Marx, Greta Garbo, and Albert Einstein. Maybe it really was for the best, I thought, that in an age of total dislocation our time was represented in the American popular imagination not only by film stars but by a holy man of science. I stared up at the face, recalling how moved, how humbly respectful I had been, when many years ago I had made his acquaintance at Princeton. To me he was not only a scientist; he had stepped quite suddenly from the pages of *Ars Magna* and *Les Arcanes*.

36

Since the Middle Ages, the Roman Church has never been favorably disposed toward chiliastic creeds, toward doctrines announcing the coming of the millennium. The Church hierarchy reacted coolly to *Les Arcanes*, and not without cause, as will be seen from the following. But before I present Milosz's vision of the future, I must briefly address the twentieth century as I now view it, reflecting on my life in retrospect.

I have labored hard to put a good face on it, but it is a joyless fate to have been born in an age of decline. Since to utter the word "decline" or "decadence" is to summon the devil himself—history, after all, has a way of becoming what people make of it—I have tried to be cautious in my pronouncements, but without much effect; and so now, in a world disdainful of moderation, I can afford to be honest. If I use the word "decline," it does not mean that I am envious of the generation of my parents or grandparents. The nineteenth century is hardly deserving of veneration; and when, with the outbreak of the First World War (I was three at the time), the fabric began to give, some of the stuffing was bound to spill. Only the blood of millions of soldiers was real: the revered statue of a humanitarian, rational, unimpeded progress had proved a straw man. The revelation was not made immediately manifest, due to the largely unwritten law of historical time lag: whatever is dealt a *coup de grâce* in one set of events will live on in parallel sets. Not only were the same noble-sounding slogans—borrowed mainly from that hotbed of rhetoric such as was France on the European continent—parroted. Ideas conceived of the nineteenth-century spirit, and devoutly loyal to its cults, now took on a mass character. Philosophy, literature, and art became increasingly progressive, humanitarian, Freudian, socialist, pacifist, and altogether more fervid in proclaiming the individual's right to happiness, meaning to greater consumption. True, some movements of the twenties—Surrealism, for one, combining the two nineteenth-century cults of Freudianism and Marxism—may have given pause by their potentially nihilistic urge. But this was an age of avant-garde movements, as diverse as they were profuse, and what self-respecting critic would have dared to raise questions of the old-fashioned, moral kind? In defense of what? Even I, in provincial Wilno, grew up brushed by the winds of progress, I in my rebellion against Father Chomski, that fanatic dictator of our schoolboy consciences. Here I see another historical law, little known but of considerable moment: the process of decline affects people in ways unknown to them, beneath the threshold of their consciousness. On this subject I command a wealth of personal observation, collected in the course of my American years, and I can testify to the range of its effects, extending to the most intimate of human relations, including the erotic. In other words, the collapse of values in a given society not only affects individuals in their attitudes and conscious choices but encroaches on what was once considered a private domain, with the result that distressed individualists vainly seek the help of psychiatrists trained in the same individualist school.

But the law by which people are unknowingly affected complicates the task of re-creating the past, because it is hard to tell, in retrospect, what was experienced consciously and what unconsciously. There is yet another difficulty: those who have stayed long in the belly of the leviathan do not necessarily know what a whale looks like; that is, our age might better be summed up by those inhabiting another century. Nonetheless, I think I can detect a certain logic pervading the age as a whole. Unfortunately, it is the logic of precipitous decline, one so remarkable in its constancy as to be without historical analogy. That society and civilization endure, I would contend, is due to those minute particles of virtue residing in specific individuals, who affect the whole through a complex process whereby each particle, or grain, is multiplied by others (on such a process, for example, is founded the ethics of well-executed work). In European civilization these grains were nurtured on an ontological soil. By the law of retardation, previously cited, the influence of religion has proved far more durable than religion itself; it has sustained customs and institutions in the face of universal or nearly universal secularization. In the nineteenth century the slogans of liberty, equality, and fraternity, of such civil rights as freedom of assembly, speech, etc., were only partially dependent on reality, which was economic in nature. They owed a measure of their effectiveness, as did economic progress itself, to a tradition rooted in an ethics of self-discipline, self-denial, and sacrifice. By themselves, deprived of religious sanction, they not only proclaimed their vacancy; eventually they would become an object of contempt among the young, those whose education had given them nothing but that void. No one of sound mind, who has lived long in a country of the West, can have any illusions as to the utter failure of secular humanism, a failure sponsored by the very successes of that same humanism.

The spectacular feats of the age—of its science, technology, medicine—have been reciprocally related to the decline. The emancipated mind needed a few centuries to legitimize its privileges. But when that day finally came, the process began to accelerate as in fast motion. In a world where every cause has a multiplicity of effects and every effect redounds on the cause, no computer could possibly compute all the intersecting series; similarly, it would be naïve to wish only for civilization's "blessings." They could not exist without the aberrations, the mass psychoses, and the malignancies that are the penalties of a power more absolute than the power exerted by the kings of old.

Milosz abetted my skeptical attitude toward the West, and everything, from the early thirties to the present, with minor deviations, was borne out by time, which gives little cause for joy and recalls rather a recurrent and familiar nightmare. Today I can well appreciate the motives which persuaded Milosz to seek an addressee in the distant future. And I must confess that as a young man I inherited much of his faith in a felicitous era awaiting a mankind reborn, and that it sustained me in times of despair. My "catastrophist" poetry, after all, was not devoid of hope.

Milosz, as I have said, was not indifferent to the age; on the contrary, he remained its vigilant observer—how could he have been otherwise if he acknowledged Goethe as his master? Nor did he dismiss the whole of materialistic science, as evidenced by his belief that modern physics held the promise of a new science; the belief, in other words, that the decline was an inevitable, and in a way necessary, phase. The treatment of space in *Epître à Storge* is entirely in the spirit of the theory of relativity. Then, in Einsteinian physics, or rather in its metaphysical implications, he found the promise of a radical realignment. The refutation of absolute Newtonian space signaled, in his view, a freeing of the imagination from mechanistic laws; it meant that man would cease to look on himself as an unmeaning thing of momentary duration, in an infinite space and infinite time; that the mind would return to its homeland, would find a point of reference outside the space-time-matter triad born of movement. It thus approximates the Blakean vision, and is based on the same anti-Newtonian postulate: man's release from Ulro. In the "metaphysical poems" one can almost infer a belief in a return to a preternatural, Edenic vision of the cosmos, a belief in the remediable nature of Adam's "prevarication." With the return of science to alchemic principles, to a theory of archetypes and the law of analogy, the great schism would be healed and a reconciliation of religion, science, philosophy, and art achieved. And of politics. Hiram—that "King of the unified world, Architect of the effective Catholic Church of tomorrow," to whom the poem in *Les Arcanes* is addressed—will bear no resemblance to rulers of the past. In his commentary to the Hiram verset, the author relates how one morning on the Métro, as he contemplated the Parisian workers on their way to work, he indulged in daydreams (*rêveries*) of the future:

But when the Holy Spirit makes itself heard in Rome, the necessary men will be present to answer the summons.

The society they will create will rest upon the alliance of faith, of science, and of beauty, that is, upon individual and collective freedom acquired at the price of surrendering one's most intimate essence, of a total sacrifice, of a transmutation of law into love. The immortal vanity of the mediocre, purged of its present materialistic barbarity, will undergo a most severe moral discipline. The utilization of this inexhaustible force will no longer devolve upon schemers, but upon a council of psychologists nominated by a Congregation of Initiates, placed on the summit of the hierarchy and at the base of the spiritual Monarchy. It will rule over the United

States of the World. Nevertheless, each State would possess its own dynasty, as far as possible rooted in old national traditions. Scientific, aesthetic, and moral competition will open to the instinct of combativeness a field embracing all the world. Nationalities will wage against each other a magnificent war without mercy in the realm of the intellect. The commandments of the Church will be observed with utmost rigor, and the Catholic anniversaries celebrated with indescribable splendor, both of them recognized as symbolizing the highest truths of science and philosophy. The first day of the universal Reign will be marked by the conversion of the ancient Elected people to Christianity: but the noble Jewish race will be carefully preserved in its purity without intermixture. The last vestiges of old aristocracies will be honored, too, because a democracy, even monarchic and theocratic, always has something to learn from people who know their origins and respect their traditions.

—*Les Arcanes*, commentary to verset 81

Before this theocratic order is established, human history will have to pass through horror, whence will come a "unification of the small planet Earth." Meanwhile, it must await the disasters foretold in St. John's Revelation.

Milosz's eschatological vision once again refers us back to the past, to the period of Romanticism. The comparison would elicit little protest on his part, for he himself saw the analogies of his own time with that age marking the beginning of the decline: the eighteenth century. In 1921 he wrote: "In the spiritual manifestations of our age we find, as we do in the eighteenth century, unbridled negation on the surface and deep down a creative affirmation" (from an article entitled "La vraie question de Vilna," published in the periodical *L'Europe nouvelle*). Such a vision, of catastrophe and fulfillment, could only alienate him from his French contemporaries, as if his presence among them were not sufficiently alien. The secular humanism of the West had done with such visions. The disaffection can be observed in the evolution of the genre later known as science fiction, particularly in the genre's earliest phase, from Jules Verne to H. G. Wells. In its dismissal of Divine Providence and the Last Judgment, which effectively reduced History to a purely worldly enterprise, the genre records the gradual shift from an optimistic faith in evolutionary progress to increasingly pessimistic previsions—and nowhere more so than in H. G. Wells, whose last book and testament, *Mind at the End of Its Tether*, is a work of perfect despair. The thematic concern of these writers is always the same: the adventures of man as a social animal, relieved of any compact with superhuman forces.

As I was quoting from the Milosz passage on the coming theocratic monarchy, I could not help recalling a different eschatological tradition, that found in Russia, where eschatology does not subside with Romanticism but emerges only in the post-Romantic era. The awesome achievement of Dostoevsky, an epileptic with a lung condition, a man debt-ridden and forced to write in serial form under deadline, would not have been possible, as all who have studied his biography know, but for the certitude of his appointed mission, religiously motivated, on behalf of Russia and mankind. Dostoevsky believed that a resurrection of bodies awaited the human race in a new eon, when, according to the creed of the Church, "time will be no more"; but he also believed in a millennium to close History, in a theocratic State destined to succeed a civilization based on mutual animosity, after a terrifying war of all against all and an epidemic unleashed by the "microbe" of self-deification—as foretold in Raskolnikov's dream in the

Siberian penal colony. As in Milosz, the theocracy of the future would be based on a voluntary repudiation of egoism, on unconditional human sacrifice of the ego in the name of brotherly love. That for Dostoevsky this faith was synonymous with a messianic faith in Russia is irrelevant, for it must be seen that this august hope served the novelist's imagination as a guiding and sustaining force. The Dostoevskian idea of Godmanhood, along with the vision of its realization in History, was later elaborated by Vladimir Solovyov. Solovyov, who unlike Dostoevsky was not a chauvinist of Russian Orthodoxy, saw in ecumenism a hope for Europe, a way of expediting Europe's unification under theocratic rule. Not until his last, and possibly his best, work, *Tri rozgovora* (*Three Conversations*, written in 1899), did he transfer his theocracy to the millennium foretold in the Apocalypse. Of salient importance in *Three Conversations* is the tale of the Antichrist, prophesying events of the twentieth and twenty-first centuries: a Chinese conquest of Russia and Europe, a fifty-year Chinese occupation, the advent of the Antichrist who becomes president and then emperor of the United Nations of Earth. Solovyov's Antichrist achieves a pseudo-reconciliation of Catholicism, Protestantism, and Orthodoxy, after which, in the course of events announced in St. John—the events are set in Palestine, with a Jewish army a million strong—a genuine unification of churches is effected and the theocratic millennium initiated. Solovyov was not the only Symbolist to promote an eschatological fervor (which seems to be what distinguishes Russian literature of the pre-revolutionary decades from the literature of the West). The combination of native influences (i.e., Polish Romanticism) and a susceptibility to Russian intellectual currents explains how two such disparate Polish writers as Brzozowski and Witkiewicz, both nurtured in the decades before the First World War, could remain loyal to the eschatological spirit, however different their respective visions. My interest in the work of Milosz, who was in some sense a man of "Eastern European" sensibility, was therefore not coincidental.

Here I must touch on a painful dilemma. That which is most crucial to the human imagination, indeed, that which Blake took to be its very essence, namely, a rebellious attitude toward Nature in the name of an august hope, is also fraught with peril because it verges constantly on folly, on a mania for self-destruction, on mental illness. I am inclined to believe that Dostoevsky's epilepsy had a salutary effect in releasing the tensions of nervous energy that might otherwise have driven him to madness; that only Słowacki's prodigious literary facility saved him from landing in the madhouse when he began to believe in his own exceptional mission on behalf of Poland and the world.

Let us be candid: Milosz's essays published after *Ars Magna* and *Les Arcanes*, that is, in the last decade of his life, greatly surpass the wildest self-exaltations of a Słowacki, and could only have issued from the pen of a man in possession of a sick mind. Yet there was nothing in his appearance, speech, or professional conduct to suggest any mental disturbance. Indeed, this was the period of his most successful diplomatic efforts. As often as I met with him in 1934–35 during my academic year in Paris, I can testify that I detected no outward signs to justify diagnosing him as a schizophrenic in the company of Hölderlin and Van Gogh. How to explain the disparity?

On the night of December 14, 1914, Milosz had a vision which radically altered his outlook, and which, since there is no reason to dispute the faithfulness of that version recorded in *Epître à Storge*, belongs to the great wonders of the visionary experience. To quote that version out of context would be an injustice. Milosz saw a luminous sphere, which he first called a "Spiritual Sun," invoking Swedenborg, and then "an angel of Jehovah." It was an experience comparable to Pascal's by now archetypal vision of November 23, 1654. From that day forward, Pascal carried a card, sewn into his clothing, as a constant reminder of what he had experienced. It was found on him after his death. It bore an inscription, which read in part: "From about half past ten in the evening until about half past twelve. / FIRE / God of Abraham, God of Isaac, God of Jacob, / not of the philosophers and savants. / Certitude. Certitude. Feeling. Joy. Peace. / God of Jesus Christ. *Deum meum et Deum vestrum.*" Swedenborg's internal crisis of 1743–45 was also accompanied by visions, the most crucial of which, by his own testimony, occurred while he was dining at a London inn. Toward the end of his life Blake reported to Crabb Robinson of having beheld a "spiritual sun." Such moments of illumination serve a common purpose: they confer on the one who has experienced them the certitude of his mission and provide invincible proof of his ordination. Milosz would allude frequently to that December night, and if at first the received *sacra* eluded him, then in due time, inspired by his readings of Swedenborg, he would become the latter's self-appointed successor. Swedenborg, as I have said, divided the history of mankind into "Churches"—or successive civilizations—the fourth being the Christian Church. The decline of that Church begot events in the spiritual world, events concealed from human eyes: the Last Judgment in 1757 and the coming of the Paraclete in the guise of Swedenborg's writings, which, on June 19, 1770, inaugurated the fifth Church. Milosz, in turn, regarded himself as the as yet unknown founder of a sixth Church, instituted on December 14–15, 1914.

In the 1930s Milosz became more and more immersed in his cabalistic studies and in his anthropological research. This research was centered on various hypotheses relating to the neolithic civilization of the Mediterranean basin. The neolithic period is still clouded by considerable conjecture, despite recent excavations, and some of Milosz's intuitions may one day be vindicated. Yet to rely on such intuitions for the purpose of "decoding" St. John's Revelation was, to say the least, a dubious procedure. The Apocalypse, as we know, has attracted scores of commentators, each interpreting its symbols according to events contemporaneous with the commentator. Milosz's treatise *L'Apocalypse de Saint Jean déchiffrée* (1933) belongs to this tradition.

Vladimir Solovyov was in earnest when he prophesied the coming of the Antichrist, even if in *Three Conversations* that prophecy, allegedly discovered in a medieval manuscript written by a monk named Pansopheus, was cast in the form of science fiction. Milosz's treatise, issued in a small printing as a *confidentiel*, as a work intended for private circulation, is agonizingly serious and is addressed to those entrusted with the world's imminent future. Both the style and the substance of its formulations stand in contrast to the author's extreme political acuity. As a diplomat Milosz was prescient of the imminent outbreak of an apocalyptic war as a consequence of Germany's withdrawal from the League of Nations in 1933, even of the fact that it would be provoked by German claims on Gdańsk and Gdynia. Still other details are a faithful rendering of the author's views on the balance of power in the twentieth century. The "Beast rising up from the sea," whose power is conferred by "the dragon," is America, the world capital of materialism and technology. The fall of Babylon, the harlot borne along by the sea Beast, symbolizes the fall of the British Empire, now dependent on the United States. The "Beast rising up from the earth" is Russia: she it is who commands earth's inhabitants to worship the first beast, i.e., technology and materialism. By the 1930s Milosz had even disavowed his earlier vision of a global monarchy, which the "metaphysical poems" had posited for the indefinite future. Now it was nothing less than the end of the world, the passing of an eon, a "new earth and a new sky," with Milosz himself cast as the angel of the Apocalypse, holding in his hand an open book, with one foot resting on the sea and the other on the earth. The war prophesied by St. John would come to pass in the thirties and would culminate in the year 1944. At that time a part of the moon would drop into the Black Sea and destroy all of southern Russia, England would be destroyed by fire and water, and America by fire. In 1944 all of reality as we know it would come to an end, and the world would once again revert to the "vision of God."

"*Pauvre Milosz.*" Whenever his friends alluded to him thus in his final years, it bespoke a deep humanity and sympathy. In this they showed themselves to be the sons of an older civilization which had seen much and consequently understood much. They saw nothing comical in what was so manifestly eloquent of a pain, of a prolonged struggle with life, impossible to bear. In the end, they, like I, had to concede that a mind as riven as his must elude conventional norms. Milosz not only continued to comport himself with skill, to exercise good judgment in political and literary matters, but he never lost the power of poetic expression, as demonstrated by his last poem (an exception, in view of his disavowal of poetry), called

"Psaume de l'Etoile du Matin" ("Psalm of the Morning Star"), a short lyric of uncommon beauty, revealing a rhythmic inventiveness never before attempted in the French language. Even so, to anyone unfamiliar with the author's exegetical work, the poem remains inscrutable, just as Słowacki's *King Spirit* cannot be disengaged from his mystical doctrine.

God had mercy on Oscar V. de L. Milosz and spared him from having to wait for the year 1944 and the truly apocalyptic miseries of the war, perhaps even the concentration camp. He died suddenly at Fontainebleau in 1939. That which was fulfilled, the exploding of the first atomic bomb in 1945, has signaled, even to this day, neither a rebirth of Nature nor the end of an eon.

37

IT IS TIME FOR MY MOSAIC to show the rudiments of a design; I come, in other words, to the book's final part. And I hear a voice which addresses me in the following words:

"Motivated by some vague impulse, no doubt to punish yourself and to undo the very thing you love, you have marshaled a variety of arguments in support of our allegiance to the Land of Ulro. Never has Ulro's power been so vindicated, its enemies so humiliated. For what can be more humiliating than for a writer, a man of ideas, or an artist to win the favor of posterity for something other than what he held to be most precious, what he tried to defend with his work? And lo, he finds himself in the museum, admired by tourists for his 'aesthetic values,' while his most sacred beliefs are treated with respect—his poems or paintings or novels performed a service, after all —but also with indulgence, like the religious beliefs of his cousin in New Guinea."

> Ghosts are a myth
> Of ale-wife and blacksmith.
> Clodhoppers! This is treason
> Against King Reason.

No longer would the crowd risk "treason against King Reason." Mickiewicz lost the argument, as did his more modern comrades, the militant ironists, Dostoevsky among them. But failure was also the lot of those visionary reformers of science, whether it be Goethe, Blake, or Milosz; at best their arguments are of interest only to a chosen few. If a civilization is retrievable through its works, anyone wishing to plumb the essence of our modern civilization should turn to its most honest writer, Samuel Beckett. It is a tribute to the capitalist West, despite what has been said of its decline, that it could produce such a writer and acknowledge that writer as its own—that it could endorse the naked truth, in other words. Beckett, like his literary contemporaries in the West, has proclaimed *urbi et orbi* what in the nineteenth century was known only to a handful, and which was the message of Nietzsche's invective directed at the Europeans: So you killed God and think you can get away with it? Now, on a mass scale, was born the realization of man's new metaphysical condition, summarized by a single word: *NO*. No voice reaching from the cosmos, no good and evil, no fulfillment of the promise, no Kingdom. But that was not all. The individual, proudly pointing to himself as "I," proved just as much an illusion, a bundle of reflexes covered by a uniform epidermis. Love was an illusion, friendship an illusion—because both were premised on the possibility of communication, and how to communicate when language is reduced to a babble bespeaking the solitariness of each? So what is left in the presence of this huge *NO*? Only time, absolute time, rushing nowhere out of nowhere; time measured by the gradual deterioration of organic cells. Whatever man does in the face of time, death's portent, amounts to a *divertissement*. Of the many kinds of *divertissement*, the most effective is the salvaging of past moments, before both they and we are consumed by nothingness. (Beckett is in many ways descended from Proust, on whom he has written an essay.) Progressing in time is a progression toward nothingness, which is why in Beckett and his imitators time is always circular: if Beckett's tape is continually rewinding, it is to show that no "is" or "will be" promises anything more than what "was." And let us bear in mind that the human condition so defined, and it is a definition entirely consistent with the lessons of Ulro, is not limited to one corner of the planet; rather, it is applicable wherever the human mind has been scientifically conditioned, which is to say, everywhere. It matters little that extremists like Jacques Monod are not tolerated wherever ideologies—relics of the "animistic tradition," Monod would call them—are in force. The literary counterpart of this scientific radicalism is Beckett, whose motto would seem to be: "Better the ugliest truth than the most beautiful lie." No country is immune to the ruthless severity of "objective truth"; sooner or later, people will realize that the curtain adorned with pretty social models is a cheat.

From the preceding discussion, one thing is evident: the burden of disinheritance is a painful one. Secular humanism has become so consumed by its own vacancy that it must prostrate itself before the bearers of revolutionary slogans. But what is crucial and, again, a tribute to the West is the self-admission contained in Beckett's one-word title: *Endgame*. And this endgame means not only the death of the individual, which can be stoically borne. It is the radical and pitiless proposition that the human imagination, which in the course of millennia has begot religious myths, poems, dreams carved in stone, visions painted on wood and canvas, may yet stir our emotions with its childlike faith, but that we can only reflect nostalgically on a gift irretrievably lost. Since the eighteenth century, the imagination has tried to wage a defense by fortifying itself on its own territory, that of art and literature, through the cultivation of a multi-layered irony; in time, however, it became impaired from within and stripped of any ontological support. The endgame is the end of literature and art, and, insofar as these have always attached to any civilization, of civilization itself. Yet, when art can thrive on the end of art, as it does in Beckett and those like him, then that, too, is worthy of tribute.

38

A LOGICAL ENOUGH ARGUMENT, if not of great relevance to me personally. I would not deny that from the moment I saw *Waiting for Godot* in Paris in 1952 I have found Beckett disturbing, almost to the point of being an obsession. I have always sensed that behind my resistance lay much that was concealed; that if I had analyzed the reasons, I might have better understood where I belonged, both intellectually and emotionally. Permit me now to address those reasons. Beckett wishes to tease us with the obvious; he is like a man who sidles up to a hunchback and begins to needle him: "Hunchback, you're a hunchback; you'd rather not be reminded of it, but I shall see to it that you are reminded." As for me, I know I am a hunchback; I make no pretense to the contrary; that is, I know full well the poverty of my human existence. Yes, there were times when I felt like howling, ramming my head against the wall, but from sheer exertion of will, from sheer necessity, I buckled down and went to work. Then along comes this man, boasting to me of his "discovery," and I say there is something not quite right about it, the hound teaching the fox how to hunt, while I, the fox, have been using all my cunning and trickery to kill the painful awareness in myself.

For generations a quarrel has been waged between the innovators and a conservative public opinion, the former appealing to the right of total striptease, the latter to decorum. At issue was the whole question of man's animal needs and drives. Gradually the line of defense retreated and the argument of the defenders of decorum—that there is no point in telling people what they already know—lost its credibility. Yet the game could continue to be played so long as there was something to "profane," so long as the few existing prohibitions remained in force. Now, when there are no more prohibitions, when sexual license and sadism have become the stuff of mass entertainment, of the less sophisticated genres in general, little is left those authors in search of brutally shocking effects. In the treatment of man's metaphysical condition, "total striptease" takes always the same form and is congruent with the gradual reduction of human nature. So were lifted the last prohibitions which once safeguarded the feelings of believers—which were designed to counteract the "profanation" of what was sacred. My hostility to Beckett and kindred writers would appear to spring from strong conservative impulses, which I accept for what they are, without imposing any value judgment. Blasphemy, when it is held up as the only means left of recapturing a lost sense of the sacred, is not to my taste, not because I am personally incapable of it, but just because it comes naturally, in a way, to a part of the human spirit I regard as inferior. I would be curious as to what extent my aversion is dictated by purely "aesthetic preferences" (to a large extent, I should think), by a taste for order and measure, which (and here I am only conjecturing) may have prejudiced many of my life's decisions.

Under the pretext of truth, this literature would have us assent to an unproved assertion. Its Man is man in general, abstract, without any historical memory, appearing on a stage that is nowhere and everywhere; Man with a capital "M," like the Sinner of the medieval morality play. Yet this grandiose claim is refuted by what we know of man's versatility, of the summits to which he can rise and the depths to which he can sink, of the saints, the heroes, the criminals, the wise men, the fools, the born leaders and born slaves; by what we know of the variable historical temperatures to which he can be subjected. And they would have none of this: one man, and he more like a vegetable than a man. Painful as the absurdity of individual life may be, and the mere certitude of inescapable death is enough to reduce everything to a vanity of vanities, these are only moments; and not only because the mind clings frantically to its *divertissements* but also because our will (a minor detail) has a say in our lives. Man has been mired in Ulro by the successes of science—of the "eye and the lenses"—and this fact has to be acknowledged; but the ultimate proof of the crippling power of

Ulro (a civilization at war with itself) lies in the passivity of those vegeto-animals, those pale Elysian shades that are its literary "figures" (formerly called "heroes").

If I had steeped myself in matters of ideology without regard for the particulars of my own biography, that of a Polish poet thrust into a civilization incommensurate with the rural, provincial ways of his childhood and adolescence, I might have surrendered to countless arguments that, explicitly or implicitly, were aimed at reducing me in my own eyes to an abstraction. Now, after long consideration, I can summon the courage to offer my own vision of man, which is neither that of a Beckett nor possibly that of any other writer practicing in the West today.

For the sake of verbal rigor, to ensure that my words correspond to reality, I shall speak of only one member of the human family, i.e., myself. And this man, by no means exceptional, knows that he is far from strong and that he must exercise a vigilant self-mastery. By imposing a certain order—by rising every morning, say, at seven—he does so on the assumption that he is inwardly vulnerable, prey to the phantom of despondency. Routine, therefore, becomes for my representative man a basic philosophical postulate, the premise for any sort of discourse. Our mind, after all, is contingent on our motor centers, which in turn are affected by our division of the day's labor. Here we should be reminded that man is above all an organizer of space, both internal and external, and that this in fact is what is meant by imagination. We are that pulsation of blood, that rhythm, that organism which transposes external spatial structures into internal spaces; on this point, Blake and Milosz were perfectly correct. Whenever a conflict arises between our fragile, constantly restored internal order and the injunctions of Ulro, we must never hesitate; this is what Blake meant when he wrote that the earth was flat, while the spheres orbiting in space were merely an illusion of Ulroland. Practicality as a criterion of truth? Why, that's pragmatism! they will clamor in protest. Yes, practicality, more, *necessity*, like eating and drinking—and can one be accused of pragmatism for saying that a man must eat and drink in order not to perish?

I can state it more concisely. When my guardian angel (who resides in an internalized external space) is triumphant, the earth looks precious to me and I live in ecstasy; I am perfectly at ease because I am surrounded by a divine protection, my health is good, I feel within me the rush of a mighty rhythm, my dreams are of magically rich landscapes, and I forget about death, because whether it comes in a month or five years it will be done as it was decreed, not by the God of the philosophers but by the God of Abraham, Isaac, and Jacob. When the devil triumphs, I am appalled when I look at trees in bloom as they blindly repeat every spring what has been willed by the law of natural selection; the sea evokes in me a battleground of monstrous, antediluvian crustaceans, I am oppressed by the randomness and absurdity of my individual existence, and I feel excluded from the world's rhythm, cast up from it, a piece of detritus, and then the terror: my life is over, I won't get another, only death now.

To speak of angels and devils is not in good taste. Perhaps, but then who of us is not guilty of an impropriety. Our self-image is but the reflection of ourselves in the eyes of others, and its embellishment means more to us than anything; but when that image begins to lose its pretty colors, some cope better and some worse. I wanted a respectable, honorable life, among friends and relatives, on my native territory and in a town that I could call my own. From brief moments of felicity I constructed, years later, an imaginary life as it might have been, among familiar sights and familiar faces, where there was no having to explain who one was or what one did. But my fate, that of an exile, got the better of me. Exile carries with it two onerous circumstances: anonymity and distortion. Anonymity, like the assuming of an alias, sunders what we were from what we are; it forces a man to indulge in complex strategies of adaptation, because no more can he appeal to past achievements—in this case, to a body of poetry written once upon a time. But vexing as this may be to one's vanity, distortion is even worse. By that I mean the sort of partial image imposed on us by the foreign press, by articles so distortive as to provoke only a shrug of despair. I had to learn to live like a pariah, in self-exile from the "respectable society" of Western intellectuals, because I dared to offend their most hallowed assumptions, which I took to be a compilation of historical, geographical, and political ignorance.

In my younger Wilno days I set out to conquer the world, only to find myself now, despite my "successes," a cripple who has mastered the art of getting around on crutches. So why should not such a man, lamed, judge himself leniently, and if with disapproval, then friendly disapproval? If he feels both the devil and the angel within (" 'Yet the girl loves,' I reply diffidently"), how, in the name of what, is he to stop from admitting to the duality? Is he such a god or titan that he can be consistently "up to standards"? Whose standards? Those of his scientific age? Some hypothetical posterity? But when it is all he can do to make it through the day, what good is the general consensus, what does he care how he is remembered by posterity? It defies comprehension how the citizens of Ulro can be so solicitous of their bodies—by dieting, by avoiding certain foods, by not bathing in polluted waters—yet seem to take for granted that their souls are vigorously healthy, that it is uncivil to decline some literary or philosophical fare with a polite "I'm sorry, it's bad for me."

Thus, my representative man, free because isolated, cultivates a strict self-stewardship, as opposed to a Beckettian radicalism of nothingness. But he also differs from Beckett's man in that he is not descended from nowhere, that he is indebted to a tradition. If I were asked to name the source of my poetry, I would have to answer: my childhood, which was a childhood of carols, Month of Mary devotions, vespers—and of the Protestant Bible, the only one then available. And I truthfully could not say whether for me the guardian angel's song in *Forefathers' Eve* is a liturgical text or one of the pinnacles of world poetry.

To make my case even clearer, I would now make two side trips, one into the realm of atheism and the other into Catholicism.

39

MY LIFETIME HAS SEEN the collapse of many columns and arches in the Christian edifice. It was a long and steady process, quickened in the course of the last couple of centuries even if the clergy affected otherwise. The havoc caused by German liberal theology of the last century must be given its due, though never was the damage inflicted so great as in the postwar years, notably in the sixties. This was a time when theologians, Catholics included, casting themselves as clowns, gleefully proclaimed that Christianity, hitherto in opposition to the world, was now both with and in the world. Meanwhile, their audience, beholders of a spectacle more pathetic than funny, took this to mean that Christians wished to be "the same as others," that is, to give up their Christianity. Sophistry, perfected by generations of superior minds, for the sake of self-annihilation has been pursued with such vengeance as to fill even unbelievers with unease. Not that we should have any illusions about time-honored practices of the Church hierarchy, turning to the seats of temporal power as naturally as a sunflower to the sun. But this time the surrender was overt; now the power before which they prostrated themselves was an anti-Christian mentality urged upon the masses by science. And if figures of intellectual and even ecclesiastical prominence performed in the distance, a nearby church building made the "abomination of desolation" only too credible. In my case, the building was Newman Hall, the Catholic student chapel bordering the Berkeley campus. As a visitor there, I was a spectator to those hucksters in the temple, those purveyors of popular ideas, corruptors of young minds, who, to pack the church, sweetened their sermons with phrases as woolly as, on closer examination, they were inadmissible for a Christian. Thus did I witness the effects of science (above all, those of anthropology, much in vogue today), as noted by a little-known English author in the following quote—I apologize for its length:

> A superficial study of the life-patterns, myths and rituals of "primitive" peoples played a significant part in undermining the religious faith of Christians in the second half of the nineteenth century. First, it was taken for granted that these other races were "lower on the evolutionary scale" than Europeans. (What, after all, had they invented? Where were their railway trains?) Secondly, it was assumed by people who had completely lost the capacity for analogical and symbolical thinking that the myths by which those races lived were meant to be taken

quite literally and represented no more than the first gropings of the rational animal towards a scientific explanation of the universe. On this basis, since it was impossible to miss the parallels between "primitive religion" and the most "advanced" of religions, Christianity, the question had to be asked whether the latter also should not be classified as a pre-scientific effort to account for observed facts.

If these arguments were sound, then either of two conclusions might be drawn from them. It could be assumed that religion is a phenomenon which evolves in step with human "evolution," provided it is constantly purged of its "primitive" and "unscientific" elements and kept up-to-date; or else that religion as such, including Christianity, is no more than a vestige of the pre-scientific age and should be discarded together with all other superstitions that we have inherited from the times of ignorance. Protestant sects, constantly on the defensive, are only too ready to adopt the first of these conclusions in the mistaken notion that it offers their religion some hope of survival, and we have recently seen the hierarchy of the Catholic Church stumbling into this very pitfall. They imagine that Christianity might be allowed to survive on a modest scale if it can be proved to be "useful" to society, that is, to make men better citizens, more decent neighbors, more conscientious taxpayers; and they are ready to abandon everything that smacks of "otherworldliness," of metaphysics or of ritualism. The more ground they give, the harder they are pressed by their enemies.

—Gai Eaton, "The Only Heritage We Have,"
Studies in Comparative Religion, Spring 1974

Among my students, very few think of themselves as Christians. The majority are indifferent toward Christianity, so that in teaching Dostoevsky I have always been aware of a paradox: for some, that course was a first encounter with matters of religion, yet nearly all shared something with those Russian intellectuals whose attitudes Dostoevsky abhorred. If a professor is not there to fashion students in his own image, he must at least show them, clearly and unequivocally, where the oppositions lie and what the acceptance of a given thesis entails; he must grant them the freedom of choice, make them aware of what they are choosing. Only once did we come into serious conflict, and that was when I openly acknowledged the existence of good and evil, a stance they dismissed as irredeemably reactionary. They took it as given that human behavior was governed by certain social and psychological "determinants," that, in other words, all values were relative. Just so, Russian intellectuals of the last century shifted moral responsibility onto the "environment": change the society and you change the man. And it was precisely this denial of individual responsibility that Dostoevsky took as depressing proof of Christianity's decline among educated Russians.

I will not push the analogy. An advanced technology, coupled with the application of scientific methods—anthropological, psychological, linguistic, etc.—to the humanities, has added something new. And that something is an atmosphere of tolerance vis-à-vis all creeds, cults, persuasions of thought, provided they be sufficiently loose, syncretic. Thus does the average mind surrender to a noncommittal, areligious and aphilosophical trance, unconsciously assimilating a certain fund of the cultural inheritance. The homage nowadays rendered "creativity," for example, is nothing but a modern version of the glorification of art for art's sake, though by "creativity" is meant excretion for the sake of excretion, the more tempting for being conducted outside of truth and falsehood, good and evil, beauty and ugliness—where the doing, in other words, counts for more than what is done. If such a self-evasive mind could at least be made to take a consciously atheistic stand, that in itself would be a feat.

A true atheist, I believe, is a rare bird, one who is constantly shedding the vestiges of old creeds in himself. One such relic is an unconfessed faith in the benign effects of evolution in Nature and of the history of the human race as an extension of that evolution. Unfortunately, such a faith presumes a covenant between two contracting parties —in this case, between man and a providential force. If man evolved on earth by random mutation over billions of years, then attributing a benign will to the universe constitutes another version of religious mythmaking. To put it another way, if nothing binds human values to the inviolable laws of the universe, then there is nothing to protect mankind from extreme cataclysms and calamities. Then even the passion for truth, so precious to the man of science, remains inexplicable, ungrounded. The authentic, radical atheism of our century differs appreciably from its predecessors, and this difference is due largely to anthropology, in the broadest sense, as it encompasses the history of art and religion. If we reflect on man's solitary condition in the universe, on his "unnaturalness," then those nineteenth-century progressive-atheists appear as promoters of the old religious triad of Paradise, Paradise Lost, and Paradise Regained, having merely transposed the movement of Sacred History to the history of human societies. The positing of a human life in harmony with Nature, the cosmos, or universal Reason merits as much credence as a belief in water nymphs and sprites, is no less a vestige of the "animistic tradition." Man is alone; and if other planets are inhabited by beings endowed with intelligence, then they too are the product of chance, are just as alien to the universe. And this very estrangement of man as *intellect* imposes its own special obligations.

Let us consider. The highest moral ideals, the most exquisite works of poetry, painting, music, architecture; the most ingenious intellectual constructions—from philosophical systems to the mathematical models applied in technology—all are the work of man. So why should he not revere his own genius, his own brothers, not only those who excel in it but those who partake of it? But man is also anti-Nature, divided, at war with the animal in him, afflicted by not being able to live without the means to assuage his existence, whatever name we give to those means. Deserving of wonder, yes, but also pity, immense pity, the greater in that man can be pitied only by man.

A true atheist must concede that Dostoevsky, and not Russia's nineteenth-century progressives, was right. The latter were wrong in believing that the collapse of the tsarist regime would mean the end of willful arrogance, greed, the lust for power, guile, servility, and inhumanity whether through cruelty or quiescence. The prescient analyses contained in those tragedies, those morality plays of good versus evil, whether in *The Possessed* or *The Brothers Karamazov*, have been validated by time. Nor can any theory propounding the relativity of ethical norms diminish the impact of *Forefathers' Eve*, an effect premised on the audience's love of good and hatred of evil. Strip good and evil of any metaphysical sanction: they only gain for being human, for being a challenge hurled into the anti-human void, for answering to a humanly rooted need. To a true atheist, mindful of what is at stake, a belief in good and evil can never be "reactionary." Rather, he will say with Gombrowicz: "Don't make a petty demon of me.

Until the end of my days, even as I die, I shall always side with the human estate (even with God—I, an unbeliever!)" (*Diary*, 1957). And he will define, with him, the aim of literature as "giving voice to our simplest, most ordinary moral impulse" (*Conversations with Dominique de Roux*).

Where there is no posthumous reparation, when his brothers are at the mercy of the good or bad will of others, a true atheist is bound by the strictest ethical code. Nothing, not even the most noble-sounding slogan, truth, or vision can ever justify the paining of an individual being. That is why, for the true atheist, Russian communism is guilty of the most awesome crimes, both physical, inflicted on millions of defenseless beings, and spiritual tortures in the form of terror and, through terror, the repudiation of ordinary moral impulses and religious practice. In its persecution of religion, which the atheist must grant as an admirable product of the human imagination, as a palliative against the severity of life and death, communism reveals itself as a decidedly anti-human system.

True atheists are so scarce that there must be an explanation. There is. History deprived of the assurance of progress, Nature devoid of any preordained harmony—not a mother but a stepmother—seem to run counter to our needs (our genetic code?). From this radical opposition between the human and the extrahuman arises its variant: man feels pressed by forces and laws not so much natural as malignant, and a demonic presence begins to loom behind the curtain of an immutable, blind, inert order.

Gombrowicz—to my mind, a true atheist—was susceptible to this variant whenever he construed existence as Pain—which is, ultimately, Gombrowicz at his most serious, his most essential. But Pain attacks man from without, is a violence done to him: Nature, the suffering of myriads of bugs, fish, animals, and abiding in man as well, retaliates for all his religions, philosophies, sculptures, paintings, poems. Here is Gombrowicz:

> I am afraid of the devil, very afraid. A strange admission coming from an unbeliever. Still, I am unable to free myself from the concept . . . From that terrifying presence haunting my most intimate surroundings . . . What are police, laws, safety measures against the Freak that moves among us with such impunity, against which there is no protection, nothing, nothing, no barrier between us and it. It has a free hand among us, the freest! What distances the festive leisure of the afternoon stroller from that nether region rent by the screams of suffering men? Nothing, only empty space, a void . . . The earth we tread is spread with pain, we wade in it—the pain of today, of yesterday, of the day before yesterday, of past millennia. But let's not deceive ourselves: it does not fade with time, the child's cry of thirty centuries ago is no different from that of three days ago. It is the pain of every generation and every being—not only man.

> —*Diary*, 1960

Here Gombrowicz, sounding almost like a Manichaean, is my kinsman. And now it is I who must make a confession. There is no doubt in my mind that I hold a deep hatred for life, for its having been created just so, subject to these laws and no other. Such a conviction was always at the heart of Manichaeanism. Today those who do not believe in God are vastly outnumbered by those who, by reason of historical experiences, assent to the devil. I have personally known those who accepted the consequences, who chose to cooperate with the devil—as only he can prevail—thus imitating the choice made by Dostoevsky's

Grand Inquisitor. But that is no choice for a poet. Just because they are anti-Nature, there is something in those "divine works of the imagination" to protect us.

Among twentieth-century authors, one who laid particular stress on existence as pain was Simone Weil. I have rendered her into Polish, written about her, and taught her—my course on Manichaeanism was mainly devoted to her and to her attraction for the medieval Manichaeans (the Catharists, or Albigensians). Weil's Christianity, heavily laden with dualism, both in its Platonic and Manichaean versions, is by no means palatable to all, yet it gains enormously in importance as the exact opposite, as the counterbalance to that new theology which prostrates itself before the world. But if most students were familiar with the name of Teilhard de Chardin—whose authority that theology was fond of invoking—it was the first they had ever heard of Simone Weil, and for some the discovery of her work was an event. Through her lucidity of thought and style, she towers above those Christians acceding to the "demands of the age," so that readers of today will find in her a powerful counterpoise.

"La distance infinie que sépare le nécessaire et le bien." If we were to put this one sentence from Weil on the blackboard and spend an hour elucidating it, we would have, in outline, the essence of her system. One of its aspects is a radical atheism; one could even say that Weil, well versed in mathematics and physics, verges on "the scientific world-view." As used by her, the word "necessity" (*le nécessaire*) refers to the entire universe, the earth, and the history of man as a system of causes and effects subject to a mathematical determinism (whose variant is contingency). In that infinite number of causalities, there is not a trace of what we call good, and her favorite counterargument against progressives of all stamps, against lay

humanists, was that they confused two irreconcilable orders, placing the good on a level where there is only blind necessity. But the universe is also free of what we call evil: Nature (which equals necessity), though cruel in our eyes, is innocent. God, having created the world, withheld dominion over it, letting it take its own course, as untenable as that may be to human reason. God is good incarnate, yet He wanted a world without good, that is, a world below good and evil. He (the good) distanced Himself from the world (necessity) by an infinity. Another version of that indifferent God the Clockmaker of the eighteenth-century Deists? No: Weil's God is tragic, loving, the dying God on the cross. The words spoken by Christ before his death, "Lord, why hast Thou forsaken me," were, for her, the most powerful affirmation of Christianity, and of humanity, which occupies the lowest of all levels, above the innocence of Nature but bound by her laws, longing for the good "not of this world." By way of qualifying our blackboard inscription, one would have to add another of Weil's maxims: "Contradiction is the instrument of transcendence." Man must conceive of God as retiring, absent, yet sustain a belief in Providence; the belief that the good, infinitely distanced, finds ways of intervening ("through persuasion," says Weil with Plato); that He abides in men's souls as that tiniest of seeds (the Kingdom of God likened to a mustard seed). And how else, except to call it an insoluble contradiction, are we to reconcile, as Weil does, exultation at Nature's harmony and innocence—for Weil, the Virgin Mother of God made flesh—with the proposition that God surrendered His sovereignty to the Prince of this World?

I would be neglectful of the truth if in a book about my spiritual adventures I omitted the name of Simone Weil. To be sure, I bridled at her extreme Platonism, at her heroic self-renunciation bordering on hysteria, culminating in her suicidal death by fasting, reminiscent in many ways of the *endura* of the Catharists. But just as Cervantes's Knight of La Mancha, by his being an extreme case verging on clinical madness, makes manifest the absurd temerity of visionary adventures, so, too, that "Red Virgin," that *monstrum horrendum* in the eyes of her university colleagues, would not have been capable of such incredible rigor of thought had she been one to compromise. If the present book has a dominant theme, it is this "morbidity" intrinsic to man, this balancing of the human weight on the very edge of the scale so that one pinch dropped on the other is enough to tip it. Simone Weil taught me that my hatred for life was not deserving of absolute condemnation, that a longing for purity may disguise itself as morbidity. And that my love of life, equally strong, is no less real, since we live by way of contradictions. Ultimately, her elucidation of the role of contradictions, even logical contradictions, is one of the most valuable lessons to be gained from reading her works.

Christians in great legions are going—to a drumroll, bearing flags, and commanded by their theologians—and will be going over to the camp of the Man-god, either ignorant or forgetful of the reverse route taken by Dostoevsky. This does not yet signal the triumph of Ulro. The earth is not a honeyed abode, and the advocacy of scientific equations, unimpassioned, neither hot nor cold, must still contend with obstacles, not least with those erected by that pestering intruder, Pain. Therein, perhaps, lay the hidden motives for my offering a course on Manichaeanism, at a time when just up the way, on what is known in Berkeley as Theological Hill, home for the graduate departments of various religions, people were testifying to the genius of Teilhard de Chardin amid a mutual swelling of social

fervor. This does not mean I wish to cast myself as a prose-
lytizer of Manichaeanism in any of its traditional forms. I
only think that a certain measure of it is both necessary
and unavoidable.

40

I AM VERY EMBARRASSED. And I feel obliged to explore the
reasons for this embarrassment, which comes over me
whenever I try to explain my religious persuasion. Not so
when I am queried about my religious affiliation, in which
case I reply: Roman Catholic—in the manner of my Irish
and Italian colleagues. Can an Italian be anything else but
a Roman Catholic? But in the fluid, unfixed American
world in which I live, where no one would bat an eye if
I added that I was actually a Buddhist, rigid distinctions
are rarely invoked, and so for this reason I must return to
my Polish childhood, to my Polish inheritance.

Roman Catholic: a concept rich in virtuous connotations. A full-blooded Pole, a patriot, a Catholic since time
immemorial; next, righteousness and old Polish hospitality
and brotherly love and *sto lat* and the ceremonial stirrup
cup. I would be guilty of a deception if I were to assume
the robe of national custom. All my books testify to my
conflict with the national ethos, which even for me remains
something mysterious, painful, and to this day inexplicable. And deep down I am still not certain but that this
quarrel was not a rationalization of my conflict with the
human community at large, that my aversion mixed
with sympathetic attachment was not always leavened with

a sense of guilt. For surely the ideal to which I have always aspired, then as now, is membership in a human community, of the sort where communion with others comes of a shared set of values and an emotional closeness. It is indeed a healthy culture which can promote the creation of great and serious work—in art, in literature, in philosophy—while preserving the bonds of intimacy. And yet I could never genuflect before that goddess bearing the name of "Polishness," though I well understand the origin of this peculiar idolatry. Too many humiliations sustained by a proud and self-loving yet strangely vulnerable national ethos have meant the eager appropriation of anything which assisted in the recovery of its self-dignity; the judging of every work of the hand and mind by the ultimate, if largely unstated, criterion of its service to "the cause." Even religion has become a slave of this criterion, and the American professor was not wholly in error when he remarked recently that Poland was a land of unbelievers who practiced their religion out of devotion to the national tradition. For me, on the other hand, even one so exalted as Mickiewicz has always been something other than a "national bard."

But much water has flowed under European and American bridges since I proudly dissociated myself from Polish Catholicism; and my pride has been crumbled by experience. Only by comparison do we discover that "there is no bottom to evil," to borrow a phrase from one of Aleksander Wat's poems. Social structures which restrain man from extreme evil are deserving of respect. My conception of man is strangely similar to that of Gombrowicz, insofar as I, too, appreciate the role of the "lukewarm," the "medium," which seemed to have been Gombrowicz's way of resisting the process of mutual incitement by which people become prone to fits of mass hysteria. If man is a Homo ritualis, then ritual, which takes us into the realm of the sacred, is not a value to be easily dismissed. Moreover, the distinction commonly made between faith and practice is incompatible with observed reality. For the vast majority of people, certainly of those in the West, expressions such as "I believe/do not believe" are equally irrelevant; nor could it be otherwise if these same people are assailed by ubiquitous forces—of now high, now low voltage—whose deeper significance, relative to the civilization at large, exceeds their grasp. Attendance at church on Sunday, even if socially motivated, even if for propriety's sake (as with the Poles, the Irish, the Italians), may well be viewed by the Almighty, who is surely endowed with a rich sense of humor, as an act of faith. In a London church at Easter I once saw two Irishmen, both blind drunk, amuse themselves uproariously but good-naturedly by rolling a lemon back and forth across the floor, and I am certain that both stood in the sight of heavenly hosts. For a religion without a sense of humor is not to human size, while, as was pointed out long ago, genuine humor, which is never a sneer, has something truly religious about it.

It seems to me that Catholicism, despite a decline in the number of the faithful, will supply the basis, or at least the background, of any intellectual enterprise in Poland, that it holds the promise of Poland's cultural originality. Polish culture (a term which is no more adequate than "structure" and lends itself just as little to analysis) is a "believing" culture, if, as seems incontrovertible, it is most fully realized in *Pan Tadeusz*, that song of earth's blessings. And yet the memory of past customs—of the Nativity plays, of litanies sung in the circle of family and servants, of the gluttonous rites observed twice a year—will be gradually effaced, making one skeptical as to the future of a Catholicism so dependent on custom as to make of "Polishness" a religion.

Another cause for embarrassment: if a poet professes Catholicism, it is commonly interpreted as a "putting into port," a "taking comfort in religion" (even if we dismiss its traditional connotation of a "shift to the political Right")—as the mark of a right honorable gent. With me, however, the process was quite the reverse. Morally speaking, there is nothing, in my view, which argues either for Christians or against atheists. In the Middle Ages, when all professed to be Christians, the term applied to both the exalted and the base, to the pious and the impious. I would even say that if someone can be an atheist, he ought to be one. Of the two of us, Gombrowicz has always struck me as the more rational, the more consistent, and, I would now add, the more honest. My ecstatically religious childhood would have passed without leaving a trace if I had not observed, early in life, that it was not within my power to live without offering constant prayer to God. My life's tragedy was revealed to me at an early age as a tension between two equally strong and antithetical forces: affirmation, openness to the world, largesse versus negation, withdrawal, self-discipline. At times, of course, I tried to rationalize this conflict, to palliate it and make life easier for myself, yet I was sufficiently aware to realize that I was lost without Divine help. I was, then, a typical *salaud*, as defined by Sartre, one who contrives to believe in a metaphysical reason for his existence, i.e., that if he lives, he must have been preordained for something. A similar belief held by my patron, Mickiewicz, was denounced by Gombrowicz as "the philosophy of a superstitious child," and I am inclined to think that what sets me apart from the rest of twentieth-century Polish literature is the same "childish superstition."

A fine comfort, religion, for someone strangely attracted to Manichaean negation, to Pascal's *"Le moi est haïssable,"* or to Simone Weil's extraordinary admission, "Wherever I am, I befoul with my breath and my heartbeat the silence of earth and sky." For one who can identify with Oscar Milosz when (in *Les Arcanes*, commentary to verset 22) he tells of his estrangement in the presence of Nature's "sublime order"; how as a secluded child (who had suffered much), roaming his ancestral estate in Czereja, he had beheld in the things around him—a river, a cloud, a bird, an ant on the lawn—part of a harmonious mobility, each bearing the look of knowing "where one is, from where one comes, and to where one goes." A man like me, in other words, is constantly visited by a voice imputing his own deficiency as the real source of his internal maneuvers; by a voice which accuses him of *willing* belief in the absence of any real belief. And to this unquitting voice he replies with a mental shrug: So?

Studying the history of religion, long a passion of mine, disposes one rather to an agnostic point of view. One is struck, for example, by the contrast between the writings of the Evangelists and the first Apostles, i.e., the New Testament, on the one hand, and the homilies of their immediate successors, on the other—even one so early as St. Clement's Letter to the Corinthians dating from around A.D. 80. Neither St. Clement's letter nor the Jewish sect to which it is addressed inspire sympathy, and altogether one gains the impression of a gradual letdown, a subsiding. What had transpired was an event of such magnitude as to make a medium of the eyewitnesses and of those inspired by the Holy Spirit's fiery breath; but a few decades later the inspiration seems lacking, even though, at the time Clement was writing, the youngest of the disciples was still alive, the "son of thunder," Boanerges, or St. John. If the Hellenic civilization which then existed within the Roman Empire hardly merits praise, the prevailing hostility toward what was decidedly an anti-Hellenic, Eastern sect seems, in retrospect, to have been justified. Had I been around in the early centuries of Christianity, a certain sensibility, a certain cast of mind would have attracted me to the Gnostics rather than to the Christians, whose precepts were becoming more and more a moralizing rhetoric. And yet victory would belong to those simple men, not to their rivals with their rigorously trained minds, just as surely as seed must strike dark earth to bear fruit. To contemplate this diminishment (the fact that many of the faithful chose martyrdom does not invalidate the pattern, in my opinion) is to touch upon the secret of History. Since then Christianity has rarely regained the spiritual heights of those early communities; often, as during its propagation among the more barbarian peoples, it degenerated into a mouthing of magical incantations and the fabrication of talismanic charms against injuries in battle and infirmity. And the countless bigotries and superstitions; the fanaticism; the mob killings, such as occurred in Alexandria in A.D. 415 when Christians headed by obscurant monks dismembered the last philosopher of the Neoplatonist school, Hypatia; not to mention premeditated murders, such as were inflicted on the Albigensians during the French crusade in the thirteenth century. After the king's legions had captured Béziers, which had been defended by Catholics and heretics alike (there was no animosity between Catholics and Albigensians in Languedoc), the bishop purportedly exhorted the conquerors: "Massacre all of them, God will know which are His!" Whether historical legend or not, such an exhortation might have accompanied many a conversion by the sword. By professing Christianity, we assume a long legacy of spiritual and bodily oppression, of pacts between the altar and the throne, between the altar and the power of money. And yet there is the Christianity of the locomotive and the electric bulb, of the atomic bomb and the laser, in short, of that mighty technology which rules the earth. We can only theorize, of course, since no one can say what a Roman Empire without Christianity might have become; yet, judging by the stagnant civilizations of China and India, a stagnant Europe is not unimaginable—were it not for that extraordinary fusing of Judaic, Greek, and Roman elements, whence came the later exercise of mind in theological speculation, without which there would have been no philosophical or scientific hypotheses. The time has passed when people could proudly proclaim the "white man's burden," yet it is an irrefutable fact that modern science and technology, universally studied by people of all races and tribes, is the product of tiny Western Europe, whose boundaries roughly coincide with the territorial radius of ecclesiastical Latin. So it was meant to be. For the better? For the worse?

From St. Ignatius of Loyola's *Spiritual Exercises*, which I read long ago, I particularly recall those exercises involving the use of the imagination. You should, the author advises the adept—I paraphrase from memory—continually return in thought to the time when Jesus was teaching in Galilee, to the towns and roads of the region, and put yourself among His listeners, accompany Him on His earthly wanderings, be present at His death. Let us ponder this advice. Loyola, in effect, was urging the reader to swim upstream through the ages of civilization, through succeeding generations, through whole lifespans from old age to birth, surveying in reverse the multitudinous procession of human lives that makes up what we call history. Here we are at the very heart of the Christian attitude toward history as a totality relative to, and unfolding from, a single event in time and place. Whether Dostoevsky, who was brought up to fear the Jesuits as the sinister agents of Poland and the Vatican, ever read the work of their founder, I could not say. Possibly such a method—the "swimming-upstream method"—would suggest itself to someone as intimately engaged with the Gospels as Dostoevsky was in the penal colony of Omsk. In any event, by fixing his imagination on the person of Jesus, he was led to pose a question, the answer to which would spell the difference between Christian and non-Christian: Was He resurrected or was He not? In other words, was there an immutable cosmic order (Simone Weil's mathematical necessity), or was that order violated at least *once*? And Dostoevsky chose, saying in effect: Even if it be shown that truth is on the side of scientific determinism, I remain with Christ.

To swim upstream through history, reducing it not to Hegelian categories but embracing the multiplicity of human lives, in all their particularity, and then to behold the figure of the God-man and touch His garment, requires a supreme imagination. Indeed, it presumes the sort of imagination which, when written with a capital letter, signified for Blake the Divine. But because our own imagination seldom approaches that ideal imagination, the modern act of faith involves something of a wager, of *pari*, of a roulette game. The analogy is imperfect, of course, because here the placing of the bet is dictated not by a whim; in fact, we do not choose so much as we are compelled to bet on "yes" or "no" by a gut-born existential necessity. Still, in the modern religious experience, beginning with the Renaissance, this element of the wager, of *pari*, exists, and characteristically it found its first formulation, albeit in a rational-arithmetical language, in Pascal.

I mention the element of *pari* (with regret, since it arises only in the Land of Ulro) in order to make the point that the gut-born imperative of faith precludes neither dissent nor the knowledge that one is sufficiently free to bet on "no." Not infrequently the Catholic clergy of the West presents a spectacle no more appealing than when it once traded in indulgences and silently ignored the crimes of monarchs in exchange for fat benefices. One need not join the enemies of the Second Vatican Council to be outraged by the actions of many theologians and Church diplomats, or to insist that the Church hierarchy harmed legions of exiles like myself when it dispossessed us of Latin, which was native to us, and instituted English, which was foreign; when in the name of "participation" it forced us to pray in English, as if Protestantism's greatest undoing had not been precisely the *nationalizing* of religion. To claim that in the last quarter of the twentieth century, when vast numbers of nominal Catholics in the West have suddenly stopped going to church, the state of religion remains neither better nor worse than it was, say, five centuries ago, requires a truly prodigious sense of humor.

And what of those for whom heaven and earth are not enough, who cannot live except in anticipation of another heaven and earth? For those whose lives, such as they are, remain a dream, a curtain, a blank mirror, and who cannot accept that they will never understand what it really was all about? They will believe for the simple reason that the consummation of their desire can be expressed in no labile human tongue. Only one language can do justice to the highest claim of the human imagination—that of Holy Writ.

41

I COME TO THE FINAL CHAPTER of my story. Its honesty seems to me as ingenuous as it can be, which is not saying a great deal. No matter how deliberately we compose the sentences on paper, verifying them against what we know to be real, against what has been witnessed, experienced, made intelligible, we are still bound by language in its past and present forms, syntactically as well as rhythmically. Even my objections to certain tendencies in contemporary Polish, to its tendency toward untidiness and highbrow palaver, may have inadvertently brought a shift in accent, may have made me less uninhibited than I would have wished to be. I hope, however, that by alluding to this other, more hidden stream in my spiritual biography, I will have upset certain fixed and blanket opinions about myself. This is a matter of personal importance, since we strive to communicate the part of ourselves which most closely approximates our real selves—without indulging any illusions that we can ever achieve anything more than an approximation. Still, I must guard against what I would regard as the hypocrisy of undue modesty. My adventures are of more than just personal consequence, when, as here, a Polish poet from the Land of Ulro tries to deal with a wide range of inconsistencies and self-contradictions.

Where have we been? What does it all mean? What is our objective? It is not for me to say or not to say—I would reply in the manner of Gombrowicz's *Trans-Atlantic*. My purpose has been to render the facts, because who would take refuge in elegant analyses in the middle of such a cyclone? This much can be said: that Blake's Land of Ulro is not a fantasy if we ourselves have been there; that since the eighteenth century something, call it by whatever name one will, has been gaining ground, gathering force. And all who have sought exit from the "wasteland" (another of the names by which it is known) have been, in my opinion, justified in their endeavor, more, are worthy of admiration, even if their efforts ended in failure and were bought at the price of various "abnormalities."

We are in the thrall of certain habits of mind acquired over the past couple of centuries. No doubt in my writing I have betrayed, perhaps acquiesced in, some of those habits without knowing it. My attitude toward literature, for example, based on my experience as a reader, is only partially my own, and even this experience is leavened with received and inherited opinion. There is much in the history of literature, both Polish and continental, that remains obscure, inexplicable to this day; unable to name it, we merely circle around it. I have been busy with Polish literature as a poet, a critic, and a lecturer, and yet I confess that what I would call its deepest sense, its special mission, eludes me. Angelic spirit in a bumptious skull, brilliance layered with mediocrity? When I compare it to other national literatures (even as I lament the plight of the language), I detect in it a certain nuance, a certain sensibility, a special gift rarely brought to light but potentially priceless. And who knows if I could be so presumptuous toward the West if I did not assume, implicitly at least, that I can prevail—just because I write in Polish—

where they, those in the West, fail. Not because I come from the East. I am not a Russian. Russian literature belongs to the so-called great literatures; in its achievement, in its sense of form it is superior to Polish literature, yet it wants that nuance, that gift which I find so difficult to name—and so it is with consternation that I discover in myself certain traces of messianism, though not in its traditionally constituted form.

Of all the schools and tendencies recorded by Polish literature in the period 1918–39, the one closest to the spirit of the Romantic age was "catastrophism." Not because of its poetics, in which respect the poets of Skamander were the preeminent heirs of the Romantics, but through its eschatological expectations. These found expression—I think now, for example, of the poetry of Józef Czechowicz and of the Żagary group, in particular of Jerzy Zagórski's poem "The Coming of the Foe" and of my own volume *Three Winters*—in a vision of massive convulsions, cataclysms, of a crisis of cosmic proportions and of unspecified duration. "Bottoming out" became a recurrent motif, and yet, curiously, it was a vision of the Last Judgment in which not everything came to an end; it was not without hope. The work of Czechowicz, the author of a dozen lyric poems whose pristine purity assures them a permanent place in the language, poems exemplary of that special gift I mentioned, is filled with premonitions of his premature death; yet even in him a belief in the other shore, beyond the catastrophe, keeps reasserting itself. This belief is central to "catastrophism." Further, a careful reading of these texts will reveal that neither the tragedy nor its resolution can be restricted to the fate of a particular nation. The national danger, posed internally by a weakened economy and externally from both East and West, undoubtedly promoted a catastrophic bias, yet the poetic intuition went deeper. "Catastrophism" was above all engaged with the great crisis of civilization. Only later was it acknowledged, somewhat superficially, as a Cassandra-like prophecy of the events of 1939–45, even though the Second World War was but a corollary of a far more protracted crisis.

The sources of "catastrophism"? In my own case, they can be deduced from this book. The "Russian experience," here understood in the broadest sense to include not only the Revolution but its portents and consequences as expressed in the literature, also played a role. Its enormity and portentousness were no doubt better appreciated in Poland than in France or England. All the more so if one was living in Wilno, in close proximity to the border, where the almost palpable hostility of the Byelorussian countryside—which tended to associate everything Polish with the world of the "masters" and with things Western—awakened in even the less sensitive a dread of some dark element. The "catastrophists," in fact, came not from ethnic Poland but were men who, in varying degrees, had already been exposed to the East. Even Czechowicz, though Lublin-born, was greatly indebted to periods spent in Volhynia and Byelorussia. Then, too, people were well read on the subject—Russian literature of the twenties was accessible in translation and even found its imitators in the native prose and poetry. As a part of the "Russian experience" I would include the pessimistic visions of Marian Zdziechowski and Stanisław Ignacy Witkiewicz, writers belonging to different generations. The former, Zdziechowski, was to some extent nurtured by the religious-eschatological trend in Russian literature of the two pre-revolutionary decades, while the work of Witkiewicz might stand as a commentary on his experiences in wartime and revolutionary Russia.

I am inclined to view "catastrophism" not as a school

but as a current. An anthology could be compiled of those authors, poets as well as prose writers, from the twenties as well as the thirties, in whom the tendency looms either explicitly or implicitly. Excluded from it would be those works hailing the light from the East, those paeans celebrating the "dawn of an age" and the rat-a-tat-tat of machine guns. Leftist or not, "catastrophism" was chary of the near future and foresaw decades, if not centuries, of tragedy. Conversely, the version of "catastrophism" exemplified by Zdziechowski and Witkiewicz, just because it posited no other shore beyond the ultimate catastrophe (Witkiewicz's "From cattle we are born and to cattle we shall return"), would not be eligible, either. If such an anthology were to have a patron, it would be rather Krasiński's *Undivine Comedy* (1833–34), with its sudden reversal at the end.

All this was so long ago, nothing of it remains: not the country, not the people, not the person I once was. Yet there is no escaping the facts of one's fate, and in a sense I have remained a "catastrophist" all my life. Such a stance has at least one advantage: if we are always anticipating the very worst, then when the very worst happens, it comes as no surprise and we can somehow adapt. Meanwhile, the eschatological expectation of a new universal harmony, of an "age of faith and fortitude," abides with us.

I have surrendered to the law of Imagination, in the Blakean sense of the word. This is not to say that I look forward, like the medieval Joachim de Fiore and the Polish Romantics, to the advent of a Third Era, to an Age of the Spirit, or that, like Oscar Milosz in his final years, I foresee the coming of the millennium in a year or two. Words are exceedingly treacherous here, which is why there has never been a clear distinction between a yearning for the Kingdom and a yearning for the end of the world, the end of an eon.

Let us descend from the eschatological heights to the realm of the mundane, which is no less given to the workings of the imagination. In the end I am that boy who as he sat at his school desk, oblivious of the teacher's words except as a monotonous humming sound, spent hour after hour filling his notebooks with the fantastic sketches of his ideal countries. Their borders, their lakes and rivers meant not only that I was organizing space but that I was surmounting the present tense, because these were countries as they ought to have been. They were, I must confess, not so much human habitats as secluded woodlands, sanctuaries of unspoiled wilderness, trackless, with only a network of waterways fit for canoe travel. It was not incidental that I had marveled at the dugouts of blacks and the scenes of a hippopotamus hunt in the pages of that French pictorial from around the year 1840, or that I had read James Fenimore Cooper's *The Pathfinder,* Mayne Reid's *Watery Wilderness,* Maria Rodziewiczówna's *Summer of the Forest People,* and Włodzimierz Korsak's *Tracking Nature.* Today those hours stolen from mathematics and physics are for me as serious an endeavor as my present dreams of a civilization in which man will be freed from the servitude of Ulro. Once again, as in the past, I am sketching ideal realms, if not as maps on paper; and if I was then, at the age of twelve or thirteen, more concerned with preservation of the "natural environment," today my concern is rather with the "human environment." The renewal I contemplate has none of the grandeur of a millennium, and yet I am prudent enough to place it beyond my own lifetime and that of my contemporaries. Even if a new conception of science were now being nurtured in certain limited circles, there is no assurance that it would have immediate access to that sphere where the popular imagination is wrought by technology and politics. If the thirties palled by their accretion of insanity, by the spectacle of a collective fanaticism and flights into mindlessness, the seventies do not appear to me any better. So my hope, modest as it is, is not addressed to the imminent future.

If not the best of worlds, then at least a better one: my renewed civilization will not protect man from pain or personal misfortune, from illness or death; will not free him from the hard necessity of work. But that "most profound secret of the toiling masses, more alive, more receptive, and more anguished than ever," will be deciphered. Man will not be subjected to a fury of words and images designed to make him think in quantitative terms; to make him contemplate others, as well as himself, through an inverted telescope (with a corresponding diminishment, in his own eyes, to something approximating zero). Discoveries made long ago but either forgotten or banished from practice will become common knowledge: that slavery begins not where the nineteenth century sought its causes; that the lie, when made the norm of social intercourse, is rooted in something deeper than fear and the lust for power; that the human revolt against conditions of life perceived as inhuman conceals longings to which the slogans of dictators and demagogic tribunes only give lip service.

Let us try to look beyond today's parodies. A radically decentralized theocracy, as envisioned by Oscar Milosz, should not be confused with what we have occasionally witnessed here and there. Romantic dreams of an age of friendly cooperation between nations could still come true —when every nation, even the smallest, is recognized as necessary, so that all might be as colors of the rainbow. And then we shall not stand accused of having known how—of having deliberately chosen—to write only in Polish, Hungarian, or Czech, and untold treasure will be discovered in each such literature.

If I have alluded to the boy who once drew chimerical kingdoms in his notebooks, it was because we are too apt to think of the "final things" in solemn and august terms, as the province of gray-bearded sages and prophets. Yet how much of millenaristic yearning betrays a childish instinct. The song of innocence and the song of experience share a common theme. In a cruel and mean century, "catastrophism" entertained dreams of an idyllic earth where the "hay smells of the dream"; where tree, man, animal are joined in praise of the Garden's beauty. By recalling that the boy and the poet-"catastrophist" and the old professor in Berkeley are the same man, I am merely observing the guiding principle of this book, a book both childish and adult, both ethereal and earthbound. Reader, be tolerant of me. And of yourself. And of the singular aspirations of our human race.

Notes

5   Bolesław Leśmian (1878–1937). An eminent—some would say preeminent—if unclassifiable twentieth-century Polish poet. A Symbolist of sorts, in his mythmaking ballads and fables Leśmian stands closer to William Butler Yeats than to the Symbolists.

5   Skamander. A poetry group prominent in the 1920s and 1930s whose traditionalism and sanguine lyricism free of political commitment were consonant with the first decade of national independence. The supremacy of the Skamandrites—they took their name from the river in Troy—was challenged by successive waves of the avant-garde.

5   Avant-Garde (also called the First Avant-Garde, to distinguish it from the Second Avant-Garde of the 1930s). A "left-wing" reaction to the Skamandrites, it advocated a more rigorous, experimental poetry of commitment.

6   Karol Irzykowski (1873–1944). A leading literary critic between the wars and author of the highly experimental novel *Pałuba* (*The Witch*, 1903). Irzykowski's role as a polemicist culminated in his major work, *A Struggle for Contents* (1929).

10   Witold Gombrowicz (1904–69). Born in central Poland,

of gentry origin; a lawyer by training. Made his debut in the 1930s as an avant-garde prose writer and playwright. Left Poland on an ocean voyage in 1939, became expatriated in Argentina at the outbreak of World War II, and returned to Europe in 1963, eventually taking up residence in the South of France. During his thirty years of exile he continued to write in Polish, publishing his work in the Paris émigré press while remaining largely unpublished and unperformed in Poland. Unofficially acknowledged in Polish literary circles as one of the greatest Polish writers of this century. International success came late to Gombrowicz—foreign translations of his work and professional productions of his plays reached their height in the 1960s—and was crowned by the International Publishers Prize in 1967. A candidate for the Nobel Prize shortly before his death. Four novels (*Ferdydurke, Pornografia, Cosmos, The Possessed*) and three plays (*Ivona, Princess of Burgundia; The Marriage; Operetta*) have been translated into English; a fifth novel, *Trans-Atlantic,* a volume of stories, and his multi-volumed *Diaries* remain untranslated.

12 Janka Milosz. The author's wife.

12 Rita Gombrowicz. Gombrowicz's wife, née Labrosse, whom he married in 1968.

13 Stanisław Brzozowski (1878–1918). An influential and controversial philosopher, critic, and novelist. An *écrivain maudit* during his brief lifetime but one whose protean thought—he was, by turns, a Nietzschean, a Marxist revisionist, a Syndicalist, and a disciple of Cardinal Newman—has been a presence in Polish intellectual life since World War II.

13 Stanisław Ignacy Witkiewicz (1885–1939). A rediscovered avant-garde Polish playwright, novelist, philosopher, and painter. Eccentric, prophetic, on the borderline between Modernist and post-Modernist. His career falls roughly between two cataclysmic events: the Russian Revolution, which he barely survived as a tsarist officer (legend has it

that he was elected a political commissar by the soldiers of his regiment), and World War II, which he did not survive—he committed suicide on September 18, 1939. His catastrophic vision of Western civilization was conveyed in a number of prolix plays and novels. Several collections of his plays and one novel, *Insatiability* (1930), regarded by many Polish critics as a classic of "catastrophist" literature, are available in English.

14 Professor Pimko. A satirical-grotesque figure, of culturally fanatical tendencies, from Gombrowicz's novel *Ferdydurke* (1937).

15 Philomath prisoners. The Philomaths were a clandestine, semi-political Wilno literary fraternity whose youthful members (among them the poet Adam Mickiewicz) were arrested by the tsarist authorities, interned in a monastery, and later deported to Russia. Their arrest figures in Mickiewicz's drama *Forefathers' Eve* (see note for p. 97), whose Romantic hero is the prisoner, the poet-seer Konrad.

16 Żagary (from the Lithuanian, meaning "kindling"). One of several poetry groups, collectively known as the Second Avant-Garde, of the "dark decade" of the 1930s. Its antiaestheticism and apocalyptic visions laced with Marxism and metaphysics set it apart from earlier literary generations. Also called "catastrophists."

16 Ksawery Pruszyński (1907–51). A minor soldier-writer, distinguished journalist, and diplomat.

16 Jerzy Wyszomirski (1900–55). A minor poet, feuilletonist, critic, and translator of Russian literature.

17 Julian Przyboś (1901–70). One of the founders of the First Avant-Garde. His prosodic experiments and poetic studies helped to shape modern Polish verse. A kind of literary Constructivist.

18 Miss Youthful. Another satirical-grotesque from Gombrowicz's *Ferdydurke*, this one of middle-class cultural pretensions.

25 Wacław Lednicki (1891–1967). A Russian-born Polish

scholar of Russian, Polish, and comparative literature. From 1946 to 1958 he was Professor of Slavic Languages and Literatures at the University of California at Berkeley.

32 Moderna. A synonym for Young Poland (1890–1918), by analogy with Young Germany and Young Scandinavia. The Polish version of the European modernist revolt in philosophy and the arts, analogous to French Symbolism and the new aestheticism in England. Other synonyms are Modernism and Neo-Romanticism.

33 Bruno Schulz (1892–1942). A brilliant Polish-Jewish writer who with Witold Gombrowicz and Stanisław Ignacy Witkiewicz formed a lost avant-garde of inter-war prose writers rediscovered by the post-1956 generation. His stories of his native Drohobycz are available in English in two separate collections (*The Street of Crocodiles, The Sanatorium under the Sign of the Hourglass*).

36 Mikhail Bakhtin (1895–1975). An influential Russian critic and literary theorist noted for his theories of carnival literature and polyphony in the novel. The two works alluded to in the text are available in English under the titles *Problems of Dostoevsky's Poetics* and *Rabelais and His World*.

37 Henryk Sienkiewicz (1846–1916). The Nobel Prize author of *Quo Vadis?* and historical novels (i.e., *The Trilogy*) aimed at elevating Poland's feudal past into patriotic myth on a Homeric scale.

37 Nikolai Chernyshevsky (1828–89). A Russian literary critic, of the empirical school, and central figure in the Russian radical movement. Author of the didactic novel *What Is to Be Done?* (1863), whose utopian, utilitarian views were combated by Dostoevsky in *Notes from the Underground*.

37 Józef Nusbaum-Hilarowicz (1859–1917). A Polish zoologist, popularizer of Darwinism, and founder of a Polish school of evolutionists.

38 Aleksander Wat (1900–67). An outstanding Polish poet,

prose writer, critic, memoirist, and translator. Began his career as a Futurist-Dadaist and "catastrophist" in the 1920s and died in Paris as another rediscovered contemporary of the post-1956 generation. His *Mediterranean Poems* are available in English; a translation of his posthumously published memoirs of the age, comparable in their moral witnessing to those of Nadezhda Mandelstam, is forthcoming.

46   Juliusz Słowacki (1809–49). A Polish Romantic poet-in-exile and dramatist whose mystical, visionary work (*Genesis from the Spirit*, 1844; *King Spirit*, 1847) was not appreciated until the age of Symbolism. Author of a number of fine lyric poems, somewhat Shelleyan in style, and of the verse drama *Kordian* (1834), a flawed but brilliant riposte to the Romantic titanism of Mickiewicz's *Forefathers' Eve*. A rival of Mickiewicz.

48   Adam Mickiewicz. See note for p. 97.

60   Lev Shestov (1866–1938). The pseudonym of Lev Schwarzman. An original Russian philosophical essayist whose anti-rationalism was founded on arguments prefiguring those of the existentialists. Died as a political émigré in Paris.

63   Tadeusz Byrski (1906–   ). A Polish stage and radio director, and actor. Formerly associated with the Żagary group.

63   Juliusz Osterwa (1885–1947). A distinguished Polish actor, stage director, and founder of the avant-garde theater Redoubt. A director known for his experiments in modernist poetic drama in the 1930s.

65   *Forefathers' Eve*. See note for p. 97.

68   *Pan Tadeusz*. See note for p. 97.

71   Stefan Żeromski (1864–1925). A major Polish writer whose novels of social injustice and lonely idealism made him a moral authority in the first quarter of the twentieth century. The "fictitious manor of Nawłoć" is an allusion to one of Żeromski's finest novels, *Early Spring* (1925).

74   Piast. A legendary peasant in the ninth century who,

according to the earliest-known chronicle, with his wife, Rzepicha, founded the Piast dynasty (ninth to fifteenth centuries). Gave rise to the pervasive myth of the peasant-king.

82   Sapieha. The name of an ancient princely Lithuanian clan which once held sovereignty over vast territories of the country.

91   National Democrats. A powerful right-wing nationalist party—colloquially known as ND or *Endecja*—active in the political struggles before and after the emergence of independent Poland in 1918.

97   Adam Mickiewicz (1798–1855). Foremost among nine-teenth-century Polish Romantic poets, nationally revered much as Pushkin is revered in Russia. His career takes in many countries—from his native Lithuania to tsarist Russia, then Italy, Germany, France, Switzerland, ending in Turkey at the time of the Crimean War—and com-bines the not always compatible roles of poet-exile, mystic, professor, socialist editor, and revolutionary fighter. In at least three literary genres (lyric poetry, the long narrative poem, and verse drama), his legacy has stood as the measure for generations of Polish poets and dramatists. The first in Polish literature to bear the title of a *wieszcz*—a vatic bard endowed with the properties of a charismatic national leader.

The Mickiewicz works discussed in the text, in addi-tion to "The Romantic," are *Pan Tadeusz* (Paris, 1834) and *Forefathers' Eve*, Part III (Paris, 1832). The first is Mickiewicz's masterpiece in verse, which in classical Polish alexandrines re-creates a mythical Lithuania on the eve of Napoleon's invasion of Russia. A kind of "remem-brance of things past," with a smile. Its hold on the Polish literary imagination is attested by a great many works, including Milosz's own *The Issa Valley* (1955) and Gombrowicz's *Trans-Atlantic* (1952).

The second, *Forefathers' Eve* (or *Ancestors*), is the archetypal Polish Romantic drama, set in Russian-occupied Poland and based on the tsarist arrest of Wilno students in 1823. This incident, although minor compared to the national disaster of 1831, is transformed by Mickiewicz into a sacral drama of Poland's sacrificial destiny as embodied in its poet-hero Gustav reborn as the rebel Konrad. The play's climax comes in a long monologue—called the Great Improvisation—in which the poet revolts against a God indifferent to human suffering. But Konrad shrinks from committing blasphemy, thus vindicating the ancestral code, and in Father Peter's messianic prophecy he is cast as a national savior. In its vision of Poland as a "Christ of nations," *Forefathers' Eve* became a major source of the potent doctrine of Polish Messianism.

97   "The Romantic." The preface-manifesto to *Ballads and Romances* (1822), Mickiewicz's first published volume, dating from his Lithuanian period, and the work which launched Romanticism in Poland.

100   Positivists. The term is from Auguste Comte. Applies to a generation of Polish utilitarians who, in the aftermath of the failed 1863 insurrection, invoked science and economic progress over "political Romanticism," i.e., insurrectionism.

100   Andrzej Towiański (1799–1878). A Wilno-born mystic-prophet and founder of an adventist sect (called the Circle) in Paris in the 1840s. Mickiewicz's spiritual master in his later years.

101   Aleksander Chodźko (1804–91). A minor poet closely associated with Mickiewicz, whom he eventually succeeded in the Slavic Chair at the Collège de France after the poet's dismissal for his mystical excesses.

101   Józef Bohdan Zaleski (1802–86). A once popular but minor nineteenth-century poet associated with the exoticism of the Ukrainian school.

101   Andrzej Niemojewski (1864–1921). A self-taught religious scholar and minor poet, novelist, and playwright. Began his career as a socialist active in the 1905 Russian Revolu-

tion before turning to freethinking and the study of religion. A disciple of Ernest Renan (1823–92), whose *Life of Jesus* he translated in 1904.

102　Piotr Chmielowski (1848–1904). A preeminent Polish literary historian and critic, of the Positivist generation.

103　Stanisław Augustus Poniatowski (1732–98). The last reigning monarch of Poland. His reign (1764–95) coincided with the partitioning of Poland and the end of the Republic.

104　Śniadecki brothers: Jan Śniadecki (1756–1830) and Jędrzej Śniadecki (1768–1838), the one a mathematician, the other a natural scientist. Professors at the University of Wilno at the time of Mickiewicz and prominent in the Polish Enlightenment. Jan Śniadecki, who combated Romanticism, appears as the "man with a learned air" in Mickiewicz's poem "The Romantic."

105　Wincenty Lutosławski (1863–1954). A Polish philosopher known for his commentaries in English on Plato.

111　Seweryn Goszczyński (1801–76). A minor Romantic poet, insurgent, and radical critic-activist among the Polish émigrés.

113　Armand Lévy (1827–91). A French journalist and friend of Mickiewicz who joined the poet on his military mission to Constantinople during the Crimean War.

115　Stanisław Pigoń (1886–1968). A distinguished Polish literary scholar noted for his studies of Mickiewicz.

123　Zygmunt Krasiński (1812–59). The third member of the triad of Polish poets-in-exile that included Juliusz Słowacki and Adam Mickiewicz. An aristocrat by origin and a Hegelian by disposition. Remembered today less as a poet than as the author of the drama *The Undivine Comedy* (1833–34), a symbolic treatment of revolution in modern, universal terms, in which the violent class conflict between the Christian, aristocratic order and the atheistic, materialist mass remains unresolved within the play. The vision of the cross which is visited on the dying revolutionary leader in the play's final moments is a stunning *coup de théâtre*.

123 Cyprian Norwid (1821–83). A late-Romantic poet, play-wright, prose writer, and draftsman. A poet of universal vision whose intellectual irony, innovative diction, and elliptical style alienated his Polish contemporaries but have since earned him a place as a pre-Modern and poet-thinker of the highest order.

125 Praga massacre. On November 4, 1794, in the final days of the Kościuszko Insurrection, the Russian General Alexander Suvorov ordered the massacre of some ten thousand civilians in the eastern suburb of Warsaw. The fall of the capital led to the Third Partition in 1795 and ultimately to the fall of the Republic.

129 Leon Schiller (1887–1954). A major twentieth-century Polish theater director and stage reformer whose theory of "monumental theater" fulfilled the promise of Mickie-wicz and Wyspiański.

130 Longinus Podbipięta. A popular, Bunyanesque knight-hero of Henryk Sienkiewicz's historical *Trilogy*.

130 Wokulski. The tragic capitalist-hero of a late nineteenth-century novel, *The Doll* (1890), written by a disillusioned Positivist and outstanding literary figure of the period, Bolesław Prus (1847–1912).

132 Stanisław Wyspiański (1869–1907). Preeminent play-wright, stage reformer, poet, and Impressionist painter of the Moderna. His surreal folk drama in verse, *The Wedding* (1901), launched a tradition in the modern Polish drama.

132 Stańczyk; Szela. The first is the name of a court jester from the sixteenth century; the second is an allusion to Jakub Szela (1787–1866), the leader of a peasant rebellion in Galicia in 1846. Both are among the apparitions who haunt the living in Wyspiański's *The Wedding*—i.e., as "things of the soul's own staging."

133 Mikołaj Sęp-Szarzyński (1550–81). A Polish Renaissance

poet whose metaphysical sonnets prefigure the Baroque and continue to inspire modern Polish poetry with their highly wrought contemplative lyricism. The lines cited in the text are from Sęp-Szarzyński's "Epitaph to Rome," and are given in Milosz's translation.

134 Józef Hoene-Wroński (1778–1853). A Polish mathematician, physicist, and philosopher. Wrote in French during his self-imposed exile and supplied the philosophical premises of Polish Romanticism and Messianism.

161 Tadeusz Kroński (1907–58). A Polish philosopher and Hegelian; portrayed as Tiger in the author's *Native Realm* (1958).

187 Vladimir Solovyov (1853–1900). A Russian religious philosopher and poet inspirational to the Russian Symbolists. Fathered a renaissance of Russian religious thought which culminated in the later work of such figures as Nikolai Berdyaev (1874–1948)—quoted in the text on pp. 126–27—Lev Shestov, and Sergei Bulgakov (1871–1944).

195 Leopold Staff (1878–1957). A Polish poet, translator, and editor. Led a long and protean career, overlapping the Young Poland movement, Skamander, and the "naked poetry" of the postwar period.

206 Józef Kraszewski (1812–1887). A popular and immensely prolific master of the historical novel. His oeuvre numbers some seven hundred titles, among them a multi-volumed fictionalized history of Poland.

222 Polish . . . Arians. Named after the fourth-century Greek heretic Arius. A radical Protestant sect which seceded from Calvinism in 1569–70 to advocate a rationalist theology and primitive Christianity. Christian communists; forerunners of the Unitarian Church.

223 Socinianism. A later phase of Arianism; named after the Italian theologian Socinus (1539–1604). His doctrine, an extreme theological rationalism combined with a mitigated social radicalism, was propagated by the Arian commune in the Polish town of Raków.

270 Józef Czechowicz (1903–39). An avant-gardist of the second wave. Czechowicz's madrigal-like poems evoke an older tradition even as they share in the metaphysical obsessions and Cassandra-like visions of the 1930s. Killed in an air raid on his native Lublin.

270 Jerzy Zagórski (1907–   ). A poet, co-founder of Żagary, editor of an anti-Nazi anthology, essayist, and translator.

271 Marian Zdziechowski (1861–1938). A Polish cultural and literary historian influenced by Vladimir Solovyov and Nikolai Berdyaev. Voiced his "catastrophism" in such essayistic works as *The Specter of the Future* (1936) and *The End Envisaged* (1938).

272 Krasiński's *The Undivine Comedy*. See note for p. 123.

L. I.